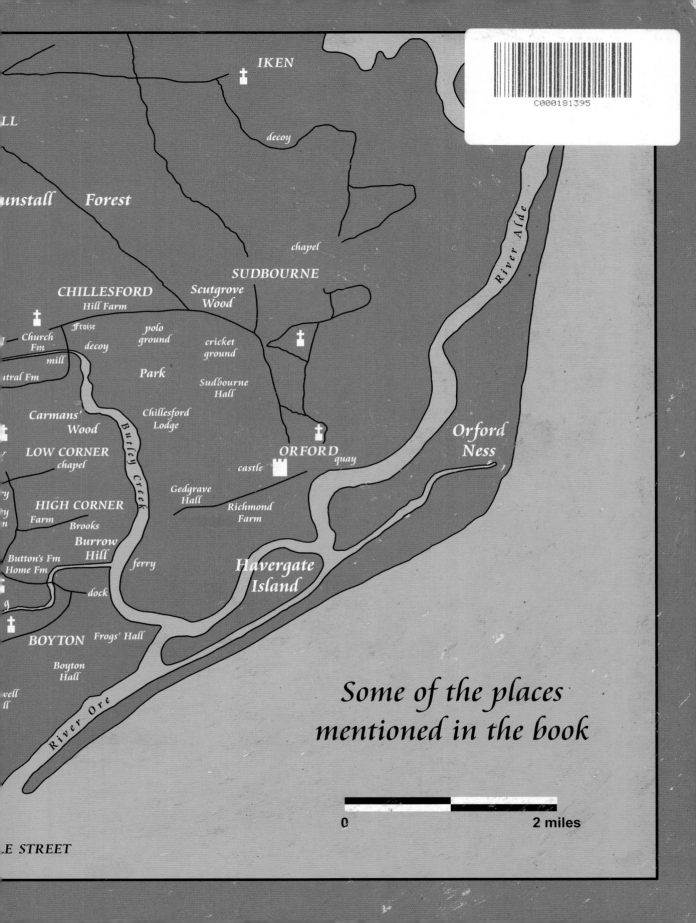

IKEN

decoy

unstall   Forest

chapel

SUDBOURNE

CHILLESFORD   Scutgrove
Hill Farm   Wood

Froize
Church   polo
Fm   decoy   ground   cricket
mill   ground
utral Fm   Park
                Sudbourne
Carmans'   Hall
Wood   Chillesford
          Lodge   Orford
LOW CORNER   Ness
          chapel   ORFORD
                   castle   quay
HIGH CORNER   Gedgrave
Farm   Hall
          Brooks   Richmond
Burrow   Farm
Button's Fm Hill
Home Fm   ferry
          dock   Havergate
                             Island
BOYTON   Frogs' Hall

Boyton
Hall
vell

River Ore

River Alde

Butley Creek

**Some of the places
mentioned in the book**

0   2 miles

LE STREET

Untold Tales from the Suffolk Sandlings

Untold Tales from the Suffolk Sandlings

Valerie Fenwick
Vic Harrup

Published by the Butley Research Group

Copyright © Valerie Fenwick and Vic Harrup 2009.

The right of Valerie Fenwick and Vic Harrup to be identified as the authors of this work has been asserted in accordance with sections 77 and 78 of the Copyright, Designs and Patents Act 1988.

© Copyright in illustrations with Valerie Fenwick and the individual owners listed.

All Rights Reserved. Except as permitted under current legislation no part of this work may be photocopied, stored in a retrieval system, published, performed in public, adapted, broadcast, transmitted, recorded or reproduced in any form or by any means, without the prior permission of the copyright owners.

First published 2009
Butley Research Group, Church Farm House, Blaxhall, Woodbridge IP12 2DH.

ISBN 978-0-9562829-0-3

British Library Cataloguing-in-Publication data.

Fenwick, Valerie and Harrup, Vic
   Untold Tales from the Suffolk Sandlings
   1. — England — History — Suffolk — Archaeology — Landscape — Archival research — Oral history

   Title
   Untold Tales from the Suffolk Sandlings

A catalogue record for this book is available from the British Library.

The publication is printed on FSC paper.

Design and layout in Perpetua and Galliard by Chris Farmer.

Clipart: Corel ©200_ Chris Farmer and its licensors. All rights reserved.

Printed and bound in Great Britain by The Lavenham Press Ltd, Suffolk.

Contents

Illustrations

Acknowledgements

Numerous friends and colleagues have provided information, or access to documents in their care.

Particular thanks are due to: the staff of Ipswich Record Office for their courtesy and unfailing assistance; Marcus Bennett for much help in deciphering troublesome records; Peter Northeast for making available his transcriptions of early wills; and Chris Farmer for creating the design and layout out of this book.

We are most grateful to the following:
The Greenwell family who have been most helpful in allowing access to their archives and fields; John and Rachel Massey and Glyn Evans for information and loan of photographs from their collection; Alan Calver for permission to publish some of his metal-detected discoveries; Margaret Poulter for access to the Emmeline Rope archive; to Roy and Marion Collins, Sam Foreman, Joyce Hazelwood, George Gardiner, Claude Read, George and Freda Smith, and Florence Warne for reminiscences and loan of photographs; to the vicar and churchwardens of Stowmarket church for access to the Tyrell monument; to Reg Snowdon for loan of his horseman's notebook, reminiscences and photographs; to Desmond Herring for details of unpublished Hearth Tax returns and alehouse licences; to Sue Andrews for access to the Hadleigh Archive and Valerie Norrington for guidance in tracing Quaker records; to the Large family in Australia for copies of documents and photographs; to Norman Scarfe whose writings enliven Suffolk history; to John Blatchly for help and advice and David Dymond for his inspired course on local history; to Jack and Bill Kemball for access to Staverton Park and Dale Farm; to the Keeper of Armour, Leeds Royal Armouries for elucidating Almain rivets, the Company of Watermen and Lightermen for information, and the Society of Antiquaries of London for permission to reproduce items in their collections; and to Jane Allen, Peter Barber, Gary Battell, David Boast, John Cross, John and Angie Gardiner, Steven Plunkett, Bertram Rope, David Sherlock and Margaret Williams, for help, advice, or loan of material.

Sources of Illustrations

Illustrations are by, or in the collection of Valerie Fenwick, or reproduced courtesy of the following:

Robert Blake, 101, 172; John Blatchly, 19, 71; Trustees of the British Library, 6, 20, 69, 70; Christchurch Mansion, Ipswich, 46, 72; Glyn Evans and Rachel Massey, 129, 136, 140, 147, 150, 155, 161, 167, 173; Chris Farmer, 10 (top); Sam Foreman, 148; George Gardiner, 62, 63; Getmapping plc, 123; Greenwell Family, 13, 51, 74, 80, 81, 83, 132, 146, 160; Joyce Hazelwood, 127, 130, 145, 155, 188; Desmond Herring, 114; Honor Hussey, 165; The Large family, 128, 175, 181; Lennoxlove. ©Lennoxlove House Ltd. Licensor www.scran.ac.uk, 135; Longleat: by permission of the Marquess of Bath, 37; the Librarian of Mrylebone Cricket Club, 66; courtesy of the Master and Wardens of the Mercer's Company, 22; New Orford Town Trust and Orford Museum, 62, 64, 121, 165, 185; Norfolk Record Office, 38; Paddy O'Beirnes, 153, Ordnance Survey, 63, 113, 115, 125, 126, Society of Antiquaries of London, 1,31, 35, 49, 55, 72; Steven Plunkett, X, 64; Freda Smith, 119, Reg Snowdon, 139, 151; Mike Stammers, 188; Suffolk Record Office, Ipswich, 12, 40, 58, 67, 71, 79, 88, 174, 187; Florence Warne, 63, 114, 155; Woburn Abbey: by kind permission of His Grace the Duke of Bedford and the Trustees of the Bedford Estates, 13; Sally Willow, 84; Woodbridge Museum, 167.

Foreword

Down the eastern side of Suffolk, as you near the coast, the country becomes sandy and heathy, and crossed by tidal waterways. Between them the peninsulas have each evolved their own stories and character. The scene of this book is Butley, with its neighbouring villages and manors east of the Deben estuary. The soil blends into rusty crag sands from a Pleistocene sea, warm against brick and tiled cottages and summer vegetation.

Leaving aside the ancient history, where better to begin than with old Ranulph Glanville, who died in the siege of Acre led by King Richard? Ranulph founded Butley Priory in 1171. There is always a fresh thrill when one glimpses its gatehouse through the trees, encrusted with solemn heraldry. The powers of that aristocracy waned many centuries ago, but the grandiose building still dominates the farms and fields. It is as if past ages are playing hide-and-seek with the present.

It is a pleasant adventure that leads us seamlessly from the last years of the Priory to the village characters we knew as children – and from them to ourselves. These tales, brought to light from the most varied original sources, thread their way in and out of the lives of villagers and landowners, successors to the Priory's estates and the employments of its servant household. From each chapter to the next we follow the thread, in stories of love and disappointment, religious devotion and fervour, bonds made or broken, and occupations and pastimes.

They lead us far afield and back again, into new worlds and circumstances, but that former grandeur was never quite forgotten. Just as the stones of the old Priory found their way into cottage walls, so the idea of its forsaken dignity assumed new meanings for later generations. That history is by no means ended:

> 'Time present and time past
> Are both perhaps contained in time future,
> And time future contained in time past.'

Ipswich, June 2009

Preface

Two of us, both old enough to have childhood memories of the Second World War and to have listened to the reminiscences of rural folk born before the First, set out to record our understanding of the past. For neither of us does the Suffolk Sandlings represent our 'roots', but it is where we have lived and worked. With retirement has come time to delve into its history and to write about some of the people who made it what it is today. Here we commemorate the dramatic and tragic events in the lives of some of the men and women who lived in this little-known part of Suffolk.

Two necessities guided us. The first was dependency on the concentration of archaeological and documentary evidence from the monastery and later estate of Butley for a chronological framework for our stories and to permit certain topics to be developed. The second was the need to use small landscape features, even smaller metal-detector finds, and memories of local people to illuminate the past and to make it more immediate for the people who live here today. We were mindful of the need to counteract the deadening effect of reliance on wills as a major source of information.

The dearth of images of even gentryfolk was frustrating. Recorded portraits of Samuel and Joyce Clyatt have disappeared; a miniature of Anne Spencer painted by Zincke at the time of her marriage is inaccessible; and the portrait of her eldest son had to be tracked down in Edinburgh. For this reason pictures of contemporaries and funeral images are used to give an indication of the fashions worn by our main characters. Wherever possible we have selected informal archive photographs. A particular joy was a large photograph of villagers gathered outside *The Oyster Inn* for the arrival of the carter's 'Wild West' wagon, which justified the digital work required to

restore it. It was also our aim to enhance the text with paintings by local artists.

While research into family history is an increasingly popular hobby, comparatively few people have been confronted with ancient documents, strange handwriting and stranger spelling. Our selection of extracts with attention drawn to key words will hopefully tempt readers to puzzle them out. The authors are entirely self-taught in this regard.

If we expected to find continuity in the families who lived here, we were disappointed. After the Dissolution the Butley, Tangham and Boyton estates remained in the Forth family for 87 years, after which Boyton was left in trust to fund almshouses while female descendants owned residual fragments of the other manors. At the beginning of the 18th century the Spencers of Rendlesham gradually reassembled Butley and Tangham, only for Edward Spencer's grandson, the Duke of Hamilton, to have to sell them one hundred years later. From that time they remained in the hands of the Barons Rendlesham until the collapse of farming after the First World War. In the 1930s the estate was again recreated by Sir Bernard Greenwell and is still being farmed by his grandsons.

We did hope to be able to trace many generations of ordinary folk who appear as freeholders or tenants in manorial records, but found that after three or four generations invariably holdings were either given up or there was no male heir to inherit. However, despite the evidence of a changing population, East Suffolk has continued to be less affected than many other parts of the South-East lying within commuter range of the Capital. It has preserved traces of a past world in its scattered villages and undeveloped coast.

It is important to question the landscape round us – to seek for explanations of what is happening today. In the summer months unmanned machines, with monstrous arms and coils of hose, inexorably move across artificially-fertilized arable, spraying even the unwary passer-by. Equally large are the machines which harvest the crops, and whisk them away in lorries and trailers down unsuitably narrow lanes. For modern farming to be economic large fields are essential, so much is clear. It is equally clear that fields used to be smaller years ago, but was this always the case? What about the

washed into watercourses by heavy rain. The slowly rising sea-level restricted the flow of the streams which dropped ever more sediment, with the result that little watercourses and estuaries became choked with alluvium, a process accelerated by the growth of reeds. Inevitably exceptional tides and storm surges flooded low-lying land. The process continued until – some time after the Norman Conquest – people started to build earth banks and sluices to keep salt water out.

Impression from a recently discovered seal depicting a sheep's head below the open castle gates with the legend:

S´ NOVAE : CUSTOMAE : ORFORD´

[Seal of the new custom of Orford]

The 'new custom' was an extra duty on wool introduced by Edward I in 1303. Orford was an established wool port; a century earlier it paid 71% more 'ancient custom' than Ipswich. The Low Countries were the centre of the medieval cloth industry in northern Europe.

An East Anglian monk delighted in the minutiae of farming when he illuminated the Luttrell Psalter for his patron.

Like Mary's little lamb, the wether reared by the shepherd has followed him, and the flock has followed the bell suspended between its horns. Closely folded, the ewes are milked and tended while their droppings (the tathe) enrich a chosen patch of soil.

medieval three-field system? Was the land at one time all open fields? It cannot have been possible to irrigate crops in the past. Is this evidence that the climate has changed, or are there other factors?

The changes to Butley Creek make a case in point. Some 6,000 years ago its valley was deeper, receiving faster-moving water from numerous small streams. At that time high tides were unrestrained and the river flowed directly into the North Sea a mile or more east of today's coastline. The first farmers exacerbated a process which continues to this day - the ploughed soil can form dust clouds in strong winds ('blows'), or be

The silts on the low-lying land were ideal for grazing animals. Rich pasture resulted in a good lactation with milk to spare from raising calves. The best arable was where a clay stratum prevented the light soil from drying out so quickly, while sheep could be grazed on the drier heaths. If a pattern of scattered settlement and threefold division of husbandry, based on the three types of soil in the area, developed with the first farmers, it was one which persisted until well into the last century.

For hundreds of years the exceptional prosperity of this part of the Sandlings - the 'Triangle' formed by Bromeswell, Orford and Bawdsey – rested on sheep bred for their wool, but also to provide milk and cheese and fertilizer. The flocks of the Black Canons of Butley and their tenant farmers were shepherded by day over 3,000 acres of sheep walks and the miles of river walls, but folded each night in different parts of fallow fields.

As late as the 20th century the contribution sheep could make to the light lands was appreciated by John Hewitt. He farmed at Butley Mills and described his Suffolks as *'four-legged muck-carters and spreaders as they stamped and consolidated the soil'*.

The watercourses conferred other benefits: the first of these was the year-round availability of protein from oysters, eels, fish and wild fowl; secondly, building materials in the form of reed thatch, willow hurdles, wattles and the clay with which to daub them; and, lastly, the means to transport heavy materials. The apparent disadvantages of the Sandlings were turned to advantage. Fields were cleared of flint to construct walls and to metal roads. Reed thatch lasted much longer than straw, and reed fences made frost barriers around garden plots. Seasonal flooding by fresh water enriched marsh pasture, while salt, evaporated from brine channelled on the highest tides into pans, enabled gluts of herring and cod to be preserved. On the heaths grey and black rabbits were raised in warrens and provided meat as well as fur and felt to keep out biting winds.

What went wrong? Cycles of plague and murrain, poor harvests, exceptional floods, high taxation, wars, agricultural depressions and unrest, combined with human failings form the setting for some of our tales. However, the backdrop remains unchanged – a gentle landscape of enclosed fields, scattered settlements, flint-walled churches, small cottages, modest farmhouses and expanses of heath. The few grand houses were either demolished or burnt down.

Continuity and change, the Yin and Yang of its past, are set to become unbalanced in the third millennium, now that traditional farming has disappeared and townsfolk replace inhabitants dependant on rural occupations. What is the point of trying to explain and commemorate an agriculturally-based way of life when it has all but vanished? The justification has to be that understanding remains a key to influencing the pace and direction of change – none of us need to be led blindly in the rush.

The Prior's Tale
Chapter 1

The 12th century was a period in which many monasteries were founded by wealthy men and women, who saw in this massive expenditure a means of ensuring perpetual prayer, and thus salvation, for themselves and their families.

Butley Priory was founded in the momentous year of 1171. It was the year when the Christian country was rocked by a clash between Church and State which culminated in the murder of its able archbishop, Thomas Becket. Whether or not Henry II was directly responsible, he made visible atonement and established a number of religious foundations. That same year, his courtier, Ranulph de Glanville, founded Butley Priory, no doubt copying the royal lead in the aftermath of the murder. Ranulph was rising rapidly in favour, both as a successful general and as a constitutional lawyer. The King rewarded him with manors, including that of Benhall. Ranulph in turn continued to enrich his religious and charitable foundations until his death at Acre in 1190 whilst accompanying Henry's son, Richard I, on a crusade to recapture Jerusalem.

On the priors of Butley fell the administration of large and scattered possessions acquired piecemeal through donations and purchases. On them lay responsibility for riding political storms and ensuring that successive kings and popes ratified the grants made by their predecessors. Over a span of 357 years there were both able and lax priors, priors who struggled with mounting debts, a prior who committed suicide and a prior who gave supper to the devil in the form of Thomas Cromwell, in order to secure his own future.

The founder

Two devout Norman families which had received land-grants in east Suffolk from William the Conqueror were the de Valoines and the de Glanvilles. They were forerunners of the Suffolk gentry who, in later centuries, are found intermarrying and consolidating their estates.

When Ranulph de Glanville and his wife, Bertha, planned their first monastery they had a number of properties in east Suffolk to choose from. One, part of Bertha's dowry from her wealthy father, Theobald de Valoines, was ideal. It lay in the Hundred of Plomesgate on the overland coastal route from the port of Ipswich to the king's new castle at Orford. A relative, Bartholomew de Glanville, was its Constable and it lay comfortably close in the event of civil unrest or seaborne attack. Orford was set to develop rapidly as a port and haven. It had a market, and was easily accessible for travellers. On a practical level Butley Creek would enable building stone to be brought close to the site, whilst proximity to both salt and fresh water would guarantee fish, a staple protein in a monastic diet.

Ranulph and Bertha had decided on a house, not of monks, but of ordained priests, known as Black Canons, living under the rules laid down by St Augustine. In Ranulph's view, the black monks were too gluttonous and the white too avaricious. The house was to be under the supervision of the Bishop of Norwich and headed by his deputy – thus known as prior, not abbot. Its *raisons d'etre* would be: interceding with God through prayer; training priests; giving succour; and providing hospitality.

The actual site needed to be carefully selected if the religious foundation was to prosper. The couple chose an existing farm of 22 acres gently sloping southwards to a brook which meandered across meadows and marshes to join a tidal creek. The fertile soil had previously been cultivated by Roger de Ermingeston who had built a house there, appropriately known as *Brochous*, or Brook House. This brook was no doubt already known by its later name of Okeland Brook and its water utilised to turn a small mill-wheel. Pure water for monastic hygiene trickled from a spring near the already-existing village church. There were reeds growing beside the watercourses and they could be used for thatch in the initial phase of building. Later, the Priory church would be roofed in lead – unlike the nave of the village church which is still thatched with reeds. As in all new monasteries, the first and greatest task was construction of a place for worship. Meanwhile Brochous and its farm-buildings could be utilised.

Gilbert, the first prior

However, in order to achieve the Glanville couple's dream of a great and successful religious foundation, one which would enhance their own status in this life and ensure daily prayers for their own souls after they were dead, they required advice from an established Augustinian house like St Osyth in Essex. They needed help to choose a really able canon to be its first prior and master-mind the years of building work ahead. As it happened the ideal man was available at Blythburgh, a small offshoot of St Osyth's Priory where, it was said, troublesome canons might be sent. Blythburgh Priory was small, but no doubt Ranulph was tipped off that Gilbert, the Precentor in charge of church services, had the expertise he was looking for. An added advantage was that Blythburgh's topography and location was so similar to Butley's that Gilbert would have a ready understanding of the technical and logistical problems of importing stone and building on sand.

An essential step was the paperwork – on vellum of course. The key document was the 'foundation charter', beautifully written in legal Latin.

It was Ranulph's vision that Butley Priory would house 36 canons. For this reason, the buildings were planned on a large scale. The methods used can be deduced. Sunrise over Gedgrave established the east-west axis of the church for which a nave length of 132 ft was initially allocated. It was shaped like a

The 'convent' was dedicated to St Mary and its seal appropriately depicted the Virgin and Child under a Gothic canopy with an adoring monk below. Impression from a small seal matrix of the same design found in the Priory precinct by Alan Calver.

cross in plan with a tower over the crossing. Work on the church had priority. The layout of all the buildings will have been marked on the ground using string and pegs. As construction necessarily extended over decades, the width of walls to be built in the coming years could be made clear by shallow trenches filled with crushed chalk, rather like a giant tennis-court. There was no usable local stone and so limestone was imported from northern France and dark marble from Purbeck. Shallow-draft ships brought it up Butley Creek as far as Rielie Green (Butley High Corner). From there it was a short distance to the building-site. The limestone chippings and offcuts were burnt to make lime mortar, and the common to the north of the Precinct acquired its name of Killhill (Kiln Hill) Green from the lime-kilns sited there.

At an early stage Bishop William Turbe will have visited and given his blessing, but he did not live to see the completion of the first church. It was officially dedicated in 1198 by his successor, John de Oxford, at the request of Ranulph. Prior Gilbert retired in 1192.

The layout of the Priory

The Church lay along the north side of an open space surrounded by a cloister, and was in use at intervals both day and night. On the east side of the Cloister, at first floor level, sleeping accommodation was reached by a flight of steps, known as the Day Stairs. Another flight, the Night Stairs, enabled the canons to descend directly into the church for nocturnal services. Below the Dormitory were a series of rooms, the most important of which was the Chapter House, a beautifully vaulted chamber in which all the day-to-day business of the monastery was conducted before the assembled convent. Visiting dignitaries and benefactors were received there, and it also functioned as the school-room for novices. Between the Chapter House and the Church there was the Sacristy, lined with large cupboards and chests in which the monastery's books, vestments and religious vessels were kept safe. A passage, known as the Slype, gave access to their cemetery to the east of the Cloister.

Monastic plans were fairly standard and Butley's was no exception. Excavations by Dr J.N.L. Myres (left) aided by schoolboys, between 1931 and 1933, when the Abbey farmyard was derelict, established the layout and phases of construction of the cloistral buildings. His fossicking fell well below archaeological standards.

Coming down the Day Stairs in the morning, the canons moved to the south side of the Cloister where, set in the rear wall, there was a linen cupboard for towels and a long trough fed by a lead water-pipe. The concept of cleanliness being next to godliness was made manifest here and in the water-flushed latrine-block, or Reredorter, beyond the Dormitory. After washing their hands canons and novices entered the refectory, or Frater. This long hall extended along most of the south side of the Cloister. The canons sat on benches round the walls with tables in front of them. The high table was set on a dais and there was a pulpit from which one of the brethren read religious texts at meal times.

The west side of the Cloister was taken up with service buildings, known as the Cellarer's Range, with wine cellars and food stores. Between it and the Refectory was the Kitchen. Above these rooms lay-brothers and servants could be accommodated. At the north end of the Cellarer's Range there was an entrance into the Cloister for visitors. Buildings were enlarged, added or rebuilt during the next three centuries.

This then was the core structure of the monastery, but by no means comprised all of it. Of the 22 acres enclosed by the Precinct wall, some 13 were needed to service and supply the monastery. To the east of the church and cloistral buildings lay a 30-acre park. The name survives in the arable field known today as 'Parks'.

Precinct walls were massive. This one at Bungay, founded by another Glanville, Gundreda, still survives to a height of 10 feet.

A substantial gateway, flanked by a porter's lodge and a room where alms were dispensed, controlled access, not only to the monastery, but also to its farmyards and domestic buildings. Not far from the entrance lay the school-house where male children could receive education. Some of the pupils would be fee-paying, but the poorest were free, *'kept of alms to learning'*.

The porter checked all arrivals before opening the small door for pedestrians, or the big double doors to admit wagons, carriages and carts. The visitor then had a view of the north flank of the huge Church immediately ahead of him. Proceeding down the Way he was able to enter by its large west door, since the nave was open to lay folk. Further along the driveway there was a projecting porch sheltering traders and tenants awaiting access to the Cellarer's offices. Beyond the cloistral buildings he will have noticed on his left: the canons' personal gardens and orchards, and two detached convent buildings, namely, the Prior's Lodging and the Infirmary where sick canons were accommodated.

Farm traffic forked right into a huge farmyard forming the western half of the Precinct. It contained barns for storage, its own brew-house, a dovecote, large bakery and numerous farm buildings, also poultry houses, a dairy-house where cheese was made, stables, and numerous ponds.

The Way ran in a straight line south from the Gatehouse to terminate at the convent's own Mill built across Okeland Brook. Its undershot wheel was worked by the combined water from three streams regulated by sluices. Today visible evidence for the monastic mill survives as two millstones in the flowerbed facing its site. Grain grown on the demesne was ground as required to make bread, the staple carbohydrate for everyone before potatoes were brought back from the New World. For security both grain and fleeces from its sheep were stored within the Precinct in large barns. They were similar in size and identical in purpose to the barns created centuries later by the Forth family out of the ruins of the Reredorter and Refectory, and still standing today.

A document prepared immediately after the Priory was closed down lists several gardens within the Precinct. The Prior had a garden and orchard covering about one and a half acres. It no doubt provided vegetables and fruit for his own kitchen. The Subprior had a half-acre garden and the Cellarer an eighth. There was a three-acre garden for the hops needed to flavour beer brewed on the

Timber piles excavated in 1934 will have supported the mill at the southern end of the Priory precinct for which documentary evidence exists. However, John Ward-Perkins identified the badly eroded stumps as a wharf for sea-going vessels, since at that time the river-walls were assumed to be of post-medieval date. Following the East Coast Floods of 1953 the stream was enlarged by the estate ditcher and drainer, Stanley King, adding to the mythology, and in recent publications being mistaken for a monastic 'canal'.

Butley Priory Precinct

layout deduced from documentary and archaeological information

1. Rabbit warren with pillow mounds and guard-house
2. Spring which provided running water
3. Lime-kilns for mortar production
4. Common known as Killhill [Kiln Hill] Green
5. Gatehouse, dispensary and guest accommodation
6. Roadway to a dock on the tidal creek
7. Ash coppice for tools, trades and kindling
8. Sluices to distribute the water supply
9. Pond Yard with fish pond and poultry houses
10. Main Way bisecting the Precinct
11. Bake-house
12. Infirmary
13. Stables
14. Dovecote
15. Garden
16. Barn to store tithe-corn and grain from the demesne
17. Church with crossing tower, stained glass windows
18. Lady Chapel with crypt
19. Cemetery for canons and lay brothers
20. Entrance to administrative and catering block
21. Cloister and garth
22. Chapter House
23. Refectory or Frater
24. Dormitory over warming rooms
25. Latrine block or Reredorter
26. Vineyard for wine or verjuice production
27. Barn for storage of fleeces
28. Prior's lodging
29. Main drain
30. Orchard and garden
31. Retting pits and sheds for hemp processing
32. Brew-house and ponds
33. Tenter yard for stretching finished cloth
34. House for dyeing and finishing cloth
35. Mill for making flour and fulling cloth
36. Bridge over brook to field known as 'Bruers Entry'
37. Jetty over Okeland Brook
38. Home Park, also known as Convent Garden

premises, and another called Drues Garden comprising three ponds within an acre of land. Yards of about half an acre served the Kitchen and Infirmary, the latter lying between the Gatehouse and Bakehouse. No less than one acre was set aside for stretching out lengths of woollen cloth after weaving and finishing and the mill is likely to have been used for fulling them.

Funding and management

The creation from scratch of this large establishment must have daunted Gilbert. Fortunately additional endowments by the Glanvilles provided funds for labour and materials: oak for beams, alder for scaffolding, reeds for thatching, faggots for firing. Masons carved the imported stone, while local men, women and children collected flints from the fields to be used for the core of the walls. Later priors continued the work of building and rebuilding: enlarging the church until it was 235 feet long, its aisles built out to the full width of the original transepts; casting bells for the tower; installing stained glass in the traceried windows; and setting up kilns for firing coloured and patterned floor-tiles. Walls, ceilings and carvings in the convent were plastered and painted, then picked out in gold, roofs were covered in lead, and glazed roof-tiles replaced thatch. At the

Exquisite 13th-century floor tiles with the design in relief. Simpler designs were also excavated in the 1930s.

height of its prosperity, some 25 years before the Black Death, a new gatehouse was built, its frieze welcoming visitors in a blaze of armorial colours [chapter 2].

For Gilbert there was another responsibility: to provide inspiration and guidance for the first intake of canons and to train a successor. Books borrowed from other monasteries enabled copies to be made; in an age before printing the only way was to laboriously copy by hand on parchment. Through the coming years this task was performed on the north side of the Cloister where there was a row of writing desks and a cupboard for materials. Although it was originally unglazed, the Cloister gave shelter from the elements and good southern light came through the tracery, the sun warming the wall of the church at their backs. In summer it could prove uncomfortably hot to sit there in the black habits of their Order and there was pressure for permission to wear white vestments.

The importance of the written word

Butley accumulated an impressive library in which not only bound volumes, but also rolled-up documents and charters with wax seals depending from them, were placed on shelves in compartments carefully marked with Roman numerals. The canons were especially proud of their foundation charter

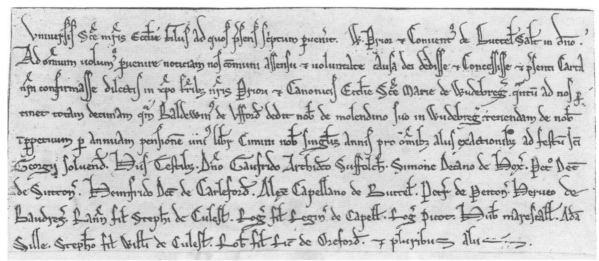

An exchange is recorded. A tiny document, beautifully written, names Gilbert's successor, William. Butley was endowed with a tithe of the profit of Woodbridge Mill, but exchanged this with Woodbridge Priory for one pound of cumin yearly. The imported spice was valued in a vegetarian diet because it reduced flatulence, which must have been an embarrassment in church.

with its Glanville seal stored in pride of place *'in primo loco inter cartas'*. They were proud, too, of the charter which Ranulph sealed two or three years later in the presence of Bishop Turbe and his Glanville and Valoines relatives to endow the fledgling Priory with further land and churches in Suffolk. Ranulph's sister, Gutha, granted the church of Weybread, and his brother, Osbert, the church of Harleston. To the 22-acre site of Brochous was soon added other land: *all the land of Relera. And all the land which belonged to Roger son of Toly in Butteley. And the land which belonged to Ernald the priest in the same ville.* As soon as the Priory was granted the parish church, Ernald's holding could be transferred to it; henceforward the Priory would supply its chaplain. 'Relera' or 'Reileia' has puzzled historians, but a 16th-century survey enables Rielie Green to be identified as the hamlet of Butley High Corner. Ranulph gave them the patronage of the neighbouring churches of Capel and Wantisden, and Gilbert Colville donated that of Gedgrave.

In the spring of 1173 the King granted Ranulph the large wealthy manor of Leiston, plus Upton Manor and 52 shillings annual rent but it required *the service of half a knight*. With a quick legal brain Ranulph promptly rewarded his own steward, Reiner, with Upton and devolved the knight service on him. This move enabled him to endow Butley Priory with the income from Leiston Manor without the military obligation. In 1186 Butley surrendered its income from the churches of Leiston and Aldringham to enable Ranulph to grant them to his new Premonstratensian abbey down on Leiston marshes.

Alongside numerous smaller bequests were placed in coming years vital royal charters in which successive kings (as the ultimate owners of all land) confirmed the legitimacy of the Priory's title to its property. Two of these have survived: Henry II's of 1184-5 issued in his court at Westminster, and Richard Coeur de Lion's of August 1190. The latter was granted on Ranulph's personal petition, while both crusaders were waiting at Marseille for the fleet to take them east to the Holy Land, where Ranulph was to die. Both are in Latin of course but are sprinkled with wonderful Anglo-Saxon words – *'infangentheof'*, *'socha et sacha et thol et theam'*, *'de ferdwita et de hengenwita et de flemenefrenthe et de hamsoca et de warpeni et de blodwit et de fichtwit et de leirwit..'*

Then there were papal documents known as bulls because of their distinctive lead seals, or *bullae*, with images of Saints Peter and Paul on one side and the name of the pope on the other. There were many of these, since the pope exercised ultimate control over the activities of monasteries.

A local man, William of Boyton, was elected by the canons on Gilbert's death in 1195. When Pope Celestine III confirmed the election he granted permission for the canons to hold free elections in future, a permission which contravened the rights of the Priory's secular patrons and was later hotly contested, first by Ranulph's great grandson, William de Auberville. The charter in which de Auberville agreed to grant it to the Priory for ever was safely filed *on the 2nd shelf in the 30th place.*

This was not the end of the matter. The quarrel erupted again after de Auberville's great grandson, Nicholas Kyryell, sold the family's core manor of Benhall. His sole heir, also Nicholas, lived in Kent and was the last direct descendant of Ranulph's eldest daughter, dying just before the Black Death, as one of its manuscripts records. The new owner's widow, Alianore Ferre, appealed to the king in 1334 for restitution of the privileges that had belonged to the manor. At this juncture there was a dramatic scene outside the doors of the newly-built Gatehouse. Helped by three canons, the hot-tempered Prior Matthew de Pakenham refused entry to Alianore. Matthew is the least attractive prior on record. Nine years later he had to pay 100 shillings to be pardoned *for all manner of oppressions, extortions and excesses committed by colour of his office,* some no doubt committed while he had been a taxation commissioner for Suffolk in 1334.

It seems that, although Matthew was allowed to continue in office, the Crown subsequently ignored Pope Celestine's grant of free election, for we find that patronage of the Priory was restored to the owner of Benhall Manor.

Plough-damaged 'bulla' of Gregory IX found near the Priory by Alan Calver.

Bronze padlock from a medieval casket, found on the Priory demesne by David Boast.

14th century enamelled harness mount with the arms of an Ufford lord or lady, benefactors of the Priory, found in its park by Alan Calver.

Consolidating the Priory estates

Slowly land was added; a most important addition was *the gift of Hugh, son of Peter, of the whole part of the Bruer which belongs to his feod of Capell next to the grove of Staverton.* This was possibly the single largest acreage added to the home farm, since it comprised more than a thousand acres of sheepwalks on the 'bruer' or heathland. During the next two centuries monastic exports of wool to Flanders were hugely profitable and the Priory's large flocks shepherded over heaths, marshes and river walls will have helped to fund its ambitious building programme.

Some time in the 13th century the Priory received a benefaction from John de Capel which consolidated their local landholdings. A document in their archives recorded that homage was paid to the Earl of Suffolk for lands which John de Capel formerly held from him. Another document showed that his daughter had subsequently relinquished any claim to the land on payment of two marks yearly. However, in 1341, Thomas Belhomme applied to the Court at Westminster to reclaim property which his grandfather, Thomas Belhomme, had possessed when he died. Canon William de Elyngham attended the Court to defend the Priory's interests. He counterclaimed that Thomas Belhomme was the great grandson of John de Capel who had granted to the canons of Butley in perpetuity *all his messuage with buildings in the town of Capel with land and appurtenances in Capel, Tangham, Wantisden, Butley, Boyton and Laneburgh with all freemen, villeins and villein tenements . . . to the said canons . . . forever.*

The importance of the monastic archive now becomes apparent. Elyngham was able to produce the original charter granting the lands to the Priory: *I, the said John ... will guarantee to the said canons ... all the prenoted land, including all heirs both Christians and Jews, as a measure of eternal mercy...* The phrase, *'heredes tam Christianos quam Judeos'*, is so unusual that an explanation is needed. In 1275 Jews, already barred from Heaven by Pope Gregory IX, were barred by an English statute from being *'levant and couchant'* among the general population. By 1290 writs required all Jews to leave England on pain of death. The specific mention of Jewish heirs implies that John's father had married a Jewess and their son had sought to save the souls of his family by means of the gift of his estate.

Scandal at the leper hospital

From time to time scandals impinged on even the apparently calm atmosphere of Butley Priory. One was sufficiently serious to reach the King's Bench during the reign of Edward I and another had to be referred to the Pope's representative.

An unfortunate result of the Crusades was the scourge of leprosy brought to England by returning crusaders. Benefactors set up hospitals to cater for them; Orford as a port had need of two. At West Somerton north of Yarmouth, Ranulph and Bertha founded a hospital for 13 lepers. Ranulph entrusted its management to the priors of his monastery at Butley, and provided a generous endowment in the form of the Manor of West Somerton. Its income was later valued as sufficient for 30 lepers.

However, towards the end of the 13th century there was mounting concern at the way the hospital was mismanaged. Following charges laid at the King's Bench, the king took over direct patronage of the hospital. Prior Thomas had to undertake to maintain as many lepers there as the manor could support, and no longer charge them for admission. The manor's value was £60 7s 9¼d, sufficient to support and maintain at least 13 lepers with a staff of guardian, chaplain and clerk.

Despite royal supervision, conditions in the hospital continued to be kept hidden from the outside world. Lepers were not allowed out; they were forced to take an oath not to complain, nor *to climb trees to talk to their friends,* while the Prior's guard dog deterred visitors. The building was inadequately maintained and a dovecote in the cloister had collapsed. The Prior proceeded to ignore a court order requiring him to rectify these matters and to admit poor and needy lepers. How far some of the accusations can be taken seriously is a moot point, but for them to have been made at all suggests that they were not beyond belief. It appears that a separate house within the hospital was used by the Prior and some of the canons for all-night parties with local officials, their staff and womenfolk – all at the lepers' expense. The house had a hall, chamber, solar and chapel and the Prior's retinue included named squires and pages with their horses and greyhounds.

The lepers found a champion in the person of Roger, the parson of Mutford, who incited them to take matters into their own hands in October 1297. Outsiders helped to expel the canon in charge. Provisions and chattels were seized: 15 quarters of wheat, 30 quarters of barley, 8 silver spoons, 2 wooden bowls, 9 swans, 80 hams, bread, beer and fish. In addition they dismantled a nub of contention, namely, the canon's private chapel, removing vestments, a chalice and a missal. There they found the chest in which were kept key documents relating to the hospital: 30 court rolls, 30 charters and a rental, all evidence of their collective ownership of the manor. These they sent to the literate champion of their cause, the parson Roger. The lepers next took control of the manorial court, raising 100 shillings from the customary tenants, confident that under *Magna Carta* they could not be convicted of stealing what was their own property.

Despite the lepers' action, it is clear from what ensued that conditions at their hospital did not improve: the Prior failed to present proper accounts; he was accused of appropriating for his own use £100 of the profits of the manor; and was convicted and fined 100 marks in January 1298. The sorry tale of neglect continued. A century later the hospital was derelict and said to be worth no more than 10 marks a year. Corruption apart, the vignette presented by West Somerton illustrates both the difficulty of managing distant properties and the worldly life-style of prelates whose main pre-occupation was necessarily administrative and not spiritual.

The corpse that moved

A scandal that divided clergy occurred late in the life of the Priory. One of the brethren kept a chronicle where the incident is described in rather muddled Latin. The then prior, Robert Brommer, was absent on 25 May 1509 and hanged himself in the house of Richard Cardon in Ipswich. No reason was given for his suicide, and Cardon

The Priory servants included women who worked in the laundry and dairy. Miniature from a medieval East Anglian manuscript showing women carrying sheep's milk. Medieval jug from the Priory stream, 12 ins high.

is otherwise unknown, but perhaps the Priory's mounting debts were weighing on his mind. The prior's deputy, William Woodbridge, took over and, since it was out of the question for Brommer to be buried alongside his predecessors within the Priory church, or even in its graveyard, he ordered interment in the parish churchyard next to the path on its west side.

Robert Brommer must have been a respected Christian, for the Prior of Tortyngton and one of the canons appealed to the Pope. The following June they obtained authority to remove the corpse and inter it in a better position close to the south door of the church. This caused an uproar in the village and parishioners appealed to their bishop, who was of course the titular head of the Priory. On 26 September they received a mandate from Bishop Nix and at 7 a.m. marched up to the cemetery to exhume Prior Brommer.

His final resting-place was outside the consecrated ground on the wide verge beside the road to Haughfen Street, the settlement at the west end of Mill Lane. Unfortunately, this historic site is now being damaged by farm vehicles. There is a reference to a cross here at the end of the 16th century. No doubt it was erected to mark the grave where he still lies.

The last priors

Augustine Rivers was Robert Brommer's successor. Despite the exactions of Henry VIII, he managed to leave its finances on a sound footing when he died in 1528. He was succeeded by the last prior of Butley, Thomas Manning, who took the name Sudbourne, and appears to have been more concerned with his own preferment than the well-being of the convent.

As his story is intimately involved with its closure by Thomas Cromwell it appears in the next chapter.

The second largest church in Suffolk

In Butley the only visible clues to the former existence of its great church and cloister are a single arch, visible from the bend in the road by Abbey Farm, and a few fragments of masonry, now scattered in village gardens or incorporated in old flint walls.

The surviving south transept arch at Butley.

Orford Church: remains of Norman chancel.

Remains of the crossing tower of Orford church (above) which was contemporary with that at Butley. From a Butley rockery a single surviving voussoir is of the same design (above left).

Column bases of Purbeck marble from the cloister built about 30 years after the Priory was founded.

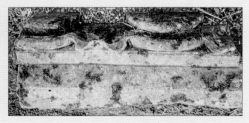

Continuity and Change:
the last Priors and their Servants

Chapter 2

The most enduring legacy of Butley Priory is its Gatehouse which has survived as a dwelling for 625 years. At the height of its prosperity, some 25 years before the Black Death, a great gatehouse was built at Butley Priory.

In an age before hotels it lodged travellers and visiting dignitaries, a blaze of brightly-coloured shields advertised royal, ecclesiastical and noble benefactors, while the Virgin Mary and other saints occupying its niches conferred a heavenly protection. The paint and pinnacles have long gone and the original parapet can only be conjectured.

The suicide of Prior Brommer must have cast a shadow over the monastery which was in any case beset by other problems. Marsh pasture was the key to dairy farming and butter and cheese were essentials in a monastic diet and also profitable merchandise. For hundreds of years the Priory maintained earth banks to keep out the rising sea-level while its salt marshes were managed for the production of sea-salt by the evaporation of brine. However, the low-lying pastures were increasingly damaged by high tides which overtopped the banks. In 1516 flood water even reached the Precinct walls. Consequent diminution of income, combined perhaps with poor management, led to a burden of debt, while the huge old buildings required upkeep now beyond its resources.

Against this background the final decades of life at the Priory took place. Following Henry VIII's confiscation of all its lands, there were successive changes of ownership. Scheming noblemen were soon succeeded by 'new men' ambitious to become estate owners. To what extent did these men displace existing staff or alter the way the lands were managed and farmed?

Rich pickings

The year 1509 when Henry VIII came to the throne coincided with a time of crisis for Butley Priory. The bishop must have realised this, for he overturned the brethren's choice of William Woodbridge as successor to Prior Brommer in favour of a brilliant administrator. This was Augustine Rivers, a Butley canon who had been promoted, and was head of the Woodbridge Augustinian priory. His return to manage Butley was doubtless prompted by Thomas Rush, a wheeler-dealer married to the Prior's own sister and already advancing himself as *'servant of the King'*. Rush took an increasing role in monastic

Detail from John Norden's survey of the Sudbourne Estate. Thomas Rush had a country house called Chapmans just across the river, on the site of the later mansion. He was thus in a position to know what was going on in the Priory.

affairs, acting as Thomas Cromwell's agent and making inventories of valuables. In 1528 he brought to the Priory a rich casket, a gift from the King's sister. Seven years later he was recorded at the hub of the Priory's management, as chief steward with the then large stipend of four pounds.

Prior Rivers was in office from 1509 until 1528 and deservedly popular. He encouraged benefactors, such as his neighbouring Suffolk magnate, Lord Willoughby, and brought in as his administrative assistant the wealthy layman, Henry Baret, making available to him as residence the old prior's

> Henry Baret died in 1516. From his will we gain an image of the man. He left all his property to the Priory with bequests for glazing the south windows of the new hall, for whitening both sides of the Refectory and for the construction of Butley Bridge. He asked to be buried in the nave of its church next to his wealthy friend, William Pakeman. Henry's handwriting survives as beautiful accounts which as bailiff from 1493-1508, he had kept for Wantisden and outlying monastic properties.

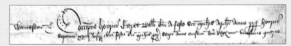

Wantesden   Account of Henry Baret Bailiff there from the feast of St Michael the Archangel in the XXIIIrd year of the reign of King Henry VII to the following feast of St Michael in the twenty fourth year of his reign.

quarters. He did much to put the house's finances in order, spending 100 marks of his own money on the repair of buildings, granges and manors. He will also have had to embark on a programme of strengthening and raising the centuries-old flood defences.

Perhaps Rivers' most important achievement was in the sphere of public relations. He placed the splendid Gatehouse accommodation at the service of a number of distinguished and influential people, such as Charles Brandon, Duke of Suffolk.

A less welcome guest was Brandon's rival, the Duke of Norfolk and his heir, the Earl of Surrey. The Howards were lords of the neighbouring manors of Hollesley and Staverton, and visited for wild-fowling and fox-hunting. In 1528 he pressed the Prior to expend £240 to buy Staverton Park from

The most prestigious guests were Henry VIII's own sister Mary, ex-Queen of France, and her second husband, Charles Brandon, Duke of Suffolk, who had holidays there. Their first visit in June 1516 was the occasion of a most elaborate welcome, described at gushing length in the Priory's Chronicle. *In 1518 the Duke and Duchess became lay members of the Augustininan Order along with the King, Queen and Princess Mary. From this time a special relationship was fostered by Prior Rivers. Charles Brandon was to find this relationship equally useful for his schemes to develop his power-base in Suffolk.*

Records of visitations by the blind old Bishop Nix supplement the *Chronicle*'s description of the unceasing struggle to maintain the buildings. Damp penetrated the lead roof of the church for years and in 1524 the rood was so rotten that it crashed to the floor. The canons took comfort in the fact that the image of the Crucified Christ suffered only slight damage from its fall. To add to continuing troubles both the parochial church and the Priory were burgled in 1534 and many valuables stolen.

The last prior and his family

Thomas Manning was instituted to a specially-created bishopric of Ipswich two years before the closure of the Priory in 1538. His enthronement in 1536 together with other perks induced him to surrender peacefully the second largest monastic house in the county. The King's commissioners received the surrender on 1 March and the Prior, anxious about his pension, quickly wrote to Thomas Cromwell. To accompany the letter to the Lord Privy Seal his servant took a present of '*vj fesaunt cokkes & iij herynsuys*'.

The suffragan bishopric included no stipend, but Manning was granted the occupation of the splendid Ipswich mansion of Lord Curson who had recently died. His income was further supplemented by the mastership of Mettingham College. It had been the practice for the Priory's canons to serve as priests in its churches and as vicars of the prosperous parish of Debenham. However, in 1529 the Prior had had himself instituted as vicar of Chillesford. His wealth was sufficient for him to make several purchases before his death in 1544. He left the annual profits of his manor of Mendham, his houses in Orford and Woodhouse Close in

him, an amount the Priory could ill afford at this time. The Prior was trapped in the uneasy relationship between the rival dukes, and needed to keep on the right side of both.

Through his brother-in-law, Prior Rivers will have been privy at an early stage to Cardinal Wolsey's plans to close down poor and failing monasteries in order to release capital from their property. The funds were to be used for Wolsey's proposed new ecclesiastical college at Oxford University and grammar school at Ipswich. From the Priory's *Chronicle*, which covers the whole of this period, it is clear that, as far as Butley was concerned, there was no initial disapproval for this step. Indeed the run-down monastery at Snape had been foisted on Butley Priory at the King's behest, and one of the first actions Rivers took when he became prior was to divest Butley of the burden of running it.

Central medallion from an Italian majolica dish found in the Priory precinct is likely to have belonged to one of its wealthy lay residents, such as William Pakeman or Henry Baret. The sherd was trimmed by its finder, Leonard Kittle.

Butley to relatives. His nephews Thomas and Augustine Brooke, who had attended the priory school, each received 20s per annum. His lands in Westleton were to be sold to provide for the education of his many nephews' children. Chillesford Church benefited from the gift of a red satin vestment depicting the Tree of Jesse, and the churches of Butley, Wantisden and Capel were left 13s 4d each. This shows that the church at Capel was functioning as late as 1544. He also gave 13s 4d for the repair of Chillesford Mill.

Manning's main property was the Manor of Russells in Chillesford. He purchased it from William Waller and bequeathed it to his nephew John Haughfen.

He asked to be buried in Orford Church *directly before the Blessed Sacrament at the choir door'* were he to die within three or four miles of the town. Orford church received £5, a book called a coucher, a grail and a cope of white satin. Manning was a local man and his brother Robert, other relations and ancestors were buried in Orford or its mother church of Sudbourne. The close connection of whole families with the Priory and of some with the Prior himself is shown in the *Household List* and in the will of the first employee known to have died after the Dissolution. Subsequent employment of the Mannings and Haughfens and the schooling of the Brooke children at the Priory show how blood relatives were given places there.

Robert Haughfen was the brother-in-law of Prior Manning and died 14 months after the Priory closed. He had been one of those attending the cattle or responsible for the sheep, that is, a sheepreeve rather than a shepherd. His wife Joan worked in the Laundry and Dairy. His son John was a *'servant in husbandry'*, that is, a farm labourer. Robert lived in Chillesford and owned a house and farm in Sudbourne which he let complete with mares, beasts, ploughs, harrows, carts, plough harness, cart harness and harvested corn to James Marett when he began to run the ex-prior's newly purchased Manor of Russells. Rent arrears of £4-12s-4d, stock and equipment were to be recovered for the benefit of his son, John. He asked his executors, his wife and son, to act with the *'counsel and advice of my lord suffragan'*.

Russells Manor, Chillesford, was mapped by Norden in 1601. Its moated manor-house lay conveniently for Manning opposite the church. William Waller esquire of Ipswich died in 1516. He was wealthy, owning Peyton Hall Manor in Ramsholt as well as the manors of Russells in Falkenham and Chillesford. After the death of his widow, his son was to inherit the properties apart from the Chillesford manor, the profits of which were to be employed for 20 years to fund the dowry of his daughter. Manning must have taken on the encumbrance of the dowry when he purchased Russells.

The Priory priests

In March 1538 when the Surrender of the Priory took place, the names of the resident canons eligible for pensions were listed, as were the staff who numbered sixty seven. We lack evidence that any of the 12 canons continued to serve the local churches as priests. However, one of them, Nicholas Oxburgh, was still around to write the will of William Barfote of Boyton in May 1539.

Occasionally original wills contain information not transcribed into the probate registers. For example, in 1529 as a young man, Nicholas Oxburgh appended a note to the diocesan official to deal kindly with the widow of Thomas Grey:

'Master Sente, I honestly recommend me to you and pray you be good friend to this poor woman for it is the first will that ever I made and therefore I would do her good in it if I could. Wherefore I pray you honestly for to be good friend to her at this time.'

In 1542 John Sone, Lord of the Manor of Chillesford, noted at the foot of John Awod's will that he had called at his house in Boyton where he lay sick:

'When I lighted off my horse and went to speak with him and demanded whether he had made his will or not. And he said "I hath sent for John Jaye and will make him and my wife my executors".'

He described himself as Syr Nicholas Palmer, using the name he was given at birth, and he was asked to sing a trental at the church for the soul of the deceased. Later he became the rector of Sternfield. Monks were offered pensions of five or six pounds, payable by those who had profited by the Dissolution and had been granted monastic lands. However, if the new owner could present the ex-monk to a living, the pension would be rescinded. Monks who found livings in some other way would retain their pension plus a stipend. It is difficult to trace the Butley canons after they dispersed because they no longer used their priestly

Canons lodged at the Priory in 1538	
John Bawdesey	John Norwiche
Robert Chipnam	Nicholas Oxborowe
John Colcestr'	Thomas Ryvers
Henry Denyngton	Reynold Westerfeld
Jamys Denyngton	Thomas Woodebregge
Johannes Harwiche	Robert Yngham

name based upon their place of birth. This explains how Prior Thomas Sudbourne born Manning in Sudbourne became Bishop Thomas Manning.

For a while the churches at Capel and Gedgrave continued to be places of worship. The only clues as to who served them are to be found in wills of the period. The scrivener writing William Cokeson's will in 1540 used both the term 'clarke' and 'Syr', which is how the canons and non-graduate priests had been titled. Thus Reynold Blanchflower was probably the minister at Capel and may equate with Reginald Westerfield, one of the

Canons known to have served as priests in local parishes in the 16th century	
BUTLEY	
1518	Robert Chippenham
1528	Thomas Sudbourne
1528	Denis Metcalfe
1529-34	Robert Chippenham
CAPEL	
1508	William Woodbridge
1519	James Dennington
1540	Richard Nicholson
1540	Reynold Blanchflower
GEDGRAVE	
1510	Robert Chippenham
1518	Reynold Westerfield

resident canons who signed the Surrender. In the same year, Thomas Punt of Capel gave Syr Richard Nycholson *'for his labour'* twenty pence. As both the testators had been previously employed at the Priory, he will have been familiar to them.

The Priory servants

The cellarers of Butley Priory had managed its accounts. For instance, during 1469 the cellarer, John Hollond, had to undertake major repairs to the Priory malt-house; his payments to three craftsmen survive. The carpenter William Camewold charged 5s for 12 days repairing the woodwork; Henry Chapman supplied 48lb of iron for this work and charged 6s 5d for labour and iron; he also supplied 200 'resewenayll' costing 8d and 3,000 lath nails for 3s 8d; and William

Lath construction once universal in the Sandlings exposed during repair work to The Forge in Tunstall during 2007.

Stebbing charged 5s 10d for the lathing of the building.

For 350 years a Prior had retained direct control of the manors comprising the demesne. Surrender to the Commissioner, William Petre, took place without resistance, unlike some other places. Henry VIII took all the monastic assets into his own hands and set up a Court of Augmentations to administer them. For nobles, the richer gentry and merchants the next decade provided an extraordinary opportunity to acquire large tracts of land which had been out of circulation and to make quick profits

When the Priory closed in 1538 a list was made of the entire household. It included men and women whose skills continued to be needed in the three parishes.

Alen	John	baker & brewer
Barfoote	Joan	laundress & dairymaid
Bastyan	William	in the pantry & buttery
Bekett	Thomas	carver
Bene	Thomas	horseman
Bestowe	Robert	kitchen boy
Bryghtwell	John	plough-maker, wheelwright
Burwell	Edmund	keeper of the granaries
Byngley	Robert	baker & brewer
Chaundeler	John	in charge of farm-workers
Chaundeler	Austeyn	farm-worker
Chaundler	Henry	carter
Clerke	Thomas	smith
Cokett	William	farm-worker
Cooke	William	cooper
Cooke	Joan	laundress & dairymaid
Cookeson	William	surveyor & outrider
Dawson	Alexander	slaughterman
Denny	Richard	in the pantry & buttery
Derker	Thomas	farm-worker
Drue	William	keeper of gardens & ponds
Eve	Robert	farm-worker
Fereby	Bartholomew	under cook
Fox	John	carpenter
Furton	Thomas	warrener
Gawge	John	plough-maker, wheelwright
Halowtree	Robert	shepherd
Haughfen	Robert	sheep reeve, overseer of pasture
Haughfen	Joan	laundress & dairymaid
Haughfen	John	farm-worker
Hethe	Robert	carter
Heywood	Marget	laundress & dairymaid
Hill	William	malster
Ingram	John	candle maker, keeper of the fish-house
Jay	Thomas	shepherd
Jaye	John	sheep reeve, overseer of pasture
Kempster	Austeyn	farm-worker
Knott	John	chief cook
Kyng	Henry	carter
Leche	John	carter
Legge	Thomas	carpenter
Lyon	Richard	in the pantry & buttery
Mallyng	John	usher of the hall
Maners	John	keeper of the swans & pullets
Mannyng	Thomas	barber
Mannyng	Robert	farm-worker
Matthewe	Joan	laundress & dairymaid
Mersshe	Robert	farm-worker
Munday	Thomas	malster
Nevell	William	boat-keeper, fisherman
Parker	William	farm-worker
Pawling	William	lame & feeble
Pullen	Simmon	boat-keeper, fisherman
Pullen	Thomas	boat-keeper, fisherman
Punt	Thomas	warrener
Punte	Henry	candle-maker, keeper of fish-house
Pyke	Robert	horseman
Reve	Robert	boat-keeper
Royston	William	understeward
Sampson	William	baker & brewer
Shelle	William	keeper of the swine
Smyth	Robert	carter
Stoker	Richard	keeper of the infirmary
Stookes	William	farm-worker
Studham	John	boat-keeper, fisherman
Sympson	William	porter
Vynterer	Robert	shepherd
Wheteley	William	farm-worker
Woodcrofte	Kateryn	laundress & dairymaid

from their resale. In the case of the Priory its outlying manors of Wantisden, Chillesford, Gedgrave, Boyton and Bawdsey and properties further away were disposed of separately from the core manors of Butley and Tangham.

The Duke of Suffolk obtained the site of the monastery with the Butley and Tangham manors and granted a twenty-one year lease to William Naunton, his household treasurer, although the full term was not completed. Within months the Duke exchanged these manors for others in Lincolnshire, and the Duke of Norfolk acquired them, to relinquish them some six years later. Was this rapid change of ownership matched by disruptions to the lives and jobs of the employees?

Those working on the land must have continued much as before and names occur in the *Household List* which can be related to surviving wills, from which it appears many staff farmed in their own right as well as serving the Priory.

From a valuation of 1535 comes the information that John Jaye, Richard Denny and Edmond Burwell were Priory bailiffs. Three years later they were differently described in the Household List: John Jaye as one of those *'attending to the cattle and pasture'*; Richard Denny was *'in the pantry'*; and Edmond Burwell was *'keeper of the garners'*.

A prior had a very exacting administrative job and required well-qualified managers to supervise the various farming activities and keep accounts and other records. Tithes and rents, which included poultry and eggs, needed to be collected and the duties required of tenants, such as to keep their hedges and ditches maintained, had to be supervised.

The description of their responsibilities in the *Household List* may sound lowly to modern ears, unused to the vital role that subsistence farming played in catering for a large community. John Jaye will have had responsibility for the monastic livestock bred not primarily to provide meat but rather milk, cheese, wool, hides and oxen for the demesne plough-teams. He will have directed the sheep-reeves and the shepherds in the movement of flocks and herds over marsh pasture, river embankment and heath, controlled the dipping of sheep and division into flocks of wool-producing wethers and of breeding ewes. He had to summon owners of sheep on the commons to attend and mark their animals. The sale and purchase of livestock will have been another responsibility. Most importantly, for the fertility of the demesne ploughland he needed to ensure that the sheep were folded where their manure was most needed.

For Richard Denny being *'in the pantry'* meant that he was working under the Cellarer, the canon with responsibility for the fabric of the monastery and for feeding inmates and providing beer and wine which were consumed daily. Beer was brewed on the premises from barley fermented there and flavoured with the produce of its adjacent hop yards. While there was a vineyard in the Precinct, most wine must have been imported as were spices and delicacies. Richard will have gained experience of

---

Spices were extremely expensive

One prior received 1lb of cumin annually *in lieu* of his tithe of Woodbridge Mill.

In the early 14th century Leiston Abbey was buying, per pound, liquorice at 6d, sugar at 1s, ginger at 1s 8d, and cloves at 3s.

As a price guide, in the same accounts a pig cost 4s.

---

catering for the Infirmary sick, the Prior and his guests, for all of whom meat dishes would be required.

Edmond Burwell as *'keeper of the garners'* for the household had a huge responsibility. Grain was the staple of the monastic diet – wheat from good lands, rye from poor and barley to malt the all-important beer. Within the monastic enclosure he supervised the water-mill where corn was ground on a large scale to supply the bakehouse and the brewery. Most importantly, he had charge of the great barns in which were stored its tithe corn and the demesne grain and wool.

Two of these educated men can be traced subsequently; John Jaye was already prosperous and Richard Denny did well for himself after the Dissolution. When Jaye died in 1541 he had more substantial holdings than other recently-deceased Priory staff.

John Jaye was taxed on goods worth 20 marks in 1524. By the time of his death he occupied tenements, meadows, heaths, pasture and feedings in Wantisden and Rendlesham and left the *'third part of ten'* to his widow, Isabel. His widow was to regard the fraction as her dower and in addition she inherited four cows, 40 ewes and two horses, one his *'blake ambelyng nayge'*. The bequest of 6s 8d to repair Snape Bridge perhaps reflects his earlier career travelling around the manors.

Richard Denny purchased the lordship of Raines in Alderton. The Suffolk Chorographer writing soon after 1600 made the cryptic remark that Denny was *'a servant in Butley Abbey, which service was his making'*. Since he worked under the Cellarer one interpretation is that he gained valuable management experience; another is that he was in a good position to filch some of the Priory's catering supplies.

The incident, described on page 18, in which he was involved, hints at actual felony.

Other Priory servants

William Cokeson of Capel, who was bailiff of Finborough and Harlesden in 1535, rose to the top post in the *Household List*, being described there as the *'surveyor and outrider of lands'*. His will was written in 1540 when he was *'labouring in the extremities of death, not able to declare and express his last will and testament in writing for hastening of death'*. Therefore, in the presence of five men one of whom was John Kempster, he made his nuncupative will. Kempster was described as a *'bedeman being impotente'* in 1538, that is, he was available in the Priory to pray for others, but unable to do physical work. Like the other household staff he was eligible for a pension after the closure. The substantial sum of 3s 4d was left by Cokeson to the poor of both Capel and Butley. He bequeathed his house and lands to his wife Maude and after her death to his son Dennis who had been educated at the Priory school. He also had two daughters and to each he left a cow, three ewes, a silver spoon and a

Non fee-paying pupils at the Priory school in 1538. The schoolmaster was Robert Fale.

Brooke	Thomas
Brooke	Austeyn
Burwell	William
Cookeson	Denys
Fale	William
Hoode	Richard
Ide	John

'lockeram' sheet to have at the day of their marriage. He was one of the last people to be buried in the churchyard at Capel crossroads.

John Mawling, the usher of the hall at the Priory in 1538, did not leave a will. His widow, Agnes, who died in 1558, compensated by leaving a long and detailed one.

She mentioned many people, including Augustine Brooke 'my kinsman', to whom she bequeathed 'one able mylche cowe'. The children of Augustine and of three others were to receive 30 shillings between them. Her nephew and niece were bequeathed money also. Next came her four servants who were given a calf or ewe, or money in lieu. Amounts of sixpence were given to a whole list of people ending with 'poore Besse'. Among the recipients were Henry Punte and Widow Furton. Henry had been responsible for making candles and keeping the fish house, and Thomas Furton was a Priory warrener. Several other beneficiaries bear the same surnames as people previously employed there and they are likely to be related.

Thomas Punt, another warrener, died in 1540. He left his wife his house in Capel and his sons received cows and money. One of them was also bequeathed a young mare. Thomas Stabyll was to have back the 'gelding that I had of him', and Walter Culling a sorrel colt. The first tenant of the dissolved Priory demesne was granted 'totum profitum cuniculorum super terris dominicalibus dni' (all the profit of rabbits on the demesne) and no doubt Thomas kept his job.

Those working on the Priory lands were probably needed to continue to work the farms unlike the many vagrants who trudged the roads. Of the others listed, two of the children at the school, Augustine and Thomas Brooke, appear elsewhere, as do Richard Denny and John Malling. In the main the Priory servants seem to have formed a tightly knit community living in Butley, Capel and Boyton.

What happened to the Priory plate?

If tracing those on the *Household List* was difficult, it was a pure accident that clues to the fate of Priory valuables were found. The chance survival of a single sheet of paper from a case brought to the Court of Star Chamber before 1540 comprises a statement made by Thomas Punte, in reply to questioning. It illuminates the cryptic remark made by the Chorographer about Richard Denny. An index in The National Archives assumes that this piece of paper relates to a case of arson between Agnes Denny, and Thomas Punt and others.

However, a close reading of Punte's replies shows the real reason for the burning of a mere shed to come before one of the highest courts in the land. Punt said he understood from Agnes that she had been in the service of the late Priory of Campsey for ten years. While out at night batfowling with Richard Denny and Davy Walsham they came across a fire in the hemp house belonging to Agnes's mother. Within the thatch, which they were presumably stripping off to contain the fire, were found various goods which must have come from a monastic house. There were 15 or 16 silver spoons, one of which was a 'great gilt spoon graven with imagery', a chalice and paten, a 'knop' from a silver cross, a silver mazer, money to the value of a dozen or so pence and a couple of hollow keys.

The accidental discovery of this cache of plate was of course what had triggered a top-level court case. The outcome of the case is unknown, but their subsequent wills are proof that neither Punt nor Denny was found guilty of the theft. Punt may have been deflecting attention away from Richard Denny, most probably a relative of Agnes, by mentioning her service at Campsea Ashe Priory.

Working in the pantry and buttery of Butley Priory, Richard was perfectly placed to steal refectory plate, and to secrete these in places like the Denny family's thatch. The fact that he was able to purchase the Manor of Raynes in Alderton after the Dissolution suggests he came by some serious money from somewhere. The three men, according to Punte, were going *'a-batfowling'* that night. This nocturnal activity involved dazzling birds with a light and knocking them from where they were perched in order to catch them. Nets may have been used and the warrener would certainly possess these.

Confirmation that no silverware was found at the Dissolution comes in the Commissioner's letter stating that there was lead at Butley worth £1000, but no other riches except cattle. The inventory of Campsea Ashe Priory records its plate, so it is likely that the silver found in the hemp-house thatch was spirited away from Butley.

A further incidental discovery of the fate of a monastic vessel from Butley Priory derives from the will of Agnes, the widow of the Ipswich cutler, Thomas Sawer. She died in 1550 and left her son *'the best brass pot and kettle made of the lamp of Butley Abbey'*. Such a lamp had burned before the Rood, that is, the Crucifix flanked by Mary and John,

Two gallants using batfowling apparatus – in their case to collect butterflies. They hold a clap, or batfowling net, a deep gauze bag up to six feet long, of U-shaped section and suspended from rods.

which stood above the screen between chancel and nave.

At many levels people looked to benefit from the closure of the monastery: the King, the Dukes, Prior Manning, his family, the monastic pensioners and even an Ipswich cutler.

The fate of two monuments, formerly in the Priory church.

Some 15 years after the Dissolution, when the Catholic Mary came to the throne, the grave slab of Prior William de Geytone was salvaged by men from Hollesley. Minus its brass, it was inverted to make a stone altar, as is proved by the consecration crosses on the underside.

As soon as the Protestant Queen Elizabeth came to the throne it had to be removed. Today it can be seen in the floor at the back of the church. Prior William died in 1332. He it was who built the Gatehouse.

Freestanding limestone torso ploughed up to the south of the Priory fish-pond. It was possibly part of a monument to a Butley prior licensed after 1398 by the Pope to wear bishop's regalia, like that above.

Warrens

In medieval times the hunting of game, 'free warren' required a royal licence. The Priory obtained a licence of free warren for its Butley manor in the reign of Edward I. However, the word was also applied to the enclosed areas of arable in which rabbits were bred.

Fourteenth-century pillow mound painted by an East Anglian monk, complete with terracotta pipes and black rabbits.

Rabbits, like sheep, were an important resource for Sandlings folk: monks, burghers and peasants used coney fur to keep out bitter winds. Black and silver-grey pelts were always the most valuable. During recurring agricultural depressions or whenever crops failed, rabbit flesh, together with eels, oysters, wild birds and fish, helped people to survive. The sandy heaths provide ideal breeding grounds.

When the Normans brought conies from sunny Spain, they were not burrowing animals. 'Pillow mounds' with artificial burrows had to be constructed for them to survive the cold. Their enclosures were guarded by warreners. One of these can still be seen on Sutton Common – a circular bank enclosing 5¼ acres and a mound today some 40 by 120ft and 6ft high. Butley Priory had numerous warrens on its manors, as incidental references show. Thus Wilfred Scut and his son John were caught in 1388 poaching conies with dogs and nets in the Butley warren.

At the Dissolution in 1538 Thomas Punt and Thomas Furton were listed as warreners on the demesne. They will have tended the conies in Broom Close from a lodge recorded nearby. A pillow mound surviving there due to later incorporation as a field bank was surveyed by the authors. Today it is some 6ft high and measures about 30 by 140ft – its southern end truncated by a crag pit.

A surviving pillow mound silhouetted against conifers on Broom Hill, Butley.

Black rabbits are easy targets for shotguns but still manage to breed in the Triangle.

When the Priory closed, the lease granted to the Alderton farmer, William Naunton, included all the profit from rabbits in the demesne. Subsequently the Forths and succeeding tenant farmers continued to find warrens profitable, whether kept in hand or let to individual operators. Use of the commons for warrening had to be paid for: a Tudor manorial document records the 'cunny money' owed by men in Eyke and Bromeswell. By the later 18th century rabbits were breeding in the wild and had become a nuisance.

Chillesford's light land must always have been ideal for breeding rabbits, but unfortunately few old records survive. In the 1901 census the 26-year-old William Chittleborough described himself as 'Rabbit warrener'. He lived in a cottage at Chillesford Brickyard. Reg Snowdon was born in the village in 1921. He recalled that as soon as he left school aged 13 his father sent him to Charles Field to work catching rabbits. Field taught him to make nets and snares; they would sit in his shed and make nets 100 yards long from twine. Field would buy the right to catch rabbits on surrounding farms from September until April and might be charged as much as £50. For some farmers and workers the income from rabbits enabled them to survive downturns in agriculture.

The Forths, Winthrops and America

Chapter 3

During the 15th century the Forths of Hadleigh became very wealthy clothiers, possessing property in London, Suffolk and Essex. Redistribution of land following the Dissolution of the monasteries gave one of them the opportunity to become a landed gentleman in the Sandlings Triangle. Towards the end of the 16th century a Forth marriage led to the birth of a daughter whose marriage to a Winthrop had a profound influence on the future United States of America. The families held the same religious beliefs.

Window in Groton church, Suffolk, commemorating the marriage of John Winthrop and Mary Forth in 1605.

For family historians the challenge of tracing back generations of ancestors is an almost addictive task. For local historians the trail also runs forward; wills, parish records, manorial documents and indentures are key sources of information about ordinary folk and gentry alike. Additionally, gentry families with coats of arms were visited by College Heralds in order to update the births, deaths and marriages recorded in their voluminous *Visitations*. Other contemporary sources, such as court cases and correspondence, need to be used in conjunction with these, as even the Heralds occasionally slipped up.

Portrait of the Suffolk cloth merchant, Sir Thomas Gresham, showing the costume in vogue when William Forth purchased the Priory estate. On the left is his mark, impressed on lead seals identifying his cloths. William Forth's mark is not known.

The Hadleigh Forths

The town of Hadleigh where the Butley Forths originated was a hot-bed of radical religion. Its clergy were not under the jurisdiction of the Bishop of Norwich, whose See covered both Norfolk and Suffolk, for the reason that it was a 'Peculiar' under the Archbishop of Canterbury. This explains how after 1533 Archbishop Thomas Cranmer was able to send evangelical Protestants to Hadleigh, to the chagrin of the elderly, blind, traditionalist Bishop Nix.

When the Catholic Mary came to the throne in 1553, Cranmer and other leading Protestants were arrested and eventually burned. Many prominent Protestants fled abroad, but others lived secretly, mostly in London. Although her sister, Elizabeth, reversed Mary's religious changes, she was against Protestant extremism. The so-called Classis Movement of evangelicals that flourished in the 1580s in places like Dedham, was suppressed in 1593, after prosecution in the Court of Star Chamber.

The William Forth who died in 1504 has been called the patriarch of Suffolk clothiers. Around 1470 he ranked second only to John Stanysby of Bildeston in Suffolk in the production of woollen cloth, while the Lavenham benefactor, Thomas Spryng II, was merely seventh. William had a mansion-house on Watling Street and moved in influential City circles. His daughter Elizabeth wed Thomas Baldry, an Ipswich man who became a London Mercer and was elected Lord Mayor of London in 1523.

William left a *'holy water stoupe of silver'* to Butley Priory *'to be prayed for under such form as it shall be ordered by mine executor and his counsel'*. This evidence for the patriarch's connexion with the Priory 40 years before his grandson purchased the monastic estate surely marks an association based on the purchase of the wool, yarn or textiles produced from its 3,000 acres of sheepwalks. He was a merchant as well as a cloth manufacturer.

In addition to the cloth processed in the Priory precinct, spinning and weaving was work which could be performed by men and women in their homes. A single will shows that John Candler was probably working in Boyton on his own account as a weaver

before 1510. The five and a half yard lengths of 'blanket' which he bequeathed to his mother and daughter are likely to have been fulled at Boyton's water-mill beside which there was a Draper's Yard recorded in 1568.

In 1538 parish registers were made compulsory and on the first page of the marriage register of St Denis Backchurch, London appear the names of William Forth and Elizabeth Powell. This was the Forth whose business sense led him to purchase the Butley estates with the sheep walks and means of cloth production there. In 1540 he inherited his father Robert's house in Hadleigh, including its tenter yard.

From a search of the records held in the Hadleigh Archive, it is quite clear that William did not play an active role in the town. Perhaps he was based mostly in London, the centre of the cloth business. His name appears only once endorsing the accounts of the Hadleigh Market Feoffment Charity. This was in 1547 when he was also among the many who purchased church goods and gild property no longer required by the 'new' religion. He bought goods worth only £5 as against his brother-in-law's, £150, but the green Lenten cloth and white damask altar cloth, latten candlesticks and 45 vessels, once used by the gilds at their meals and celebrations, will have graced his dining table.

Continental weavers stretching cloth. Below, William Forth's purchase of Butley itemised the one-acre monastic tenter yard, where finished cloth would have been stretched on tenterhooks.

The dangerous years

While Edward VI was on the throne, life was good for Protestants, but everything changed when the King died young and his half-sister, the Catholic Mary, raised her banner at nearby Framlingham Castle in July 1553. For the many Suffolk Protestants the future was dangerous. Soon after Mary was crowned, William Forth was dismissed as a Justice of the Peace and his rival, Walter Clerke, who was among the first to give allegiance to Mary at Framlingham, was appointed in his place. A year or so previously servants of the two men had caused an affray over a piece of land near Hadleigh.

It was not long before Archbishop Cranmer along with Ridley and Latimer were in prison awaiting trial for heresy, having been found guilty of treason. Their trials resulted in their being burned at the stake. The same fate befell Rowland Taylor in Hadleigh, whose death led to emotional scenes in the town. The last hope for the overthrow of Mary failed with the defeat of Sir Thomas Wyatt's rebellion in Kent in February 1554. This may have prompted William Forth to make his will on 1 March, although he lived for another four years. His preamble simply bequeathes his soul to *Almighty God, my Creator*, unlike the expressions used by Catholics.

What did he do in the dangerous years while Mary was queen? He may have contemplated leaving the country as did his former business partner, Richard Morison, who was to die in Strasbourg in 1556. Although the majority of the exiles were propertied, a few poor Protestants fled abroad. Three 'poor weavers' from Hadleigh and their wives also took refuge in Switzerland, at Aarau; they must have been members of Rowland Taylor's congregation. Some Protestants remained in England, managing to escape persecution, especially in London, so William may have stayed in his town house.

There were places where those of like mind could meet secretly. Most conformed by attending church, but read their Bibles at home and took part in Protestant communion services at such places as inns under cover of attending a play. Twenty six persons of wealth, known as the Sustainers, helped finance those abroad and those leaving the country. Their names were kept secret and William may have been among them.

The Butley Forths

The creation of a market in real estate, following the wholesale confiscation of monastic lands, enabled some well-placed merchants and courtiers to become landed gentry. Richard Morison, a member of Henry VIII's household, was in such a position. He joined with William Forth in 1545 to purchase the 'reversion' of the Manor of Boyton which the King had used with other monastic property to fund Anne of Cleves' generous settlement when he divorced her.

When William Forth acquired the *'site of the late monastery of Butley'* some of the buildings survived in a more or less usable state. He might have anticipated building a residence there, but if he had intended to do so, the religious climate necessitated a low profile and in his will he describes himself as *'of Hadleigh'*. He died in December 1558, barely a month after Elizabeth became queen, but aware that for his descendants the immediate danger had passed.

Apart from his Sandlings manors he owned land in Hadleigh, Aldham and in Essex and London. He left his wife, Elizabeth, her dowry of one third of his properties and all his goods except his chain of gold weighing nine ounces, worth the huge sum of £30, and his sheep at Boyton, which he left to his eldest son, Robert. His other sons, Philologue, William, Israel and John were bequeathed lands in and around Hadleigh. His two daughters, Anne and Katherine, were left 300 marks each when aged twenty one.

Although the Butley estate was leased to a farmer, William Redham, it is clear that William Forth placed his trust in John Mawling, who had been listed as the 'usher' at the Priory in 1538. He left £20 to the poor of Butley and Capel. Out of this, trustees, of whom Mawling was one, were to purchase land for the poor. Mawling himself was left 40s yearly for the remainder of his life. This enabled him to lease a farm in Butley, choosing either Geldinglees or Clarkes. In due course the trustees purchased two further properties, Moyses and Haughes, the income from which was distributed to the poor.

Robert Forth's early success

Robert married into a long-established Suffolk family. His wife Frances Glemham came from Benhall and they married in the church there on 7 July 1562. She bore him three sons and eight daughters and outlived him. Unfortunately no portraits of the family survive, but we know that Frances owned a gown of silk and was left a taffeta gown and a satin *'forefair'* by her mother.

A lost country house

The Butley Mansion-house was described by a local historian at the beginning of the 18th century when Mrs Clyatt was living there:

'Tis an old decayed and irregular structure contiguous to the East side of the Gatehouse, having but one wing on the front and a portal adorned with four pilasters of the Doric Order, two below and as many above, all of freestone, as is likewise the Entablement. Over the door are the Arms. The Gate hath for ornament two pilasters and their pedestals of freestone of the last-mentioned Order, both on the outside and inside thereof are Arms.'

Thus in common with other Suffolk Tudor houses, such as Christchurch Mansion built by Edmund Withipoll, or Erwarton Hall built by Robert's friend, Sir Philip Parker, the house was of local brick. Its front entrance was flanked by a pair of fluted pilasters of limestone, flanking the Forth-Glemham coat of arms which will have been brightly painted. At first floor level there was another pair of columns below a pediment. To the east it was approached through Home Park and an ornamental gateway emblazoned with Forth arms. Its irregular plan resulted from its attachment to the medieval Gatehouse which provided additional accommodation on the upper floors, while the ground floor was a useful storehouse for building materials and fodder for horses. The Gatehouse continued to function as the entrance to the stable yard. Altogether there were more than 20 bedrooms.

The description of the dining room suggests that Robert Forth enjoyed entertaining (He was remembered as being *'famous for Housekeeping'* 60 years later):

'..the wainscot painted a copper colour adorned with fluted columns of the Ionic order with intercolumnar quadrangular panels on which are two small fluted pilasters supporting an arch in the centre of which is a fleur-de-lis, the whole copiously gilded, the whole said to have cost not less than £50. The ceiling has panels of crocket work and the windows have coats of arms in stained glass.'

His inventory shows that turkey and goose, oysters and claret would have appeared on his table.

The original paintwork on the front of Hengrave Hall, built by Thomas Kytson, another wool merchant contemporary with William Forth, has recently been restored.

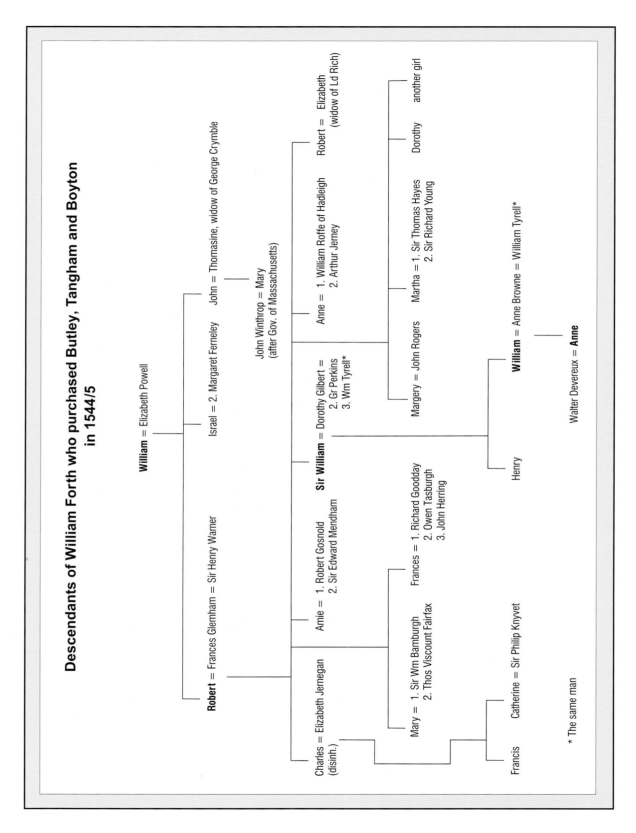

Descendants of William Forth who purchased Butley, Tangham and Boyton in 1544/5

William = Elizabeth Powell

Robert = Frances Glemham = Sir Henry Warner

Israel = 2. Margaret Ferneley

John = Thomasine, widow of George Crymble

John Winthrop = Mary
(after Gov. of Massachusetts)

Robert = Frances Glemham

Anne = 1. William Roffe of Hadleigh
2. Arthur Jerney

Robert = Elizabeth
(widow of Ld Rich)

Dorothy   another girl

Sir William = Dorothy Gilbert =
2. Gr Perkins
3. Wm Tyrell*

Margery = John Rogers

Martha = 1. Sir Thomas Hayes
2. Sir Richard Young

Henry

William = Anne Browne = William Tyrell*

Walter Devereux = **Anne**

Charles = Elizabeth Jernegan
(disinh.)

Amie = 1. Robert Gosnold
2. Sir Edward Mendham

Frances = 1. Richard Goodday
2. Owen Tasburgh
3. John Herring

Mary = 1. Sir Wm Bamburgh
2. Thos Viscount Fairfax

Francis

Catherine = Sir Philip Knyvet

* The same man

The armour and weapons in Robert Forth's hall were valued in 1601:

34 bills, 5 holbards, 3 lance staves and
1 lighthorseman's staff – £4
9 corselets, 2 Almoine ryvetts and 4 pikes
with the swords and daggers and 3 Calivers
with their flasks and butch boxes – 15s

'Almoine' or Almain rivets were comparatively inexpensive suits of armour worn by light-horsemen. Distinctive slides on the arms enabled the hand-guards to be retracted.

Robert was the first Forth to live at Butley where he built a grand house. One of Suffolk's now-lost country houses, it was attached to the east side of the old Gate-house giving it an unfashionably asymmetrical appearance. An inventory taken in 1601 shows that it was of three stories over cellars, and provides information on its furnishings. The same year John Norden happened to indicate the house and the park on which it fronted on his small-scale map drawn for Michael Stanhope. The derelict house can be glimpsed behind the ruined Gatehouse in an engraving made in 1738.

Robert's grand dining room was the setting for a meeting of Suffolk's Deputy Lieutenants on 24 January 1588. Philip Parker, Robert Jermyn and Robert Wingfield accompanied Capt. Turner to ride along the entire Suffolk coast *'in which journey most of the gentlemen appointed to be captaines in this county have travailed with us, upon which view some places show great danger . . . laying open before [the enemy] a most large and champion county to march upon with very maine and great battles.'* The chill of January will have made the warmth of the fire very welcome as they sat around Robert's table to compose their report to Sir Francis Walsingham. They urged him to ask the Queen to contribute £1,000 towards coastal defence, assuring him of their loyalty and their control of recusants.

In common with so many landowners Forth took his turn as Sheriff of Suffolk and JP, and with his eldest son Charles, was at the camp at Tilbury in 1588 when preparations were being made to defend the capital from a Spanish attack up the Thames.

He was required to furnish a lance and horse, obligated by knight service to his sovereign. This was attached to the Butley estate his father purchased from Henry VIII. The knight service for his manor of Boyton devolved upon his tenant, John Fox, as appears in the court roll entry of 1573.

In addition Acts of Parliament required gentlemen to maintain specified weapons and armour for the defence of the realm. The silk and velvet gowns of their spouses were assessed for the provision of war-horses. Justices were empowered to search and view. Robert kept five geldings in his best stable and had 41 working horses.

Robert Forth's later difficulties

The two charters granting the Butley, Tangham and Boyton manors make it possible today to compare the demesne lands at the very end of the monastic period with the terrier which Robert had made of Boyton in 1568, and the survey made of Butley, Boyton and Capel in 1594. Following this survey Robert drew up the indenture disinheriting his eldest son, Charles, whose disastrous marriage is described in another chapter.

From manorial records and his will it transpires that he placed his estate with trustees between 1588 and 1595 and again before his death in 1601. The trustees were Robert Lord Rich, Sir Philip Parker, Sir Henry Glemham, the Attorney General Edward Coke, Leonard Spencer, John Osborne, Thomas Hayes and Anthony Morse.

Of his eight daughters, six reached adulthood, and two married particularly well, requiring Robert to find marriage portions which must have placed a strain on his finances at intervals. Just how little cash was available became clear to his widow after his death. She was reduced to borrowing £60 from one of her tenants and had difficulty in proving that the estate could provide for a suitable marriage for her second son, William.

Robert Forth's extremism

Robert Forth's religious convictions were as strong, if not stronger, than those of his father. He was keen to make sure that

Boyton House, the former rectory originally built for Thomas Agas c.1560. It lies north of the site of the medieval manor-house and the main road known as the Portway.

suitable 'godly' ministers served the churches where he held the advowson. One of these was Thomas Agas, who wrote four wills for different people between 1567 and 1568. He described himself as *'minister of Butley'* or *'parson of Boyton'* and occupied the rectory built for him in Boyton. The identical preambles give a clear indication of Thomas Agas' beliefs. One will, that of Robert's servant, Margaret, was witnessed by Robert's brother Israel and is, incidentally, evidence that the Mansion-house was built by this time.

It is clear that this clergyman served all three parishes, although by this time Capel church had fallen into disrepair and was no longer used. This was not necessarily as much for reasons of economy on Robert's part as due to a shortage of educated clergy

---

Thomas Agas' successor was Daniel Devies. He was installed as rector of Boyton in 1573. He remained rector until at least 1608 and raised his family there. The spelling of the rector's name caused problems; he appears as Deiwis in the records of the military muster at Snape in 1588 when he was required to arm himself with a bill.

Robert Forth had built the rectory for Daniel's predecessor. It was described in 1568 as having rooms suitable to maintain the household. It lay on the site of the present rectory (now Boyton House), set in 16 acres bordering the Laneburgh river to the north.

---

of his religious persuasion. Long before this the Catholic trappings would have been stripped out of the little parish churches and the walls whitewashed. The Forth family replaced the glass of the east window of Butley church with clear glass inset with their coats of arms.

Robert and the Essex Forths

Robert Forth was convinced by his eldest son's precipitate marriage to a Catholic whilst away at school of the need to have his younger sons educated at home. A suitably qualified person was required to take on the

The Classis Movement comprised evangelicals in various parts of the country, who wished to do away with bishops and form groups of 12 parishes into a 'classis' to deal with local matters. They intended that delegates from these would form a provincial synod and above this would be a national synod. Even the Queen would be a mere member and not Head of the Church. The movement began around 1570 and, although suppressed in 1577, it continued under ground. Only the chance survival of the *Dedham Minute Book* begun in 1582 enables us to understand this secret organisation.

task. The obvious place to look was not far away at Dedham on the Suffolk-Essex border where he had property.

One of the houses where the Classis was in Stratford St Mary. It was shared by Anthony and Edward Morse and their mother Julian, an aunt of Robert Forth. Anthony Morse must have fancied himself as a preacher because in January 1587 he asked the Meeting whether he might preach at Mr Forth's of Butley *'to exercise his gift'*. He applied to the bishop who would not allow him to preach as he was not ordained. However, the Classis would not let the matter rest and William Tay, an ordained minister, went to Butley soon afterwards. He was prepared to take the living although it paid very little, but was uncertain whether it was safe to do so without authority. His colleagues wanted him to take it that he *'might do well to serve the Lord in that place'*. This must have fallen through, because in October 1587 Anthony Morse suggested that he should go to Butley until *'Mr Forth got himself a preacher'*.

These evangelicals placed a particular emphasis on weekly lectures, normally held on Thursdays in church. They had a strong social conscience and were prepared to make up the wages of those who could not afford to lose pay to attend the lectures. The poor were visited in their cottages and even invited to the tables of their better-off neighbours. Robert Forth did obtain a preacher a

couple of years later, and he was Thomas Reddrich who transferred from his previous parish of Hutton near Brentwood, Essex. Reddrich's major role would be as tutor to the younger Forths. He was paid £20 a year and he and his wife were accommodated at the Mansion-house. The 1601 inventory shows he had a posted bed and tester, valance and curtains of saye valued at 20 shillings. The Reddriches were allowed to reside there after Robert's death.

Robert's youngest brother John was also one of the 'godly'. He married a rich widow, named Thomasine, and settled down as a gentleman at Great Stambridge in Essex on property which was his wife's dowry. They had only one child, a daughter named Mary, who married John Winthrop early in 1605. Diaries kept by John's father, Adam Winthrop of Groton, record visits to Stambridge and return visits by John Forth, each to view the other's properties. After the financial arrangements for the forthcoming marriage were completed, Adam recorded that his son was solemnly contracted to Mary by Ezekiel Culverwell on 27 March 1605 and married on 16 April, the bridegroom *'being 17 years 3 months and 4 days old'*.

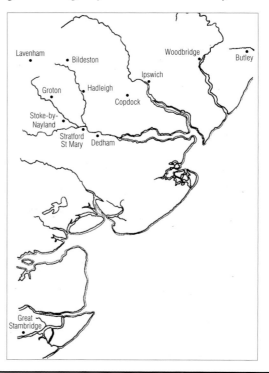

John Winthrop, a Suffolk landowner and evangelical, whose first wife Mary died before he emigrated to the New World. Their son became the first Governor of Connecticut.

This hasty marriage and young John's abandonment of his studies seems evidence of a passionate attachment. Less than a year later their first child, John was born, followed by five more children, before Mary died in childbirth in 1615. John senior married twice more, his third wife Margaret joining him in New England after his arrival there on the *Arbella* in 1630. John senior became the first governor of Massachusetts and his son, that of Connecticut. Thus the Forth family's puritanism, allied to that of the Winthrops, had a direct effect on religion in New England and the future United States of America.

The Fateful Marriage
Chapter 4

The landscape and remains of buildings or objects can recreate for us the environment and possessions of long-dead people. Old documents have to be searched to bring the past alive. Most of these are laconic records concerned with the administration of property and assets. Some, such as wills, can provide clues: sometimes a husband uses loving words for the wife he is leaving behind, at others making scant provision for her widowhood. However, buried within legal jargon covering large vellum documents, the pride and the passion – and the heartbreak – is sometimes there to be found.

This story is set in Elizabethan England and concerns the upheaval caused by a Suffolk Protestant boy's marriage to a Catholic girl in Norfolk. He was Charles Forth, heir to the Butley estates and she was a Jernegan, a branch of the family who had helped to secure the throne for the Catholic Queen Mary in 1553.

The home of the girl in this story, Somerleyton Hall (here depicted after later alterations to its facade), had an elaborate entrance like the Butley home of the boy with whom she fell in love, but of which no pictures survive.

Elizabeth showed herself to her people as no monarch had done before. In an age without mass media it was a most effective way of cementing their loyalty.

The setting

England underwent several religious changes in the 16th century. However, Queen Elizabeth trod a path between extreme Catholics and rampant Protestants. The latter, who included Robert Forth and Richard Wingfield at Wantisden, liked to be known as the 'godly', or the 'elect'. The Queen stamped down on all extremists, although her main concern was with the Catholics, because at times of impending invasion by Spain she was uncertain of their support. Thus from time to time they were imprisoned or heavily fined. Among her loyal Catholic families in East Anglia were the Jerninghams and Bedingfields who, like the Protestant gentry, normally married within their own socio-economic groups.

The process of making a valid marriage involved four stages: first, betrothal which comprised solemn promises; next the reading of banns or the acquisition of a special licence; then the wedding in church; and finally, consummation. Between the betrothal and the marriage ceremony there were usually negotiations, in the case of the propertied classes concerning jointures and dowries. A jointure was provided by the groom's family for the bride should she be left a widow, whereas a dowry was the money brought to the marriage by the bride. It was the custom for newlyweds to live with the bride's parents until the birth of their first child, but thereafter the groom's family was expected to provide them with a permanent home.

Charles and the Norwich schoolmaster

Robert Forth's heir, Charles, was baptised at Benhall, where his wife's parents lived, in July 1565. When he was about seven Charles was sent to school in Norwich, to be brought up in *'the fear of God as in learning and the knowledge of the Latin language'*. There Charles was placed with Mr Burde, *'a very reverend, grave and godly schoolmaster'*. He had been headmaster at Norwich School, but resigned during Mary's reign. He must have been an old man because he had taught at the 'Common School' in Henry VIII's time, receiving 100 shillings for half a year's salary in 1545.

Later in life Mr Burde taught privately in Norwich with a class of about 20 scholars. However, he did not keep a close watch on his pupils in the eyes of the Forths in Butley, and did not inform them of developments. When Charles was about 14, he was highly likely to have witnessed Queen Elizabeth's state tour of East Anglia. He may even have taken part in the entertainments provided by Norwich schoolboys who, attired in white, made short speeches or disported themselves as water nymphs.

Elizabeth Jernegan

Charles met Elizabeth Jernegan, who was two years his senior, while he was still at the school and they fell in love. According to his father, Charles was *'withdrawn from his love of learning'* by Elizabeth and her mother.

Elizabeth's family came from a higher social stratum than Charles'. Two of the Jerningham branch of the family had distinguished themselves as warriors in the reign of Henry VIII and had become gentlemen of the Privy Chamber, while Sir Henry Jerningham had played a prominent part in securing the throne for the Catholic Queen Mary. For his part in defeating Wyatt's rebel army when it attacked Whitehall he was rewarded with the large manor of Costessey to add to his other property in Norfolk, and Wingfield Castle in Suffolk. Sir Henry built Costessey Newhall, a manor-house where at the time of this story his widow entertained Queen Elizabeth.

The Jernegan branch of the family held the Manor of Herringfleet and their seat was at Somerleyton. The Jernegans were one of the oldest gentry families of Suffolk, having lived at Somerleyton since the mid-13th century. Elizabeth's mother was sister to Lord Cobham, later Queen Elizabeth's Lord Chamberlain. However, in 1570, 12 years or so before Elizabeth and Charles fell in love, her father John Jernegan led a disturbance in Norfolk. Surprisingly he was pardoned. A *quid pro quo* was required; he was sent to the Netherlands to spy for England, ostensibly a Catholic exile. Four years before the Spanish Armada, he warned the Queen's spymaster, Walsingham, of the *'malicious design of Spain against Her Majesty'*.

Jernegan was so useful to the Privy Council that he was twice given protection against creditors, because he had *'certain matters depending before the Lords to be determined'*. Thus it is evident that he was not only short of money but also absent on the Continent at the time Elizabeth met and married Charles. His career throws an interesting light on the part played by leading Catholics loyal to the Queen.

Charles was only 17 in 1582 and his parents knew nothing of what was happening away in Norwich. When they found out they attributed the secret union to Catholic *'cunning and sly practices'*. Some hint of the religious gulf between the two families can be gleaned from Robert's subsequent declaration that *'no earthly or worldly thing*

Oxburgh Hall. Both of the moated gentry houses to which Elizabeth fled when she was pregnant have survived. She stayed at Oxburgh Hall for four years. It was there that Frances, her older sister, lived with her husband, Thomas Bedingfield, whom she had married in 1580. They had two sons, Henry and Thomas, the 'sweet babes' to whom Elizabeth refers in her letter.

Thomas died in 1590 and, as minors, the children became wards of the Queen and were placed under a Protestant tutor in London. However, Frances' second husband, Henry Jerningham, purchased the wardship and took over the running of Oxburgh Hall. In 1607 he willed the wardship to his wife, their mother.

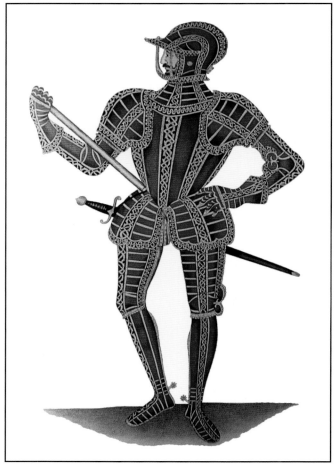

The two sets of light armour in the Forth home at Butley contrast with the exquisite inlaid German armour of Charles Forth's patron and employer, Lord Buckhurst. He was one of Queen Elizabeth's ambassadors and Charles will have accompanied him to Holland in the critical year when Spain was preparing to launch an invasion of England from there.

could more offend or discontent' him and his wife. However, it was a *fait accompli*.

Charles' future seemed assured as heir to the Butley estates, and he was also a beneficiary of his widowed grandmother, Marie Glemham of Benhall Park. He and his sister, Ann, were each left £100, Charles when aged 21 and Ann at age 19.

The boy must have been popular locally, for in his teens John Long of Capel bequeathed to him the *'sucking colt'* to be *'taken off at Hallomas from the dame'*. He had also been left by John Hatch of Butley in 1580, *'a double sovereign or double ryall in value worth twenty shillings'*.

After their marriage Charles returned with his bride to the Mansion-house at Butley

and, according to Robert Forth, they were quite content for five years, although this must be doubted. When she became pregnant the problem arose as to whether the forthcoming child should be brought up as a Catholic or not. Elizabeth and Charles went to visit her married sister, Frances Bedingfield, at Oxburgh Hall where she stayed for the birth of their daughter Catherine. In the event she remained there for four years, rather than return to Butley with Charles.

Elizabeth was at Oxburgh Hall when Thomas Bedingfield died in 1590, and must have been a comfort to her grieving sister. In his will he left his sisters-in-law, Elizabeth Forth and Katherine Jernegan, five marks to buy rings to remember him by.

Meanwhile Robert and Charles were playing a part in national events. Charles had been placed in the service of Lord Buckhurst, Queen Elizabeth's cousin, chief diplomat and former Lord Treasurer. Buckhurst had married Sir Henry Glemham's eldest daughter, Anne, and the Forths are likely to have been on intimate terms with him. In the Armada year of 1588 Robert commanded a troop of 500 and with Charles was camped at Tilbury to protect the Capital. It was an opportunity for Robert to try to persuade his daughter-in-law to return to Butley to keep company with his wife, although unlikely in view of the *'sharpness of air between them'*.

The continued separation of the couple had become something of a scandal, and in 1591 an attempt was made to resolve the matter by Lord Cobham, Elizabeth's uncle, and Lord Buckhurst. Her father-in-law agreed that she should return to Butley and be maintained with the £300 paid by the Jerninghams at the time of the marriage, while he would provide a jointure for her. Others were keen for there to be a reconciliation, and three months later, on 6 March 1592, Elizabeth was escorted back to Butley by the Bishop of Norwich, and Charles Cornwallis and his wife. Unfortunately when Elizabeth arrived Robert undid the good intentions of all parties by upbraiding and shaming her in the hearing of his friends. He said that it was *'better to come late than never'*; that he would forget and forgive

After the death of her husband, Thomas, in 1590, Frances Bedingfield married her close relative and her sister Elizabeth's supporter, Henry Jerningham. A contemporary inventory of Wingfield castle survives and lists more than 20 chambers, including those for *'my mistress'* – that is, Frances – for Henry Jerningham, and *'Mrs Forth's chamber'* with an inner chamber. Elizabeth Forth's room contained the following, *'four pairs of Arrys, a bedstead, a woolbed, a featherbed and bolster, two stitched blankets, a coverlet of Arrys lined, a livery cupboard, a Turkey carpet, an old window carpet, a chair lined with bone, a needlework cushion, a low stool covered with drops, a window cushion green silk, a pair of dog irons, a firepan and a chamber pot.'* The 'inner chamber', the only one thus positioned in the castle, must have been for Elizabeth's daughter, Catherine. Here there were *'a bedstead, a mat, a featherbed, a bolster, a red blanket, a tapestry coverlet with the Kingston's Arms, a tester of white linen, a brushing board and a necessary'.* There was little overtly Catholic in any of the rooms apart from Henry Jerningham's which contained a tester with the picture of Christ and elsewhere there was a coverlet of images.

We can picture Elizabeth in her room enclosed by the rich tapestries, teaching the four-year-old Catherine to stitch and learn her prayers. Sometimes she must have sat on the window cushion wondering whether Charles would ever return to her. The coverlet with the Kingston's Arms will have come to the castle through Henry's grandmother.

Eighteenth-century engraving; much of the castle including its gatehouse and moat survives.

her, and that she would be treated kindly if she merited it.

Not surprisingly she gave him no words of thanks, by which he concluded she was *'an obstinate person.'* Not only that, she with her *'lewd manner, abusage, but wilfully and with stomach, persisted in her disobedience and undutifulness'.* Did Robert in using the word 'stomach' in this context recall words he had heard the Queen utter at Tilbury? In her speech to the army she is claimed to have used the expression, *'I know I have the body but of a weak and feeble woman, but I have the heart and stomach of a king…'*

Elizabeth was at Butley for the next seven weeks, continuing to be a trial according to her father-in-law. She declared herself sickly and ate in her chamber and had a garden for her own use. Another child was conceived and while Robert and his wife were out of the way for two hours attending a religious lecture, Elizabeth's friends came for her and she and Charles left for the long ride to Norfolk. Her sister, Frances, now lived with her second husband at Wingfield Castle and Costessey (Cossey) Newhall. Robert knew she wanted to visit her sister to recover her health, but only Charles returned. A week before Christmas she gave birth to a son who was christened Francis.

Her father-in-law was now prepared to maintain her in his house in Butley but not elsewhere, nor would he provide a jointure should she become a widow. Her family had for their part provided for her with the dowry of £300 raised by Henry Jerningham by borrowing money from his mother, Lady Jerningham. The subsequent court-case came about because the Jerninghams wanted the dowry to be repaid in order to support Elizabeth. The loan from Lady Jerningham had to be repaid at £10 a quarter and the money applied to the relief of poor Catholic prisoners in London.

The birth of a male heir had changed everything; Robert now had the prospect of a Catholic grandchild inheriting the Butley estate. Things turned really nasty when accusations began to be made on both sides.

A law-suit was laid in London at the Court of Requests on 2 May 1593 by Elizabeth in conjunction with her brother-in-law, Henry, as her father had died the previous year. This court existed to hear cases on behalf of the poor, which Elizabeth technically was. She stated that her children were *brought to great distress and in danger to perish*. The lengthy legal documents are the source for much of this story. The complainants claimed that Elizabeth requested maintenance for herself, her children and servants, and also demanded a jointure at

various times with no response from Robert Forth. She had received nothing during the five years since she was first absent from Butley. Moreover Robert Forth had recently conveyed all his lands and tenements to his two younger sons, thus disinheriting Charles and, therefore, Elizabeth's children. They believed this was contrary to Common Law.

Since maintenance was not forthcoming, Elizabeth sought the return of the £300, which had been her dowry, so that her family could maintain her. She asked for further money to support her children (his grandchildren), and the £100 which had been given to Charles and Elizabeth by their friends for their upkeep while they were away from Butley. From her point of view the case seemed straightforward and four days later she wrote to another relative, Sir Robert Cecil. The letter reveals that Elizabeth wanted to use her uncle, Lord Cobham's name in her Bill of Complaint, because he had been *privy to payment of most of my portion*. He was unwilling and she had, therefore, withdrawn that complaint and exhibited another in the name of her brother-in-law, Henry Jerningham, and her own.

It may seem strange that she wrote to Sir Robert so soon after entering the Bill to court, but the clue is to be found in her words *for the avoiding of further expenses in suit*. In her opinion her only fault was marrying Charles without his father's consent. She wanted Sir Robert to persuade

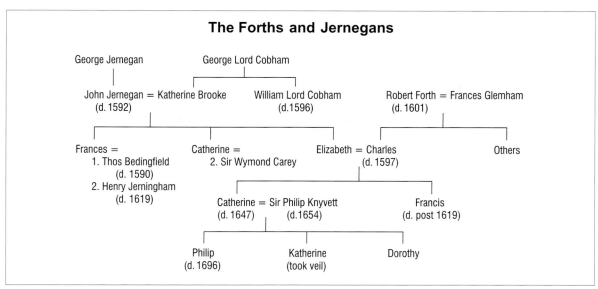

The Forths and Jernegans

George Jernegan
|
George Lord Cobham
|
John Jernegan = Katherine Brooke (d. 1592)   William Lord Cobham (d.1596)   Robert Forth = Frances Glemham (d. 1601)

Frances = 1. Thos Bedingfield (d. 1590) 2. Henry Jerningham (d. 1619)   Catherine = 2. Sir Wymond Carey   Elizabeth = Charles (d. 1597)   Others

Catherine = Sir Philip Knyvett (d. 1647) (d.1654)   Francis (d. post 1619)

Philip (d. 1696)   Katherine (took veil)   Dorothy

William Brooke, 10th Lord Cobham, was painted with his family in 1567 by an unknown artist. His second wife stands on the right and a lady, presumed to be her sister, holds baby William on her lap. They are shown supervising the children who are seated round a dining table laid with pewter plates, a gilt goblet and fruit. On the left of the bowl is a baby's rattle – four little bells on a drum.

Lady Cobham was one of the Queen's Ladies of the Bedchamber, although her frequent pregnancies necessitated absences from court. Within less than eight years of marriage she had produced the six children shown here, sons on the left and daughters on the right. The eldest girls were the five-year-old twins, Elizabeth and Frances, with their younger sister, Margaret, aged four.

Lord Cobham's nieces, the Jernegan girls, Catherine, Frances and Elizabeth, were seven, five and four years old respectively at this time. One can visualise them, similarly dressed, visiting Cobham Hall, and playing with their cousins and their exotic pets.

Years later, William was concerned at his niece's unhappy marriage and sought a reconciliation with her father-in-law. When Elizabeth next had need of him, he was too involved in affairs of state to help. Her cousin Elizabeth (centre) by this time had married Robert Cecil and it was, therefore, natural for Elizabeth also to appeal to him for help.

Nothing shows more clearly the social gulf between Robert Forth and the Jernegans than this portrait. If Robert had been able to overcome his religious prejudices, his family would have acquired connexions at court and this story a happy ending.

A letter from Elizabeth Forth to her loyal sister Frances was discovered wrongly catalogued among the Jerningham papers. Written in her own hand, it gives a candid picture of her situation.

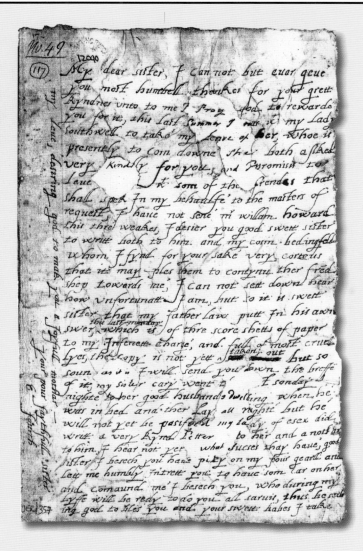

My Dear Sister,

I cannot but ever give you most humble thanks for your great kindness to me. I pray God to reward you for me.

This last Saturday I visited my Lady Southwell to take leave of her. She is presently to leave town. She has asked very kindly after you and promises to leave •••• with some of the friends who are to speak on my behalf to the Master of Requests.

I have not seen Mr William Howard for three weeks. I desire you, Good Sweet Sister, to write both to him and to my cousin Bedingfield whom I find for your sake very courteous and pleased to continue their friendship towards me.

I cannot set down here how unfortunate I am, but so it is, Sweet Sister, that my Father-in-Law submitted his own sworn testimony this last Monday. It runs to 60 sheets of paper to my infinite cost. It is full of most cruel lies. It is not yet copied, but as soon as it is I will send you a précis of it.

My sister Cary went last Sunday all night to her good husband's dwelling when he was in bed and there lay all night. However he is not yet passified. My Lady of Essex wrote a very kind letter to her and another to him. I have not yet heard what success they had.

Good Sister, I beseech you to have pity on my poor girl, and let me humbly entreat you to care for her. Command me, I beseech you. All my life I shall be ready to serve you in every way. Beseeching God to bless you and your sweet babes, I take my leave, desiring God to make you a joyful mother.

Your poor faithful sister, E Forth.

her father-in-law to settle quickly. A secretary wrote the text of the letter, and Elizabeth added her signature. Unfortunately for her another Spanish invasion loomed and both men were preoccupied: Cobham, as a Privy Councillor, Warden of the Cinque Ports and Lord Lieutenant of Kent, and Cecil, Secretary of State and the Queen's right hand *'going through the chamber like a blind man with his hands full of papers and his head full of matter.'* Parliament had to be recalled to consider two Bills against Protestant extremists and Catholics, the latter especially harsh. Robert himself had been recalled to duty.

The court ordered Robert to respond within 12 days and this he did before returning to Butley. His statement is very verbose. Elizabeth was appalled that it ran to 60 pages *'full of the most cruel lyes'*, the copying of which would involve her in additional costs. She wrote in her own hand from London. where she was with her baby son, while her sister looked after her *'pour gearll'* in Costessey. Her letters reveal that she was very well-represented by various powerful people.

The judgement made on 22 May said that Common Law decreed that Robert's eldest son, Charles, should inherit his lands, and therefore Elizabeth's son should eventually inherit them. Robert had failed to maintain Elizabeth, and so was directed to pay 100 marks in respect of the charge, £30 for Elizabeth's maintenance between Charles' last departure from her plus the £300 dowry, the latter to be paid over 18 months at Temple Church, Fleet Street. Furthermore, an injunction under Her Majesty's Privy Seal upon pain of £200 was directed at Robert for the due performance of the order.

Robert contested the judgement: he had been given too little time to respond; the Clerk was in error in entering the order before the matter was heard and debated by the learned counsels; and he himself was out of London. The case rumbled on for at least another two years, but there are only a few undated documents, including one in which Elizabeth describes herself as a widow. Charles' death changed her legal position, which had been unclear throughout. Robert had contended that Henry Jerningham should not have brought the suit and, because Charles was then alive, Elizabeth was a *feme covert* required to sue in her husband's name.

Quite apart from the legal differences between the parties various scurrilous charges were made on both sides, such as that Charles had *'a vile and most shameful disease'* and Francis was illegitimate. As a consequence Charles had gone abroad *'appalled and troubled in his mind'* where he had died. His death was recorded in January 1597 when Elizabeth was granted an Act of Administration. He had neither goods nor money. We cannot be certain what happened to Elizabeth. As coheir with her two sisters to the Somerleyton estate, she will have been a beneficiary when it was sold in 1604.

The children of Charles and Elizabeth can be traced into the next century. Catherine married the Catholic Sir Philip Knyvett of Buckenham Castle in Norfolk. He was forced to sell the castle and estate and they moved to London. She died in 1647 and was buried at St Martin's in the Fields.

The son of their heir, Philip, was childless, and a daughter, Katherine, took the veil, becoming a nun in Niewport. Another daughter, Dorothy, married James Erskine, Earl of Buchan, and their descendants continued Charles Forth's blood-line.

The discovery that Francis had reached adulthood was made in an unlikely place. It was in the court rolls of the Manor of Staverton. Although his grandfather had

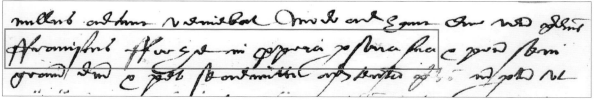

The clue that Francis had lived to reach manhood was found after a long search in an unexpected place — the records of the manor of Staverton. The entry for the 1612 Court shows that he came to Eyke in person – 'Franciscus Forthe in propria persona sua'.

disinherited him, and he is excluded from the Herald's Forth genealogy, the Lord of Staverton Manor, Sir Michael Stanhope, adhered to that manor's custom of primogeniture. In 1601 when Robert Forth died the Staverton court took no account of the fact that he had disinherited his son, declaring his grandson Francis to be his heir *by propinquity and closest by blood*. Eleven years later he was of age and came to the court to be admitted to those Staverton copyholds within the parish of Butley previously held by Robert Forth. One was called Skuttebroom and the other was part of the tenement Smoltes and Rayles. After Francis surrendered it in 1619 the trail goes dead. The 29-year-old is described as a gentleman showing that he had not been impoverished as a result of his father's disinheritance.

The young couple, Elizabeth and Charles, clearly fell in love and paid a terrible price in a society where marriages were arranged by parents. A hundred years later another Elizabeth, one of Robert's descendants, was to marry unsuitably in her father's eyes, and she, too, must have been in love.

Excess of Wives and Daughters

Chapter 5

Of the Forth family who owned the three Priory manors William, who purchased them, never lived there. His eldest son, Robert, built a fine house at Butley and his wife, Frances, bore him three sons and eight daughters. Six of the girls lived to adulthood and needed to have money or lands settled on them in order to marry. By the time he died part of the estate had been placed with trustees and his widow and his descendants were faced with financial problems thereafter.

As Robert had disinherited his eldest son, the Butley estate did not pass to his grandson, Francis, but via his second son, Sir William, to his great granddaughter, Anne. Her father, another William, died soon after the Civil War broke out.

The indomitable Dame Dorothy, a central character in this story, had a memorial in Stowmarket church erected by her doting third husband. She had children by each husband, but only two reached adulthood.

The setting

Queen Elizabeth was succeeded by the son of her cousin, Mary Queen of Scots. Thus James VI of Scotland became also James I of England in 1603. He took his time in travelling from Scotland, leaving a whole month for the sadness over the death of the late Queen to diminish. On the way he handed out knighthoods to the chief gentlemen through each county he passed, no doubt to help ensure their support.

Some people expected him to be more sympathetic to Catholics than his predecessor, but they were disappointed. After the Gunpowder Plot failed in 1605 Catholics were required to swear an Oath of Allegiance to the Crown. Most did, although Jesuits and priests who refused were banished. The Authorised Version of the Bible was published during his reign, in 1611, and is still used in some churches.

James' finances were never in a strong position, and his lavish expenditure was blamed. The splendid court functions were talked about both at home and abroad. Much fun was made of mishaps caused by intoxication. Efforts to raise more revenue included the sale of baronetcies at £1,095 each and an increase in the price of wardships. The King was offered £200,000 yearly to replace the latter, but no acceptable alternative way of raising this amount was found.

Overspending seems to have been widespread in the kingdom and debts led to the sale of long-held estates. Borrowing was fraught with danger, since a property had to be surrendered if the mortgage on it was not repaid on time. For landowners the problems were exacerbated by harvest failure due to poor weather conditions, which continued to deteriorate during his son's reign. Thus Charles I inherited financial short-falls and also needed to raise extra funds to pay the militia and maintain the navy. Forced loans and Ship Money were not popular, nor were his efforts to rule without Parliament. Charles' support of Archbishop Laud's strict Anglicanism and attitude towards landowners holding tithes and advowsons also undermined his rule.

The Civil War which followed resulted in yet further taxes on the rich to pay for the conflict. The King's defeat and execution in 1649 was followed by the Commonwealth led by Oliver Cromwell until 1660 when Charles' son returned from exile and claimed the throne.

A Forth marriage

Following Robert's death his widow endeavoured to arrange a good marriage for her eldest surviving son. However, she was unable to satisfy Lionel Tollemache in July 1602 that there were sufficient funds in the estate. It may be significant that William was not among those men with an income of £40 or more summoned to be knighted when James I was crowned the following year.

In June 1605 Frances Forth's matchmaking efforts were rewarded when her son, now Sir William, married Dorothy, the eldest daughter of Sir John Gilbert, in her home parish church of Great Finborough. She was aged 19 and he was a little older.

One of the letters which passed between Lionel and Frances shows that they were haggling over the sum of £1,600 as his daughter's portion. This cash dowry would be passed to the Forth family and would give Frances financial flexibility. Her letter is a delightful example of idiosyncratic Tudor spelling

'Good Mr Tollemach havinge bigoane a matter of such waight with you and uppon such good liking of your part as you to myself and my frinds did seme verey acceptable to yoy . . .'

She reminds him that, in a previous letter, she has dealt with the maintenance of the young couple and a jointure should the daughter become a widow. Clearly agitated over the delay she writes:

'I have sente again to you requiringe your answer eyther nowe or within shorte tyme, for I can se no good in delayinge of any such maters, specially seeinge yt semeth you have risolved in your selfe what to do. And even so I do hartely comend you and the cause in the marsy and favor of god. From Butly this XXth of July 1602, your assured frind frances fourthe'

Letter to Lionel Tollemache, 20 July 1602.

Sir Henry Warner of Mildenhall was the second husband of Frances Forth. She lost Robert in February 1601 and Henry his wife Mary, daughter of Sir Robert Wingfield, the same year. At that time Henry was MP for Thetford and a JP. He was knighted for the second time at the coronation of James I, whilst William, the second son of Frances, was knighted the following year. Frances died in 1608 and Sir Henry outlived her by nine years.

His brass is in the chancel of Mildenhall Church and he left his manors and leases to his eldest son, Edward. Henry was well-connected, asking the Lord Chief Justice, Sir Edward Coke, to supervise his will. Clauses in the will made Edward's inheritance conditional, since he had made a habit of gambling.

Edward was to be allowed *'the use of the goods and leases as long as he shall [not] lose at play at cards, dice, tables or other games above 20s in one day or night . . . and be proved by or before Sir Edward Coke . . . else Edward shall lose the benefit of the lease of the Manor of Lambholme.'* And for a second lapse Edward would lose the goods, leases, plate that remain *'as if Edward were dead.'*

Her dissolute stepson must have been anathema to the godly Frances, who had brought up 11 children.

Funding the marriage had involved financial assistance from the gentry network. The previous April Sir William and his mother had agreed with Sir John Gilbert, that six messuages and certain lands would be set aside for her jointure. The land totalled about 1,300 acres, most of it the 1,000 acres of Tangham and Capel sheepwalks. The antiquary, Hawes, said that she brought £2,000 to the marriage. This does not seem to have been sufficient to solve Sir William's financial problems entirely, because in 1612 he sold a thousand-year lease of his chief Boyton farm, called the Dairy House, to John Ferneley of West Creeting for £530. Sir William's first son, Henry, was baptised at Great Finborough on 10 July 1606, but died on 22 August 1614 when his younger brother, William, was aged five.

Meanwhile Frances Forth had remarried. Her new husband was Sir Henry Warner of Mildenhall, whose presence in the Butley area was only confirmed by discovery of a record showing he paid rent on land in Butley to Sir Michael Stanhope on behalf of his stepson.

Wards of the king

When Sir William made his will in 1613 aged only about 30 he did not describe himself as of Butley, but 'of Farnham', where he must have lived after his marriage. However, he asked to be buried at Butley. The Mansion-house was of course his mother's for life and she may have leased it after her marriage.

He left Dame Dorothy his 'head houses' at both Farnham and Butley. She also received £100 a year from his lands as her jointure, and their two daughters were each to receive £500 when aged sixteen. He directed his executor, Sir Henry Glemham, to sell some of his land in Boyton to raise £200 towards the payment of his debts. The debts included borrowing from the Butley carpenter, Richard Bradie. Bradie died in 1612 leaving £100 to his children, owed by Sir William under a penal bond. Gambling perhaps added to his financial difficulties; he and his dissolute step-brother, Edward Warner, were no doubt social companions.

Sir William's badly-drafted will was presented at the Chancellor's Court in Ipswich, but probate was not granted until 1621. In it the property he left his wife was to be hers whilst she remained a widow or until his eldest son married. This child, Henry, died soon after his father, and there was no explicit clause for his second son William to inherit should this occur. William was merely left a farm in Boyton then occupied *'by one Nitingall'*. This was the Dairy House farm already mortgaged. Dame Dorothy was therefore free to remarry and continue to possess the properties. Thus both Frances and Dame Dorothy (and subsequent husbands) continued to have the use of the family homes, precluding occupancy by their eldest sons. However, the latter's son, William, would not come of age for another 15 years. She had remarried by 1617 when Robert Brightwell of Butley made his will and made reference to *'Lady Forth and Mr Purkins'*.

Matters did not stagnate during the eight years between Sir William's death and grant of probate. There were two inquisitions *post mortem* held in Ipswich after his death and that of his eldest son. These were required because Henry was a ward of the king, being under age, and his brother William became a ward following Henry's death.

The latter enquiry confirmed that Sir William had been the legitimate holder of *'the site of the dissolved Priory, the Manors of Butley, Tangham and Boyton* [various lands, woods and mills, income from various sources including the right to give in marriage] *and also of frankpledge and free warren'*. The properties he owned were in ten parishes but most were in the core parishes that had belonged to the old Priory. There were 15 messuages and the lands comprised just over 2,200 acres, nearly half of which were gorse and heath.

The inquisition finally arrived at its main purpose: determining the rightful heir. The 15 messuages and 2,200 acres were held *in chief* from the king. Part was by fractions of knight's service with the annual value of about £50. These sums, representing two and one day's service, respectively, were payable to the king during William's wardship, thus adding to the family's financial problems. Other landowners, such as Bess of Hardwick's grandfather and Robert Forth, avoided the cost of wardship by placing their property with trustees.

Two widows to support

Robert Forth's daughters married well and their dowries must have been a severe drain on the finances of the estate. Adding to the problems was the subsequent need for it to provide for two widows. Sir William and his family lived at Farnham, no doubt because his mother, Frances, had leased the Mansion-house after her second marriage. Hawes mentions that she died in 1608, after which the estate was divided roughly as follows: young William would hold, when no longer a ward of the king, some 2,000 acres, and his mother, Dorothy, her jointure of about 1,300 acres. In due course he and his sisters were able to move into the Mansion-house with their new step-father, Gresham Perkins. The Crown, through the Master of Wards, sold wardships for lump sums to the highest bidder, although family members or friends might be given preference. Gresham Perkins is likely to have purchased William's wardship.

Gresham and Dame Dorothy were married for no more than eight years, but during this time she bore him several children, all but one of whom died young. He made his will at Butley in 1625 when he was aged forty seven. He had two surviving

> Gresham Perkins' mother was a Ferneley of Creeting and John Ferneley had purchased the lease of the chief farm in Boyton in 1612. The distinctive Christian name derived from the fact that the Ferneley family was related by marriage to Sir Thomas Gresham, founder of the Royal Exchange. Gresham's father was a Hadleigh clothier and his mother married, secondly, Israel, the brother of Robert Forth.

sons by a previous marriage and, by Dorothy, a son, Charles. He was concerned with making provision for his three sons who were to inherit only after Dorothy's death. His own property lay in nine parishes and he had made arrangements to sell much of it before he died. His eldest son was to inherit the remainder and his three boys the vast sum of £3,400 between them. The three Forth children were left £5 each to buy a ring. The burden of executing this will was given to Dorothy who was required to take out bonds to guarantee its performance. If she opted out, the bondholders were required to fulfil Gresham's wishes, while she would only have the use of Harland's Farm, Aldham, and his properties in Hadleigh, Whatfield and Elmsett. Dame Dorothy was to live to 1641 and to bring yet another husband, William Tyrell, to Butley.

Marriage and financial straits

In 1629, as soon as he had ceased to be a royal ward, a marriage was arranged between 'young' William and Anne Browne of Elsing, Norfolk. The couple lived at Elsing for most of William's life. Their first child, yet another William, was baptised there a year later, but died the same month. Their second baby, Anne, was to survive, continue the Forth blood-line and, with her mother, make her home at Butley.

It is possible that the estate had not been well managed during William's minority. Financial factors and climate change adversely affected agriculture nationally. No doubt raising a jointure in order to marry Anne had put a further strain on the estate. William initially raised money by the expedient of short-term mortgages, but his finances rapidly got out of control and he had to turn to his neighbour, John Harvy at Wantisden Hall, for a loan.

Before 1631 he had begun to convey land near the ferry to Francis Warner. He took out two mortgages with a merchant in Ipswich. In one he 'sold' 120 acres of land for £600 for a term of three years. After this period he could redeem the mortgage for the same amount. However, for each of those years the merchant would receive the rent of £60 per annum, representing ten per cent interest. If Forth failed to repay the £600 the

Boyton White House, now Valley Farm. In 1594 it was rented by Henry Chambers and had previously been called 'Greenes'. Agas noted that there was a newly-built cottage rented by Marie White and a barn on the south part. The house is likely to have taken its name from her family.

deal would be, in effect, a sale of the land. The other he redeemed in August 1632 with the father of his neighbour, Robert Harvy.

In 1633 he raised the large sum of £1,000 by a 99-year lease of valuable marshes and Boyton White House farmland to a Norfolk widow. He may have hoped that this would get him out of trouble (no doubt paying off the loan), and he must have been dismayed a year later when the Norfolk lady's new husband made a profit by selling the lease to Francis Warner, who was now bent on acquiring Boyton land. The Warner Charity papers reveal William's desperate situation and an escalating need to raise money. Next he purchased a licence from Charles I for

---

HERE LYETH BURIED ROBERT HARVIE THE SECOND SONE OF JOHN HARVIE OF ICKWORTH IN THE COUNTY OF SUFFOLK ESQUIRE WHOE DYED THE SECOND OF JULY 1633 AND MARIAN HIS WIFE WHO DIED THE [blank]

On the floor of neighbouring Wantisden church a grave-slab is evidence that, like the Wingfields in the previous century (chapter 11), the Harvys, a gentry family from central Suffolk, with younger sons to provide for, was poised to take over an estate in the Sandlings. Robert and his wife were clearly resident in Wantisden. The unfinished inscription suggests that his widow left to live elsewhere.

For a while William was a captain in the militia, known as the Trained Band. Young gentlemen, usually without military experience, were given temporary command of a troop and expected to be actively involved. A contemporary letter from Sir William Harvy shows that in the autumn of 1632 'Captain Forth' resigned. Despite this, the title looked good on the family pedigree when the Herald visited, and for modern authors it can be a useful way of distinguishing the third William.

There exists no image of young William Forth, but a portrait of a Suffolk contemporary, Tobias Bloss, depicts the dress of the leader of a Trained Band.

£10 in order to sell the Manor of Boyton outright and almost all his land in Butley and Capel. Fortunately some of the land had already been mortgaged by his mother, her husband and himself, and so was excluded from the sale. He was prepared to sell the manor along with the advowson of the church and other lands, totalling some 560 acres, for £700, including rights to the river below the ferry.

Even this was not enough. A year later he planned to sell the Boyton manor plus nearly all the Forth lands in Butley and Capel to Warner for £3,600. His mother and step-father intervened because legally he could not sell the 1,300 acres which comprised her jointure, or leased lands which formed part of a 1634 indenture made by the family. No document survives to show how this was finally resolved.

Four years later he found a way to raise money on the lands which his mother still enjoyed. In 1638 for the sum of £2,600, by an unredeemable transfer for 99 years, virtually all the residual Butley estate was passed to Sir William Harvy of Ickworth. 'Captain' William and his heirs retained the lordship rights, the advowson of Butley church and its tithes, its woodland, the Mansion-house and about 300 acres of land. Still short of money after his mother died in 1641, William Forth was forced to mortgage Burrow Hill Marsh to a mariner of Aldeburgh, named Edward Cocke, for £300, and in due course it was re-mortgaged to Viscount Hereford. He also sold Woodhouse Close to Anne Smallpiece for £420.

In the mid-17th century landowners went through some turbulent times, as did the whole country during the Civil War. The first large battle between the supporters of the King and of Parliament took place at Edgehill in October 1642, but 'Captain' William did not take part. Later historians have confused his name with that of Sir Faithful Fortescue who did participate. William's sympathies seem to have lain with Parliament, judging by the preamble to his will which was generally Puritan in tone, and he did not date it by the usual reference to the year of the king's reign. His stepfather William Tyrell was an active Parliamentarian in Suffolk, raising money and arranging the defence of Landguard Fort, while his brother Thomas actually fought against the King in the army of the Earl of Essex.

The 'Captain's' short will written in 1643 was witnessed by his mother's third hus-

BUTLEY ABBEY
Remains

William Forth's will provides the first evidence that the family were not being buried in the parish church, but in a chapel formed out of the remains of the Priory church. The antiquary Grose was informed that a chest of money had been found arched into a wall of the old chapel [of the Priory]. Corroboration of its existence is provided by the 19th-century name Chapel Field for the enclosure to the east of the site.

Pen and wash sketch by Isaac Johnston dated 1830.

band, William Tyrell. He asked to be buried in a vault in Butley *'where my ancestors lie'*.

He left his *'temporal estate'* to his *'loving and tender wife'*, Anne. Now aged 34, she inherited merely the remnants of what had been a huge estate a century earlier. Her elder daughter, Anne, was now 11 years old. They were the last Forths to live in the Mansion-house. One can imagine her watching with dismay the decline of the family's fortunes.

The marriage of Dorothy's third husband to her son's widow

In this period the need to keep property within the family could lead to extreme measures. By 1643 Dame Dorothy had been dead for two years, leaving her third husband, William Tyrell, a widower. Her son, Captain William, had also died, leaving Anne a widow with a young daughter. Later the marriage of the two bereaved persons consolidated what was left of the estate. The date of their marriage is not recorded, but a contemporary historian 'Candler', writing in 1655, wrote that a marriage took place *'in the dining room at Butley Abbey this year'*. Like many afterwards he seems to have confused

the two Anne Forths. During the Interregnum it was not obligatory for marriages to take place in church.

In 1657 William Tyrell left his property in Bury St Edmunds and personal estate to his brother, Thomas, to be sold to pay his debts. The main branch of this old gentry family lived outside Stowmarket at Gipping. His widow could live in Butley and retain that which was hers when they married, although his books kept at Butley were also to be sold. Clearly they lived in both places. His 'great debts' were occasioned, he said, in part by the 'defence' of his wife's estate. Although these were connected with a family settlement, other costly legal fees had been incurred following the death of Dorothy, William's sister. She had married Nicholas Southcott of London. Unusually she made a will in 1643 in the lifetime of her husband, albeit a nuncupative one on her deathbed. Husbands had to give permission for wives to make wills, and the subsequent court cases strongly suggest that he had an interest in a formal declaration from her that he was the sole beneficiary.

The will was challenged by William's widow on behalf of their daughters, Anne

William Tyrell commissioned this bust of himself about ten years before he married Anne Forth. It formed part of the memorial to his second wife in Stowmarket parish church and shows him to have been a devoted husband.

To complete the family memorial he included images of their three children: little Penelope flanked by two babies. In laboured Latin verse he bewails the loss of his good and devout wife and tender children, exclaiming:

Quid spectas mortem miraris symbolum amoris

What? Does it take you aback to see a representation of death? It is an expression of love.

and Dorothy, and also by his stepbrother Charles Perkins. They sought to recover the estate or money which had formed Dorothy Southcott's dowry. The case was considered by an ecclesiastical court during the Civil War with numerous lawyers representing the parties. No decision was reached and the case was referred to the Court of Arches. Unfortunately all the court records were lost in the Great Fire of London, but the Forths must have been successful because the Southcott and Perkins names feature no further in the Butley story.

Between 1642 and 1649 the English Civil Wars caused severe disruption in many parts of the country, but East Anglia was little affected militarily. Some gentry, such as Sir Thomas Glemham and his son Sackville, fought for the King in the North, but William Forth, grandson of Robert Forth, died from natural causes in 1643. He had no surviving son.

None of William and Anne Tyrell's children lived to adulthood, and young Anne Forth became heir to the Butley estate. In 1650 a suitable match had been arranged for her with a neighbouring land-owner's younger brother, Walter Devereux.

This had been followed by her mother's remarriage in 1655 and a settlement which partitioned what little was left of the estate between the Tyrell and Devereux families.

The story continues in the next chapter.

The Wily Lawyer
Chapter 6

William Forth's daughter, Anne, was the mother of the heiress in this story.

Daughters of the gentry were normally educated at home, but should their mother die when they were young, and not be replaced by a step-mother, they might be sent away to live in the household of relatives or friends. This story concerns two motherless sisters who were brought up in Ipswich, firstly at the house of their Hereford relatives and, when adult, in the house of a family servant. They were educated by two Puritan ministers. One sister died, but the other did the unthinkable, and married secretly.

Christchurch Mansion as it appeared when the sisters were living there.

The later descendants of Robert Forth

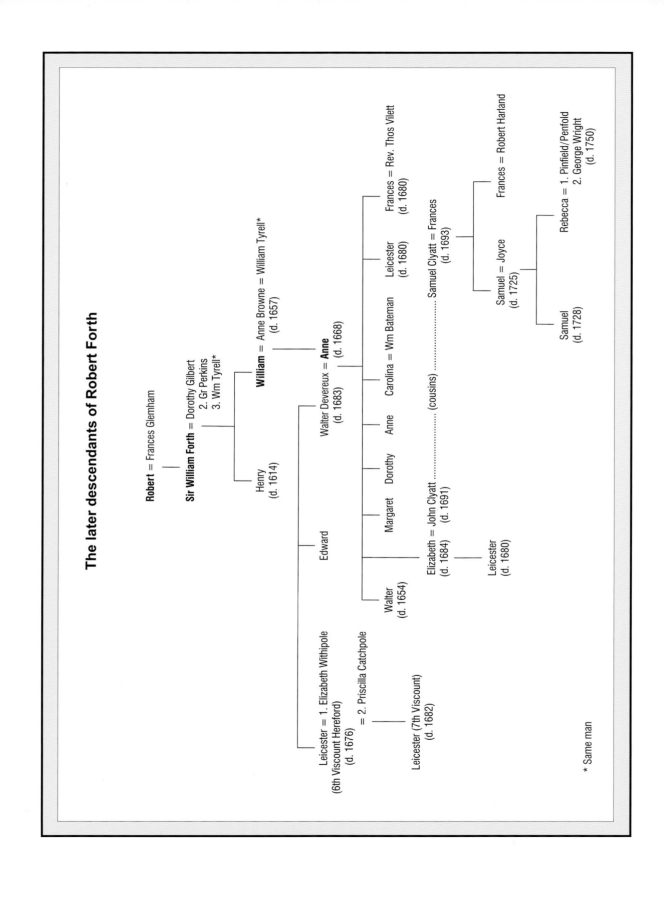

Robert Forth and Michael Stanhope were neighbours, owning the Butley and Sudbourne estates respectively. The men had little in common. Forth was a religious extremist, farming much of his estate himself, while Stanhope was a royal courtier and absentee landowner. However, their lands eventually devolved upon female descendants connected by their marriage to two brothers on the make.

In contrast to Robert's probably simple interment in the former Lady Chapel down at Butley, Sir Michael Stanhope commissioned a grandiose memorial in little Sudbourne church before he died in 1621.

The large hood his widow wears would have been all the fashion for mourners at the modest funeral of Robert Forth's son, Sir William, that same year.

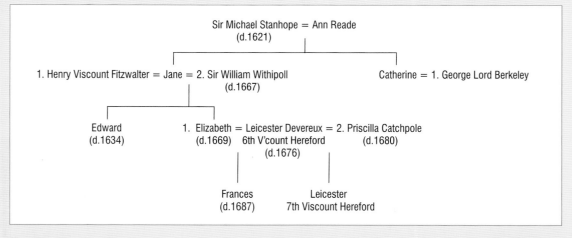

When Leicester Devereux inherited the title of 6th Viscount Hereford he was suddenly in a position to marry into money and land. He came to Suffolk, choosing Elizabeth Withipoll, heiress not only to her maternal grandfather's Sudbourne estate, but to her father's property including Christchurch Mansion in Ipswich. They married in 1642 and Leicester's younger brother, lacking both title and money, must have been pleased to contract a marriage with the heiress to the estate on the other side of Butley Creek. It is unclear whether at the time Walter realised the extent to which the Forth estate had been sold off or mortgaged.

It may explain why he appears such an embittered man in this story.

Two marriages

Anne, the surviving child of 'Captain' William Forth, had to rely on her now remarried mother to make as good a match for her as possible. Across the river at Sudbourne she married Walter Devereux on St Swithin's Day 1650. The marriage was recorded in Orford's parish register. If Walter was expecting by this means to acquire the estate which William Forth had created a century earlier, he was to be rapidly disillusioned. Five years after their wedding his brother Leicester had to come to the couple's rescue with a package by which he purchased half of the already reduced and mortgaged Butley estate.

Another humiliation was that Walter and his bride were unable to move into the Butley Mansion-house since Anne's mother and her third husband, William Tyrell, were still alive and had the use of it. Instead they rented Glemham Hall. In the event Anne was never to live in Butley as a married woman and Walter was resident only towards the end of his life. The baptismal records of St Margaret's Church in Ipswich show that their children were born in the parish where his brother had his town house.

A widower's dilemma

Walter and Anne's first daughter Elizabeth, the subject of our story, was baptised in November 1652 and her sister Margaret in April 1656. Their brother Walter died in infancy. Another brother, Leicester, baptised in 1662, died when he was 18 years old. Had either son survived his father, Elizabeth would not have become an heiress. They went on to have another four daughters: Dorothy, Anne, Carolina and Frances. Following the death of his wife in 1668,

Facade of Christchurch Mansion today. The interior is little changed since Elizabeth and Margaret lived there.

Walter did not remarry; his son, Leicester appeared to ensure a male succession. He arranged for the older girls, Elizabeth and Margaret, then aged 16 and 12, to live in their uncle's household at Christchurch Mansion. There they were educated with their cousin, Viscount Hereford's daughter Frances, the nine-year-old great-grand-daughter of Sir Michael Stanhope. Frances' mother had also died and the three girls lived with her stepmother. Here they were under the influence of John Carr, Theophilus Hook and Cave Beck, the last two being Puritan ministers. John Carr and his wife, Alice, were employed by Walter, who was later to bequeath them *'all his hats, cravats and wearing apparel'* and 40 shillings.

The Viscount died in 1676 and in a codicil to his will directed that his nieces, Elizabeth and Margaret, should have a lodging at Christchurch Mansion whilst they remained unmarried. If his second wife did not agree to this arrangement, they were to live elsewhere and receive an annuity of £25 until they were married. They went to live with the Carrs. This relieved their father of the need to provide for them until marriage portions were required. It was whilst living with the Carrs that Margaret died, leaving

Elizabeth, now aged 24, a lonely spinster without marriage prospects.

Her brother Leicester's death in 1680 was to change everything. Walter no longer had a male heir. Ipswich society would not be long unaware of the changed circumstances of Walter's eldest daughter. An opportunist, John Clyatt, saw a means of advancement and swooped on the now 30-year-old heiress. The Clyatts were prominent inhabitants and an ancestor had been a portman, one of the 12 men who governed the town.

When Walter discovered that his daughter intended to marry without his consent, he immediately made a will to disinherit her. This was in September 1682, but it did not deter John and Elizabeth from marrying secretly in Harkstead on 13 November the same year. Her father betrayed the emotions of both anger and sadness in the wording of his will. He said he wrote it *because of the uncertainty of man's life*, but in reality to disinherit Elizabeth for disobeying him regarding her marriage.

He left his manors, lands, rents, tithes, and hereditable property, *whether mortgaged or not*, to his executors and they were charged with passing them on to his two surviving unmarried daughters, Carolina and Frances, under certain terms. They were to receive half of the estate as their portion upon marriage to someone approved by the executors.

Walter Devereux's will left no doubt of his intentions where he expressed his wishes in the words, *'My principal design in disposing my said estate in this manner, is to prevent my said two daughters from ruining themselves and dishonouring their family by rash, mean and unworthy marriages'.*

A bleak future

The newly married couple were facing a bleak future together until John's cousin, a wily lawyer of Gray's Inn named Samuel Clyatt, saw a means of overturning the will. A series of court cases took place: in June 1683, Clyatt *contra* Carr, in December, Clyatt *contra* Hook, in June 1684, Clyatt *contra* Edward Devereux (Walter's brother)

Self-portrait: detail from the frontispiece of Cave Beck's *The Universal Character* (1657)

Theophilus Hook was a contemporary of Samuel Pepys at Cambridge and became rector of Sudbourne and Orford. Cave Beck was rector of St Helens, Ipswich, and the perpetual curate of St Margaret's adjacent to Christchurch Mansion. He was also Master of Ipswich Town Library for many years and thus his young pupils had access to the many learned books held there. He had accompanied his patron, the Viscount, and five other peers to bring King Charles II back from exile in Holland.

and in 1685, Clyatt *contra* Bateson, Carolina having married William Bateson.

These cases were analysed by J.J. Muskett, in his article, *The Clandestine Marriage,* published in 1889-90. He called the lawyer, Samuel Clyatt, 'wily', and accepted the exaggerated charges made against Walter Devereux, that he had: deprived his daughter of affection and sustenance during her childhood; despoiled her woods; and taken into his own hands the profits from the Butley estate. Muskett enhanced Elizabeth's status and implied that she was not much more than a girl, *'There lived in Suffolk in the latter years of King Charles II, a great heiress . . . a maiden neglected and banished from her father's house'.*

There is no doubt that Walter showed little concern for her wellbeing, failed to arrange a marriage for her and excluded her from his will, but a rereading of the court cases in conjunction with other documents reveals that she was neither a great heiress nor a girl, but was approaching what was middle age in those days.

In the first court case wild accusations were made on John's behalf by Samuel Clyatt with the intention of forcing the defendants to produce a document which they were unwilling to do. The defendants, described as 'confederates' by the Clyatts, were Walter himself, his lawyer the octogenarian Thomas Edgar, John Carr and the two ministers. The court was asked to *subpoena* the defence to produce the crucial evidence and to answer the charges. Walter was forced to produce the key document, a family settlement dated 1 October 1655. In this the estate was divided in two parts, one

The inheritance of the so-called great heiress superimposed on Isaace Johnson's draft map of Butley and Tangham manors.

granted to Viscount Hereford and the other to the use of Anne Tyrell, Elizabeth's grand-mother, for life, then to Walter and Anne Devereux for their lives and then to their eldest son or, lacking sons, to their eldest daughter. Back in 1655 the future was unknown. Walter had just lost his baby son, but at that time he must have been hopeful of another male heir.

The second case was brought in December 1683, when John Clyatt claimed the settlement of 1655 meant that his wife should inherit that part of the estate which devolved through Anne Tyrell as a result of her previous marriage to William Forth. The proceedings then stopped because Walter Devereux died that same month. He had been correct about the uncertainty of life.

John and Elizabeth Clyatt now came into her inheritance, and the subsequent cases concerned only other parts of the estate. The next heir was on his way, because Elizabeth

was pregnant in December 1683 and their son Leicester, no doubt named after her dead brother, was born in June 1684.

However, tragedy, never far away in this sad narrative, struck again and the baby died four months later. Elizabeth herself passed away not long afterwards.

The lawyer scents an opportunity

Samuel Clyatt had moved quickly. Within a month of Walter's death, in January 1684, he set in motion a legal device to secure John and Elizabeth's rights. The inheritance comprised the advowson of Butley Church, any unmortaged portions of the manors of Butley and Tangham, and the tithes belonging. These were: Broom Close; the backside of Capel Hill; the woods called Capel, Oakhill, Watery and Carmans; the Mansion-house called Butley Abbey; its watermill; the Park; Inghams alias Brewers Entry; Cowpasture Marshes; Burrow Hill;

Hawes Marsh; 20 acres between the Lesser Sheep Course and Relie Green; and small pieces of land containing a further 14 acres. These totalled only some 300 acres, plus the woods, out of an estate of more than 5,000 at the beginning of the century. There was an arrangement whereby Samuel would be able to recover his costs from various rents and profits following the death of either John or his wife.

The final two cases involved further challenges to the Clyatts' title to Burrow Hill and some other parcels of land. After all this wrangling the widowed and childless John Clyatt was to enjoy his wife's inheritance for only eight years. In his will, dated 1691, he left nearly everything to cousin Samuel. Probate was delayed until 1694. By this time the wily lawyer was dead also, but his widow Frances owned the run-down property for the next 25 years.

For the 18th century there are only scraps of information about the Clyatt family. She managed to arrange a good marriage for her daughter Frances to Robert Harland, gent. of Wherstead Park, Ipswich, where portraits of her late husband and herself hung until the house was sold in 1934. In 1706 as patron of Butley church she appealed to the Bishop of Norwich for permission to sell

one of its bells and with the money raised to repair the tower. It had been weakened by the Great Storm of 1703 which brought down one of the chimneys on the Gatehouse. The other two bells needed to be recast as the parishioners were unable to repair them *'being all poor farmers . . .'* She may have moved to London for in 1716 she wrote from Highgate to her steward, complaining about her bailiff's management of the income from the estate. Her kindly nature is revealed by the words, *'as for the poor widow that had her house burnt, I forgive her the fine and pray God make up her loss to her'*. The death of her son Samuel in 1725 was followed by the death of his only son three years later. Thus in 1728 the remnant estate descended to her granddaughter, Rebecca, whose first husband had died. She was now married to George Wright, a gentleman who had property in Norfolk and a London residence.

Ten years later the couple decided to demolish the ruinous family mansion. The medieval Gatehouse, although derelict, was saved and was converted into a property to let. John Kirby's map of 1766 provides the sole clue that the widowed Mrs Wright returned to Butley and was living there towards the end of her life.

The only representation of the old Mansion-house; it appears on the left of Samuel Buck's engraving of the roofless Gatehouse made in 1738 shortly before its refurbishment by the Wrights. Ruins of the Priory church can be seen in the distance on the far left.

The ruined gatehouse of Butley Priory was repaired in brick in the 18th century. The walls have traces of earlier windows. Below a blocked-up doorway a later buttress supports the west side.

Sport for the Master

Chapter 7

In the latter part of the 18th century the aristocratic owners of the huge estates based on Sudbourne and Rendlesham did not own them in order to generate income, but to impress guests with sporting pastimes in a rural idyll. Thus the agricultural writer, Arthur Young, observed on a visit here that hares and a profusion of rabbits were a barrier to good cultivation. The county abounded in game, especially pheasants.

The agricultural depression following World War I led to the break-up of the old estates, but left opportunities for the creation of new ones. After World War II the land which had been requisitioned for camps and air-bases led to similar opportunities.

Sir Bernard Greenwell's head gamekeeper, Fred Meadows, painted in the 1930s by T.C. Dugdale. Fred's brother Harry lived at Water Wood and features here in a personal recollection.

The Stanhope estate

A vast estate was assembled in the Triangle by Sir Michael Stanhope at the very end of Queen Elizabeth's reign. Its 15,000 acres stretched from Wilford Bridge, where there was a gibbet, to Orford where there was another. In Sudbourne Manor, with which the Queen had rewarded him, he transformed the Tudor mansion known as Chapmans where the Rush family had lived.

Much of its park survives. John Norden described it in 1601 as *'New neatly beautified and adorned with pleasant and delightful walks and shadowing trees. And plentifully stored with variety of all kind of plants of the rarest – fruits, apples, pears, plumbs, apricots and cherries, with other things delightful & profitable fish & fowl were the ponds & fleet accordingly respected and used. The woods & groves seen unto.'* That this was a sporting estate is clear from the note, *'And the hawkers, hunters, snarers and gunners banyshed without which you shall be deprived both of your pleasure and profit'.*

Norden was being unduly optimistic for poaching was ever a labourer's necessity. At times it was practised on a commercial scale as in the 1740s when Viscount Hereford, who had acquired the estate through his marriage to Stanhope's granddaughter, joined other Suffolk landowners to reduce it. They published their agreement for the preservation of game, specifically hares, pheasants, partridges and fish, in the *Ipswich Journal*. Informers would be paid £5 and all gentlemen were desired to write names and dates on any game transported.

The Spencer estate

On the opposite side of the Butley river what was left of the Forth estate was acquired by George Wright in 1729. George appears on the scene the previous year in the capacity of steward to Rebecca, the *Wily Lawyer's* granddaughter. George and his family appear to have lost money in the stock market. She had just been widowed and George snapped her up, technically becoming lord of the manors of Butley and Tangham, although the income was little more than seven pounds. Kirby's 1736 map does not name any owner at Butley. Although George had a farm in Norfolk, it is clear that the couple lived in London.

Meanwhile in the first quarter of the 18th century Henry Spencer was making a fortune in London as a merchant. He was a member of the Spencer family whose manorial home was nearby at Naunton Hall, and he bought up portions of Butley and Capel land from relatives of the Harvys, Devereux and Clyatts as they became available. Henry's nephew Edward, the owner of all Rendlesham's manors, purchased other portions and kept an eye on the new acquisitions as manorial steward to the Clyatt family until his death in 1728. In 1731 Anne Spencer inherited Henry's property to add to her father's estate and commissioned John Kirby to survey it. Before 1736 she had moved to Rendlesham Hall, which had been rebuilt after it first burnt down in 1619. It remained her main residence until 1756.

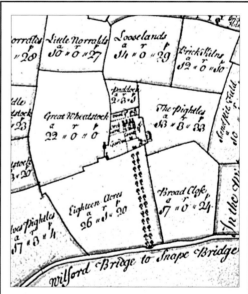

Rendlesham Hall. The house and its four acres of gardens were mapped by John Kirby when he surveyed Naunton Hall Farm prior to its transformation into Rendlesham Park by the young Anne Spencer. Note the avenue leading south in the direction of her estate in Butley and Tangham.

Unlike Elizabeth Devereux, Anne was indeed a major heiress, with a fortune of £70,000, vast at that time. She was only about 23 when she attracted the attention of Scotland's premier peer, James 5th Duke of

With a view to letting the ruined Priory Gatehouse and 148 acres of land as a shooting lodge, Wright refurbished it with flanking towers. One of the tenants, General Charles Frampton, died there in 1748. His obituary in the *Gentleman's Magazine* recorded, *'death of Lieut. Gen. Frampton at Butley Abbey; remarkable for his integrity and honour, as well as great humanity to all mankind'*. After her husband's death Rebecca Wright returned to her Butley home and was living there as late as 1766. As her children had predeceased her she bequeathed the Gatehouse to a London relative, the clockmaker Samuel Clyatt, who leased it to Arthur Chichester, the then Earl of Donegall, and his wife, sister to Archibald Hamilton.

was to die from a chill caught hunting.

After eight years of widowhood, in 1751, Anne married a neighbour, roughly her age, namely, the Hon. Richard Savage Nassau de Zuylestein, brother of the 4th Earl of Rochford, who had his seat at Easton. The Dowager Duchess thus became Anne Nassau de Zuylestein. She bore Richard two sons, Henry and George, born at her Rendlesham home in 1754 and 1756 respectively. After her second husband purchased Easton Park from his brother, they moved there, and it was at Easton that her daughter, Lady Anne Hamilton, was married in 1761.

It seems to have been a happy loving family with all the children and the new husband being on the best of terms, as is shown by their respective wills and the inscriptions on the Nassau monuments in Easton church. Lady Anne was 23 when she wed Arthur Chichester, 5th Earl of Donegall (later 1st Marquess). He was a year older, immensely rich and had a *'passion for gambling'*, as well as being a keen sportsman. Arthur leased the Gatehouse from William Strahan, and retained the lease after his brother-in-law,

Hamilton, said to have been one of the handsomest and most graceful men of his time. She became his third wife in 1737. His heirs were his two sons by his first marriage, so Anne had no reason to anticipate that her eldest son, Archibald, would inherit the title.

The Duke died six years later, aged only 41, leaving his wife, who had lost her father when she was a minor, a young dowager duchess. She had five children to care for; James her stepson, who now inherited the title, his younger brother and her own children all less than five years old. The Duke desired his heir *'to live in the most friendly way with the Duchess and his brothers and sisters'*.

The portrait of the young Archibald on page 135 shows him sitting pensively in a landscape of venerable oaks. In another, his stepbrother James, the 6th Duke, is dressed for shooting, gun in hand; the archetypal sportsman, he

The Gatehouse. The west wing and pavilions had not been completed when Archibald, now Duke of Hamilton, was obliged to auction the estate in 1802. Hay's engraving of 1819 shows that the western pavilion lay very close to Isaac Johnson's 'canal'.

Archibald, bought it and its 148 acres in 1776, spending money on enlarging its accommodation and improving its coverts. He could well afford to do so, as his Irish estates alone were said to be worth £48,000 yearly. He brought his third wife, Barbara, on visits there. She was a clergyman's daughter and made an impression on the perpetual curate of Butley, the Reverend John Black, for he celebrated her beauty in a 'pastoral song'.

Annually on the Queen's birthday the Marquess gave a dinner at the *Oyster* for the farmers of Butley and Capel with a barrel of beer for the labourers to drink the Queen's health. He also provided 50 stones of beef and 150 loaves for the parish poor on Christmas Eve 1794, and a further 60 stones

Landowners were not the only sportsmen. In 1784 the young François de la Rochefoucauld accompanied Arthur Young on a tour of Suffolk. In his diary he noted that gentlemen with landed property worth over £100 a year could shoot wherever they wished as long as they did not trespass into parks or damage crops or fences. He was paraphrasing an Act of Charles II which remained in force until Game Licences were introduced in 1831.

On Oyster Hill, Butley, a pair of three-storey cottages was extended to provide accommodation for a gentleman and his family during the shooting season. They occupied part of the two acres that had previously belonged to *The Oyster Inn* and no doubt the publican, Richard Dowsing, was the builder. It was advertised in 1784:

A Complete Sporting Box

To be let and entered upon immediately. A small, but convenient Dwelling-house, ready furnished, pleasantly situated, at Butley, together with a good stable, chaise-house, granary and other convenient offices, small pleasure garden behind the house. The premises are entirely new, and calculated for a small family. Butley is a very healthy and pleasant situation, near the sea, in a fine sporting country, abounding with game. The premises would be particularly suitable to any gentleman fond of field diversions, there being an exceeding good dog-kennel and every other convenience requisite to make the abode a complete sporting box.

The venture seems to have been poorly timed, because the Duke of Hamilton's son, Lord Archibald, placed a notice in the same newspaper warning that he would exercise his manorial rights if gentlemen continued to sport on his manors of Rendlesham, Butley, and Tangham without leave. This probably made the sporting box at High House redundant, and it was let as three labourer's cottages by 1797. Today, the stable (below left) has also been converted into a cottage and the sporting box (below centre) extended.

To be SOLD by AUCTION
By AUGUSTINE READ,
At the Oyster in Butley, on Friday, the 15th of Sept.
At Twelve o'clock,

Lot 1. A Freehold Brick-built Messuage, on a small scale, formerly the temporary residence of a sportsman, consisting of a kitchen, store-room, pantry, parlour, backhouse, 3 chambers, 3 garrets, cellar, and proper offices, stable and chaise-house, with a piece of garden ground, now let in 3 tenements; the whole at the rent of 12l. 17s. per ann. situate on a dry airy eminence in Butley, near Orford, a part of the county of Suffolk, abounding with game.

Lot 2. A range of Copyhold Buildings, now let in 5 tenements, with about an acre of garden ground, in Butley-street, at the rent of 13l. per ann.

Lot 3 A Freehold Cottage, in Chillisford, now in 3 tenements, rented by Smith, Knights, and Cook, at 7l. per ann.

Further particulars of the auctioneer, and of Mr. Waller at Butley, who will shew the premises.

of beef the following year when a diarist noted *'our poor are in the most shocking distress, absolutely in a starving condition'*.

The Marquess died in 1799, the year that – against all expectations – his sporting brother-in-law, Archibald, inherited the peerage as the 9th Duke of Hamilton. It was a mixed blessing.

Although Archibald had inherited the Spencer estate on his mother's death, it was his title which now made his adored daughter, Charlotte, attractive to a ducal suitor, and in 1802 Archibald was obliged to sell its 4,042 acres to raise a dowry of £20,000 for her to marry the Duke of Somerset. In the event it fetched £50,000. Archibald himself had married and had brought up three children, but had been saddled with a make-shift title all his life – he appears in documents as *'Mr Archibald Hamilton, commonly called Lord Archibald Hamilton'*. Aged 59 when he became the 9th Duke, he immediately made over Hamilton Palace and the Scottish estates to his eldest son. All his own life had been lived in the shadow of his ducal stepbrothers and his home was not in Scotland, but in Suffolk or on his late father's estate of Ashton Hall in Lancashire. It was there that he died in 1820.

The Thellusson estate

One man's loss was another's gain. In 1802 the auction of the Spencers' *'very desirable sporting domain well stocked with game'* in Butley and Tangham was to provide an

The second Rendlesham Hall burnt down in 1830. Samuel Gross, who farmed at Alderton and Hollesley, noted in his diary that the house was valued at £9,000, the furniture at £4,000 and the books at £3,000. The fire had started in the conservatory flues.

The will Peter Thellusson left in 1797 caused problems for his descendants. He had intended most of his fortune to accumulate during the lives of three generations. The implications were alarming; it was calculated at the time that the accumulation might reach 130 million pounds within 120 years. Within months of the will becoming public, the *Ipswich Journal* foretold the subsequent problems, declaring it would be *'the best general windfall which lawyers have known for the last century'*. The Thellusson Act of 1800 was passed to limit future wills of this type. In the event the trustees mismanaged the estate during half a century of costly litigation. The newspaper had been correct.

opportunity for Peter Isaac Thellusson to add it to Rendlesham Manor which he had purchased eight years previously. He was the son of a very wealthy naturalised Frenchman. By the 1850s it had extended to more than 20,000 acres, most of it in the hands of trustees due to the 1797 will. In 1806 Thellusson was created Baron Rendlesham and made his seat at the Hall.

He died during a shooting party in 1808. His 12-year old great grandson inherited the title in 1852 and grew up to be one of Britain's best shots, employing numerous

Buttons from gamekeepers' jackets can be found in cottage gardens.

keepers dressed in blue velvet livery. As one of the most celebrated sporting estates in East Anglia, it later attracted King Edward VII and other leading Guns.

The Rendleshams ensured that the preservation of game took pride of place on the estate, letting farms at low rents and expecting the tenants to grow crops beneficial to game birds. Each keeper was expected to rear a thousand pheasants each season. Vastly increased stocks enabled thousand-bird-days to be laid on for guests.

The owners of large sporting estates tended to be innovators, introducing new species. The raising of the red-legged partridge was pioneered by local landowners. As early as 1770 the 2nd Marquess of Hertford had brought to Sudbourne

Game bags

A single note on the game shot at Rendlesham survives: in 1807 the game bag numbered: 1,815 English partridges, 112 red-legged partridges, 1,314 pheasants, 698 hares and 44 woodcock. The high point was the last week of January when over 1,000 head of game was bagged.

When the Butley Abbey portion of the Rendlesham estate was sold in 1919 it formed *'a sporting estate of exceptional merit'*. The sale catalogue lists the game total over three years. More than 10,000 pheasants formed the chief bag. The open lands were described as *'broken here and there with small areas of heath, gorse, bracken and broom, favouring the retention of ground and other game, and, bordering the Butley River, are saltings and snipe marshes, the natural haunts of duck and wild fowl'*. In 1919 when the Reverend Luther Wanstall was occupying the Gatehouse it was still thought of as *'an ideal shooting box, inexpensive to maintain'*.

One of Richard Wallace's keepers listing game shot. An under-keeper is reporting the numbers of game, in this case, hares. Detail of painting by Alfred Decaen, 1880.

quantities of eggs from France. They thrived, unlike the four red grouse his neighbour was to bring down from Scotland in 1866, one of which was shot by mistake, stuffed and displayed in Rendlesham Hall.

The later Sudbourne estate

The enormously wealthy but illegitimate Richard Wallace inherited his Marquess father's unentailed property in 1870. The following year, in acknowledgement of his philanthropy during the siege of Paris, he was awarded a baronetcy by Queen Victoria. He moved to England, purchasing Hertford House. He then bought the entailed Sudbourne estate from the financially embarrassed 5th Marquess for £200,000.

George Gardiner with Marble Arch, a bay Arab gelding.

There he set in motion improvements, including well-built homes for the workers and for the managers. In Chillesford a fine model farm was created in 1878; adjacent to it lay the Lodge built for the farm manager. Subsequently the 7,600-acre Sudbourne estate passed through a number of hands and was broken up during the downturn after World War I. The Hon. Alastair Watson, a keen polo-player, made his home at Chillesford Lodge where his family farms today.

Our informant, George Gardiner, was born in 1921 and became a special kind of horseman, looking after the polo stable with seven girl grooms and 32 ponies. The horses were requisitioned at the start of World War II and he was called up. After the war ended he was promoted head groom and sent to the Middle East to help buy Arab ponies which were flown back to England.

The polo ground lay next to the road. There was a charge for parking cars and cycles. Pedestrians were free, so locals left their bicycles in the hedge and walked in. The superb pool in which water polo was played is now overgrown, and the changing rooms and bronze statues are long gone.

The ground was reckoned to be the finest in the country. Underground pipes irrigated the turf. A kink, which can still be seen on the drive to Chillesford Lodge, was the result of enlarging the ground. There were day stables for visiting strings of ponies and the grass was so perfect that Mrs Watson used to give a box of chocolates to anyone who could find a weed. The ponies were taken to the ground three times a week, but had a practice ground near their stables on the model farm. In the 1953 flood George bravely went down to the marsh where the grazing ponies had been stranded and he put a rope on two of them. Then, leading them, he waded through the water which came up to his chest and fortunately the others followed.

Chillesford Polo Ground. On the last day of a meeting George and his girl grooms demonstrated the skill the game required. Then local lads competed in games of bicycle polo - Butley v. Chillesford and Sudbourne v. Orford.

Other game was, and still is, shot on the estate, but for centuries rabbits have bred there and rabbit-shoots were a sport for guests of the Watson family. There was a big warren with a perimeter net. The rabbits were driven and were so closely packed that already-shot rabbits were sometimes shot again. George recalls helping to collect 700 rabbits one morning and loading them into a game cart in order to take them to Wickham Market station *en route* for Campbell, Key & Langley, London rabbit

Florrie and her sister Mary gathering spring flowers for the church. Village children used to be immaculately turned out on Sundays.

dealers, whose names were stamped on the boxes into which they were packed. The rabbits were not skinned, but had been gutted by the keepers. At that time rabbits were very cheap; you could buy one for tuppence, he recalled.

From the Tithe Map we know that the present *Froize Inn* was known as Decoy Cottages in the 19th century. The cottages took their name from a two-acre, star-shaped lake which still lies hidden within 18 acres of vegetation and surrounded by saltings and reed-beds at the head of Butley Creek. It is shown on John Kirby's 1736 map of Suffolk. Like the 16-acre decoy at Iken it was an artificial lake with narrow waterways or pipes into which wildfowl were lured as they flew inland very early in the morning. The ends of the pipes were netted to trap thousands of birds. By 1907 the annual take had dwindled to 250, suggesting that the decoy was no longer netted and the lake was used by sportsmen. Reg Snowdon confirmed this; when young he was paid to take a boat to collect ducks shot from hides there.

The gamekeeper

Standing between the masters and the men were the gamekeepers. An unusual viewpoint of their life was provided by Florrie Warne née Collins, daughter of the under game-keeper on the Butley portion of the Greenwell estate and born in 1923, *'When I was about seven we moved to the lonely little cottage by Carman's Wood. A staircase led from the tiny little living room to two bedrooms and there were six of us.*

'My father was the under game-keeper. The head game-keeper, Mr Harry Meadows, lived down at Water Wood with his wife. He used to think so much of us girls, because he did not have a family. Nowadays keepers buy the chicks in, but at the start of the season they used to go and take so many of the eggs in each nest. There'd be

Chillesford's decoy pond as it was mapped by the Ordnance Survey in 1881. Decoy Cottages, now the *Froize* public house, are at the top.

as many as sixteen. All the birds were wild round the fields and in the hedges and on Saturdays we girls would have such fun going round with my father and Mr Meadows looking up the eggs. Mr Meadows would give us a few pence for the nests we found.

'My father used to have a lot of the younger pheasants to look after. You know the gateway on the ride as you go down to Water Wood? There were no trees there then and up at the top there used to be a great big shed with all the meal and the crumbs.

'Outside there were two big coppers on a fireplace with a bar across. There would be a dozen or so rabbits stewing away and in the big

Another lost country house. The rear elevation of Sudbourne Hall; designed by James Wyatt. It was demolished after World War II.

shed there was a trestle all the length of it. When the rabbits were cooked, we girls would strip all the meat off and that would go through the huge mincer in there. We would have our sleeves rolled up mixing it with the crumbs and

Alfred Decaen: detail of a grand al fresco luncheon in the Park; the table is laid with silver and Richard Wallace watches as his butler carves a Strasbourg pie and a keeper tends his dog.

The sporting heyday of the Sudbourne estate was in the 19th century. Its absentee owners, the 3rd and 4th Marquesses of Hertford and the latter's illegitimate son, Sir Richard Wallace, held large shooting parties there. These are commemorated in a series of paintings in Orford Town Hall, The polygonal game-larder is now a house. It held some 5,000 birds on steel racks with facilities below for dressing them. Wallace's 23 keepers wore green velvet livery.

various cereals. Then that would go into baskets to feed the pheasants.

'When the young pheasants went from there to Carman's Wood, the drive would have coops each side, two to three dozen, with a hen and the baby birds in. And I've been down with my father feeding them with the basket on his arm in the late afternoon. The birds as they grow go further afield. He'd whistle and they'd come out just like that. There were just my father and Mr Meadows. All they had was a bike.

'Sir Bernard Greenwell used to have shoots once a week through the season and sometimes they'd have them at Abbey House, sometimes at Water Wood and sometimes – and that was their favourite place – they used to come to little Carman's Wood. My mother set two big tables in the little sitting room. There'd be about 12 guests and Piper, the Butler, would do every-thing. My mother would put out the tables and he'd bring the cloths and she'd help to put the glasses and the silver round. And there'd be these huge picnic baskets, absolutely beautiful, Everything was cold, but sometimes there'd be soup which Mother would heat up. They'd have pies, nice cold meats, puddings, cheese and biscuits. Piper would always leave for us what was left of the cheese and biscuits and of course that was a luxury.'

The story continues
The First World War had a catastrophic effect on land prices. When the Rendlesham estate was put on the market in 1919 some of the farms failed to attract a single bid, including Butley Abbey Farm. Boyton Hall and Cauldwell Hall with 431 acres were sold as one lot for £4,300, amounting to the same price per acre as had been paid by Edward Spencer 200 years previously. Using his wife's money Walter Boynton of Melton Grange seized the opportunity to buy some lots privately, including Abbey Farm. Despite selling off its timber he went bankrupt. When a former headmaster, Dr Rendall, bought the Gatehouse to restore in his retirement, the Abbey farm and yards were unoccupied. Indeed after World War I there had been plans to turn the derelict buildings into a carpet factory. Between 1932 and 1938 Sir Bernard Greenwell bought up farms on the light land in which only the Forestry Commission had shown an

Easton Harriers. Although a Tudor sport described in Butley's Chronicle, *fox-hunting was never prominent in later centuries. Otters and hares were pursued with dogs until recent times. When a foxhunt met at* The Oyster *in 1980 Vera recalled that that she had not seen one in Butley since her childhood. The recent Act has resulted in enthusiastic drag-hunting, maintaining a social focus and providing cross-country recreational riding.*

interest. He was determined to recreate the Butley estate and find work for all the unemployed.

Financial difficulties led Rendall to sell the Gatehouse, but Sir Bernard allowed him to continue to live there. The estate was extended into Sudbourne, Gedgrave, Iken and Tunstall and Sir Bernard lived to see relative prosperity return due to the demand for increased food production prior to World War II. His son, Sir Peter, while a prisoner-of-war in Colditz, had time to plan for the future improvement of the Butley estate. He foresaw that water management was key and after his release arranged to receive rainwater from the runways of the nearby Woodbridge airbase. In addition he had water from aquifers pumped 180 feet to high ground. It could be used to irrigate crops in summer, whilst the powerful float-ing pump he installed in 1956 lowered the water-table sufficiently for 1,000 acres of marsh land to be under-drained, levelled and ploughed.

The biggest challenge faced was in 1953 when sea water broke through the river walls in three places and flooded large areas. After the gaps had been plugged by Sir Peter and

Part of Staverton Park has been restocked with deer after a gap of perhaps 600 years and the rest is carefully managed as a wildlife reserve.

his men, the East Suffolk and Norfolk River Board raised all the walls by three feet. The wide dykes on the landward side of the walls

were the source of the clay used. His sons are farming today, and face the challenges of a downturn in agriculture and continuing rise of sea-levels.

The Wantisden estate

After the Second World War ended many acres of heath land requisitioned for military purposes provided an opportunity for Jack Kemball to create a farm centred on Wantisden Hall, the Tudor house which John Talbot was leasing when Norden surveyed the Stanhope estate way back in 1601. The heath was ploughed and with irrigation has been made productive. Padley Water has been recreated as a string of beautiful pools, the topmost formed at the junction with Drydale, a valley choked with sand many centuries ago. With his family's involvement the estate has prospered and expanded with other business enterprises.

At Campsey Ash (J. G. Sheppard, Esq.'s), in Suffolk, August 29 and 30, 1845.

Gentlemen of Suffolk.	1st Inn.		2nd Inn.
E. Layton, Esq., b Taylor	12	— b Taylor	39
Rev. W. Poley, b Lyon	7	— c Taylor, b Pickering	11
W. Blake, Esq., c Dewing, b Pickering	53	— c Taylor, b Lyon	7
Rev. T. L. French, b Taylor	11	— b Taylor	6
Rev. C. Chapman, b Lyon	9	— c Lyon, b Taylor	3
T. Blake, Esq., l b w, b Taylor	20	— l b w	8
E. Walton, Esq., b Taylor	9	— run out	6
Rev. F. Freeman, b Dewing	1	— c Pickering, b Dewing...	5
E. B. Smith, Esq., b Taylor	2	— c Nethercote, b Ponsonby	13
R. Cobbold, Esq., b Dewing	2	— not out	13
O. Oakes, Esq., not out	0	— b Taylor	18
Byes 4, wides 23	27	Byes 26, wides 12, noes 1	39
	153		168

I Zingari.	1st Inn.		2nd Inn.
Lord Glamis, b W. Blake	2	c — Blake, b ——	9
Hon. C. Lyon, run out	12		
J. G. Sheppard, Esq., b W. Blake	3		
C. G. Taylor, Esq., c W. Blake, b ——	57		
E. M. Dewing, Esq., c French, b ——	44		
E. H. Pickering, Esq., run out	58		
H. O. Nethercote, Esq., c Smith, b W. Blake	3		
Hon. F. Ponsonby, c Walton, b Cobbold	15		
W. Bolland, Esq., b Cobbold	1		
E. S. E. Hartopp, Esq., b Cobbold	10		
G. A. F. Bentinck, Esq., not out	3	— not out	7
Byes 10, wides 20	30	Byes 3, wides 4 ...	7
	238		23

I Zingari (The Gypsies)

The gentleman's game of cricket was played in the grounds of country houses in the 19th century.

The match at High House, Campsea Ashe, was contested by the Gentlemen of Suffolk v. the newly-formed amateur touring side, *I Zingari*.

It took place in August 1845 and was watched by a crowd of 2,000 entertained by *'a capital band which played during the whole day and with its lively polkas excited even the grave and sturdy yeoman.'*

The Surveyor's Tale
Chapter 8

Today the Ordnance Survey can refine and update maps using aerial survey and global positioning systems, while the Land Registry is tasked with recording the boundaries and ownership of every property in the land. It is the culmination of a thousand-year process going back to a survey ordered by William the Conqueror in 1085, which we know as *The Domesday Book*.

It was probably a monastic initiative to draw a map of landholdings. One of the earliest known was made in 1306 by the Augustinian canons of Flixton Priory near Bungay. Although none of Butley Priory's maps have survived, this part of Suffolk is rich in later estate maps and plans. Who were the surveyors and cartographers and how did they work?

A Suffolk surveyor, the gentleman John Darby, on his map of Falkenham and Kirton humorously depicted the hot reality of survey work in the field with scale and dividers. The pose he borrowed from a Breughel painting. His map of Aldeburgh, made in the same year that Radulph Agas was surveying Butley, can be seen in the Moot Hall there.

In the Middle Ages administration on a local level was in the hands of the lord of each manor; he held his 'fee' from the king, to whom he rendered regular taxes, special levies and military service. These financial obligations were, as much as possible, delegated to the holders of land in his manor, and his steward kept records in court rolls, terriers and rentals. In the absence of maps, holdings were located by description, size and what lay north, south, east and west of them – a cumbersome process which could lead to confusion. Two such medieval documents, the property of Butley Priory, have survived.

Walter Baa

The earliest existing survey made for Butley Priory is that of Boyton. It was compiled in 1383 by the canon, Walter Baa. He was receiver of rents for the manor purchased by the Priory 18 years previously. He used descriptive formulae to identify land by its abutments and its previous occupiers. Written in Latin in red and black ink the document is entitled *Register of the services and customs of the Manor of Boyton made by the whole homage in the month of October in the 7th year of the reign of Richard II* . . .

The upper course of the River Tang was known as the River Laneburgh. It runs under the Capel-Hollesley road beside Wash Cottage.

Incidental information in the document is of various kinds. The first entry gives the turbary or peatbed of Laneburgh as an abutment. This, together with a 1568 name *'Riveria de Laneburgh'* for the upper Tang,

fixes a hitherto uncertain Domesday location. It is the extension of the parish of Boyton west and south of the Tang known today as Little Scotland, a former sheepwalk of some 155 acres. A delightful name for the lost settlement at the east end of the Boyton ridge was *'Enlond'* (Land's End). The surveyor records that he was unable to measure one part of Boyton marshes because of the inundation of the sea at the time of the survey.

Walter Fulbourn

Walter lived at Wickham Market. No doubt he was educated in a monastic school. That he was well-to-do is evinced by his will and the large chapel which he built on the south side of the parish church, and where he asked to be buried. He died at an advanced age in 1489, leaving an extensive list of bequests to churches and monasteries; Leiston Abbey was a particular beneficiary, but not Butley.

Fifty years earlier Walter had made a survey of Bawdsey Manor for Sir Thomas Willoughby. A copy of Willoughby's 'Terrier or Register' (*Terrarium sive Register*) was made for Butley Priory which had been bequeathed a half-share of the manor. It is the copy that has survived, a paper ledger of 59 closely written pages, sole representative of all the long-lost administrative documents needed by the Priory for the management of its estates.

The neat abbreviated Latin lists present and past holders of each piece of land, its name and its abutments. These shed incidental light on salt production, sea defences, the extent to which the land was enclosed, its size and its comparative value. Belonging to the Priory was *'le Park'* , while *'le Est'* and *'le Clyf '* are easily identifiable today as East Street and Bawdsey Cliff.

The map-makers

During the later 16th century cartography was to develop nationally. The Woodbridge benefactor, Thomas Seckford, employed Christopher Saxton to produce the first printed atlas of counties published in 1579. At a local level landowners found an estate map to be an invaluable management tool. Sometimes they mapped their estates themselves, for example, Sir Nicholas Bacon and his son at Stiffkey in Norfolk.

Radulph Agas

The most colourful of our surveyors was crippled from his birth in about 1540. After taking holy orders he became rector of Gressinghall in Norfolk, but failed to make a success of this profession. He returned to surveying for which he had earlier shown talent, having produced a remarkable bird's eye panorama of Oxford. His disability may have made him acerbic. Unfortunately he upset some of his gentry patrons. He wrote a treatise on surveying as did his contemporary John Norden. Declaring that he had *'practised in Survey more than forty years'*, he complained that *'more abuse in concealments . . . hath been offered in these last 100 years than in the 500 before'*. He was referring particularly to lands held directly from the monarch. The lack of standard units of measurement angered him and he told his patron, Lord Burghley, that *'the great number of land meters [surveyors] with the diversity of device[s] for measuring . . . lead to infinite errors daily committed'*.

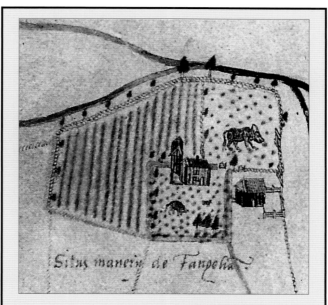

Agas' exquisite drawing of the site of Tangham Manor provides an addition to moated manors in the *Historical Atlas of Suffolk*. It is located at the head of the watercourse which, like the moat, is tinted pale mauve. The house with a central chimney stands at the north end of the 600 sq yd enclosure. Surrounding the moat are five enclosures in one of which there is a barn and, in another, a bull. By 1594 Tangham manor-house is described as *'mediocriter edificat'* – no doubt because it was timber-framed and not brick.

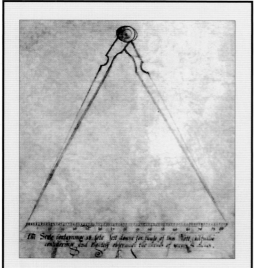

Measurements were based on the acre, divided into 4 rods and 40 perches until replaced by the metric hectare in the 20th century. Unfortunately the smallest unit was not standardised. Thus Agas used an 18ft pole for his Tangham map (above) while on the neighbouring estate Norden used a 16ft pole. Surveying instruments were basic: a compass, plane table and chain.

Radulph found a congenial employer in the extreme protestant, Robert Forth. His services were used on at least two occasions, the first when a map of Forth's Tangham sheepwalks was needed to counter a charge of encroachment headed by the Earl of Surrey. The verdict is unknown, but statements of shepherds from adjacent manors show that Forth was indeed encroaching on neighbouring commons. At the top of his map Agas states the methods he has used: *'A Description or Plott of percell the estate . . . after the testimony of many olde and wise men . . . out of an olde book dated 1 May 1457'*. Clearly the reference is to a monastic document; the date suggests a now-lost survey by Walter Fulbourn. At the bottom the self-publicist refers to his own skill and accuracy. Information is in English for the most part, but Agas occasionally employs Latin phrases. The map shows tracks intersecting across the heath and the disputed part known as Cowedale in the north-east corner. Here and there mounds are depicted,

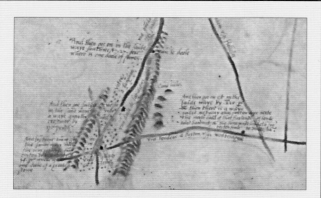

A row of five mounds, labelled 'some hilles', flanks a dry valley on the south-east boundary of Tangham Manor. They were located in 1980, but the dense vegetation and tree cover made survey at that time impossible. However, following the hurricane of 1987 the badly-damaged barrows were surveyed by Valerie Fenwick and John Cross, using a Southampton University random-plotting program.

including an adjacent pair, one of which survives as a scheduled barrow within the Forestry Commission plantation. Were there originally two here?

When Robert Forth called upon Agas again, in 1594, to produce a descriptive survey of his manors of Butley, Boyton and Tangham together with a, now lost, set of maps, it was written in the traditional way, on parchment and in Latin.

In the three manors there is very little woodland, mostly plantations, totalling 173 acres of which 129 were demesne – a mere 3.25% of the total acreage. Because much of the land had long been enclosed, its hedgerow trees were the main source of timber and coppice as in later centuries. Furze from the heaths and peat from turbaries in the valleys were other sources of fuel. Annotations in Forth's own handwriting show that he was planting woodland in the last years of his life.

John Norden
While Forth, in common with many other landowners, was in financial difficulty exacerbated by crop failures, wealthy newcomers were buying up land to create estates. Michael Stanhope rose to be a Privy Councillor under Queen Elizabeth who granted him Sudbourne Manor. The agri-cultural depression enabled him to amass around it in a very short time an estate measuring 35 miles in circuit. Like other landowners before him, he needed a surveyor to advise. He engaged an experienced cartographer who, despite his talent and years of surveying experience, had failed to attract a patron for a projected independent survey of counties.

Most fieldwork had to be undertaken in winter when vegetation had died down. One can imagine John Norden, blue with cold on the shingle of Orford Ness in March 1600 when he surveyed the breach made by recent storms and planned remedial measures. It was invariably his practice to annotate his maps with useful information and advice. In this case he was acting as a hydrographer and costing the measures he proposed.

Shortly afterwards he began the survey proper of Stanhope's estate. Clearly expense was no object. Norden himself calculated that estate maps cost twice as much as written surveys of fields with selective maps.

John Norden chose to portray himself in Tudor court dress rather than in leather breeches like John Darby.

Born in Somerset and trained in law, he became the first cartographer to insert roads on English maps. In the year 1600, when he began to work for Michael Stanhope, Norden was appointed Senior Surveyor of the Crown Woods, reflecting his knowledge of arboriculture.

A good surveyor needed many talents.

He would also have needed to charge for a team of assistants, the cost of board and hire of horses.

The end product on vellum, *An Ample and Trew Description and Survey of the Manors, Lordships, Townes and Parishes* . . . is in English throughout, and comprises beautifully coloured maps prefaced with lists of tenants and holdings identified by letters of the alphabet. Every map or 'table' has a preamble of explanatory matter. Like Agas and other surveyors, Norden has difficulties with occupants who try to conceal from him the fact that some of their land is not freehold – *'doe drowne muche of the copie lande amonge their ffree'*. When he comes to survey Tunstall he is exasperated by the obfuscation of the inhabitants. Manorial boundaries are another problem and he highlights 56 acres of demesne with the words *'usurped by Sutton'*. A further problem encountered relates to detached pieces of land in other manors. Butley proves so complex that he has to postpone dealing with it.

It was a remarkable achievement to complete the survey so rapidly. Its variable accuracy reflects this speed and the number of assistants on whom he must have depended. Two years later James I reappointed him as one of the surveyors of Crown lands. It seems his efforts in Tunstall and elsewhere had not gone unnoticed, for he was singled out for his ability to search for pieces of land which had been lost or encroached upon. The final embellishment of *An Ample and Trew Description* is a beautifully decorated and coloured title-page, highlighted in gold. Imagine Norden's dismay when just after he finished it Michael Stanhope was knighted. 'Sir' and 'knight' in black ink had to be inelegantly squeezed in beside his name.

Good maps could last a long time; Norden's map for the Duchy of Cornwall was not superseded until 1771 and the survey for Stanhope was separated into two volumes when the estate was divided in the 19th century. He was assisted by his surveyor son, John, and died in 1626 in Fulham, Middlesex. Greville Collins, who in 1686 made the first usable charts of our coastline, commented on the decline of cartography after Norden.

John Kirby

Wickham Market was home to two outstanding surveyors. Kirby has been called our first great native surveyor and mapmaker. At one time he kept a school in Orford, but after his marriage in 1714 he moved to Wickham Market where his 11 children were born. Like Isaac Johnson he supported his family by producing workmanlike estate maps and selling books. However in 1731 when he was 41, he announced that he was undertaking a survey

John Kirby chose, as the starting-point for his map of the county, his own parish church. This was perhaps his inspiration, since from its tower he was able to see *'very near (if not altogether) fifty Parish Churches'*. Two of these, in Wantisden and Tunstall, were separated by heath sufficiently level for him to lay out his measuring chain between them. In this way he created the five-furlong base-line of a triangle with Wickham's tower as the apex – the beginning of a web of bearings covering the whole county.

of the whole county. It took him and an assistant five years. At the same time he gathered data for a guide to the county, entitled *The Suffolk Traveller*, published in 1735. The maps showing the seats of gentry include occasional comments such as that on his map, published in 1766: *the Sand-land may . . . be divided into the Marsh, Arable and Heath Lands. In the Heathy part are fed great numbers of Sheep and Oxen, and sometimes it produces greater Crops of Corn than any in the County . . .*

His maps were revised and republished after his death in 1753, aged 63, by his sons, the artist, Joshua, and William, the lawyer. They have recently been reprinted by the Suffolk Records Society together with his *Suffolk Traveller*.

Transformation of the Priory Gatehouse
Miss Anne Spencer was named on Kirby's 1736 map as residing at Rendlesham Hall. Two years later she married Scotland's premier peer, becoming the Duchess of Hamilton, as is duly noted on his 1766 map. The name 'Little Scotland' for the Boyton part of her estate dates from this time. Her irascible Scottish gamekeeper, Graham, had moved boundary posts there and caused a drawn-out dispute with the Boyton Almshouse trustees. On the same map Mrs Wright was noted having her seat at Butley Abbey, showing that Rebecca was still alive and had returned to her childhood home.

The shooting lodge

Years before, the Priory Gatehouse and attached Mansion-house had become ruinous and uninhabitable. In 1738 the Harvy family's long lease expired and Rebecca Wright and her husband were in a position to take them in hand. The brick-built Tudor house was beyond repair and had to be demolished, but, although roofless, the medieval stonework of the Gatehouse was still sound. Tall flanking towers were built; the ground floor passageway was blocked up to create a large vaulted room. Sash windows and a reused staircase were installed. It was converted, not into a residence for themselves, but into a shooting lodge.

Following George Wright's death in his London home 12 years later, his only personal effects in Butley were a model of a

Born in 1754, Isaac Johnson spent his childhood in the Triangle at Alderton. He succeeded his father as bailiff of the Hollesley-cum-Sutton manor. Three years later he moved to Woodbridge. He had 12 children, whom he supported by surveying numerous estates. Like other surveyors, Isaac also worked as a painter. During his second survey of the 5,137-acre Butley estate in 1800, he made a number of drawings and watercolours of the ruined Priory, including one of himself at work. He had an extraordinarily long and active life and was buried in Woodbridge in 1835.

ship, a map of Suffolk, two pieces of old tapestry, several locks and some old pictures. Rebecca bequeathed the property to her London clockmaker relative, Samuel Clyatt. He sold it to a prominent printer, William Strahan. From the *Printer to His Majesty* the Gatehouse passed into noble ownership. A contemporary note in a copy of Grose's *Antiquities* states '*The two towers erected by Mr Wright 1737 were taken down by Lord Archibald Hamilton about 1780*'. Purchase of the Gatehouse and its 148 acres filled a gap in the estate Hamilton had inherited from his mother in 1771.

He enjoyed the relaxation afforded by sport '*in Butley, Tangham, Capel St Andrew, Boyton, Eyke and Wantisden*', but acquisition of the Gatehouse sporting lodge together with the lease held by his brother-in-law enabled the two men to embark on the creation of a sylvan setting and a stately ride from Hamilton's seat at Rendlesham. A talented surveyor with experience of Sandlings soils was at hand to advise.

Transformation of the landscape

The year 1780 marks the beginning of Isaac Johnson's very long association with an estate for which he was providing plans up to his death. As his first major commission the 25-year-old produced a survey of the Butley Estate and recommended ways in which the Gatehouse could be improved and cover for game created. He was laying out the line of the '*New Road*' before Christmas 1794. It is shown planted with trees on his 1818 map. We are fortunate that his working plans, finely drawn on patchwork sheets of paper pasted together, survive in the Butley estate archives, while his correspondence, some plans and an account book for 1791-96, are preserved in Ipswich Record Office.

The Clumps

For older local people the Clumps, that avenue which leads from the Woodbridge Road to the Gatehouse was an ancient feature of the landscape. In fact it was laid out in a straight line to connect the shooting lodge with Rendlesham Hall's original southern drive on the north side of Staverton Park.

After two hundred years the end came for the Clumps when they were deemed dangerous. Local people hope to recreate the avenue and have taken part in planting new groups of saplings.

visitors. An apparently French solution was used; on each side at intervals clumps of trees, comprising four beeches around a fir tree were planted. In the 1980s, the last surviving clump had a misshapen fir tree at its centre.

A sylvan setting

The immediate surrounds of the Gatehouse needed to be improved, too. Isaac cleared away farm buildings, yards and ruins round the Gatehouse in order to set it in *Hall Green*, a lawn of ten acres. The road which ran in front of the Gatehouse was realigned behind a screen of trees. Before this time the road connecting Butley Priory with Woodbridge ran well south of the present road. Stretches of this medieval road can be followed today as a ride, numbered 10, in Tangham Forest. At Folly Cottage it is interrupted by the perimeter fence of the old air-base. Another plantation concealed a second new road on the east side of the site. The result was firstly the Six Ways we see today and secondly, the awkward bend where his second road joined an existing track to Abbey Farm.

An avenue of more than a mile running not within a park, but across heath and arable, needed to be dignified by more than a single row of flanking trees if it was to impress

Adjacent to Rendlesham Park, the grounds of Ashe Park, previously surveyed

---

Great havoc in Staverton Park

The park is the largest and most visible area of ancient woodland in the Sandlings. Before Isaac Johnson laid out the Clumps, some of Staverton's oaks had been despoiled. In the 18th century the park was part of the estate of Loudham Hall whose owner, Robert Oneby, wrote his will in 1743, ten years before he died. Clearly he expected his heirs to inherit, but should he lack one, his estate was to pass to his brother-in-law, Sir William Chapman, and his heirs. The problem was that neither gentleman produced children who outlived them.

Sir William died in 1785 and asked to be buried in his family vault at Ufford. His effects were auctioned at Loudham Hall. The rightful heir to the estate had to be decided by a judge and special jury at Bury Assizes. Judgement was reported

in the *Ipswich Journal* in January 1786, '*The heirs at law of the late Robert Oneby esquire were put into full and quiet possession of the very valuable estate.*' Afterwards there was a grand ball to celebrate.

An explanation of the pollarding at different heights which has puzzled Oliver Rackham appears in the *Transactions of the Suffolk Natural History Society* in a report by two botanists who passed through the park the following year and recorded that '*great havoc has been lately made and many fine trees appear shamefully dismembered; the branches of which it seems were cut off and carried away during the time the estate was in litigation.*'

A story circulating in *The Oyster* as late as the 1970s echoed these events. It was said that two brothers owned the park and they fell out with each other, despoiling the other's trees by 'nipping out', that is, cutting out the leading branch.

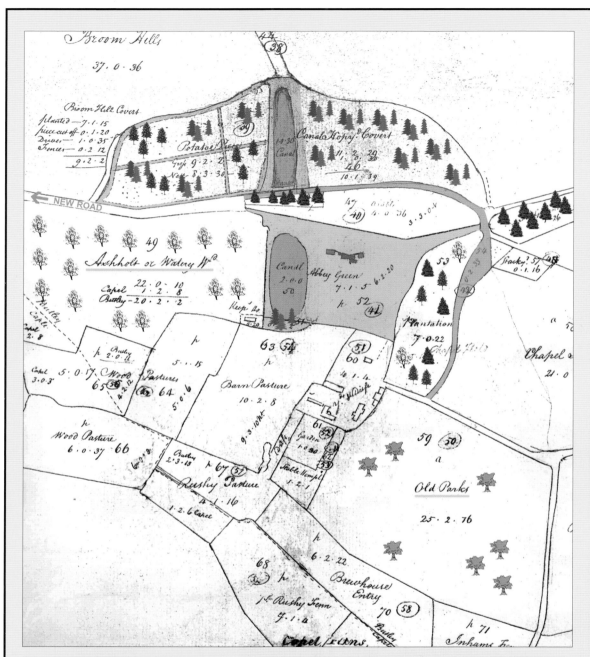

Pen and ink draft survey by Isaac Johnson shows the sylvan setting he created around the Gatehouse. He noted that his new 'inclosed' roads consumed three and a half acres of land. In addition he created the tree-lined approach, later known as 'The Clumps' (arrowed).

Colour and key have been added

Gatehouse and pavilions – red	New roads – brown
New planting shown with trees	Enlarged monastic pond and new canal – blue
Existing park and coppice underlined	Lawns – green

by Isaac, contained no fewer than three canals. Old-fashioned though these were, they suggested a solution to the problems presented by the topography round the Gatehouse. On its west side lay a narrow pond and Isaac created a 'Canal' parallel to it. However, his working drawing of 1818 shows that the pond and canal were subsequently amalgamated into the two-acre pond known today as the 'monastic fishpond'.

To the north yet another 'Canal' of more than an acre was created in 1795 by damming the stream in Hopyard Fen which fed the old pond and adjacent canal. The Gatehouse was flanked by sinuous coverts with drives, planted to obscure from view lime and brick kilns at the south end of Church Field.

A seven-acre wood, 'Abbey Plantation', had to be created down the east flank of the lawn in order to screen the brick-kilns at High Corner. This connected with a 25-acre park, 'Old Parks', to create a vista across water-meadows. The final touches were: a belt of firs closing the view to the east; and doubling the size of 'High Abbey Lawn' by sweeping away all the old barns, hempland and cinder mounds which lay between it and the brook to the south.

The Gatehouse was successively upgraded. George Wright's old-fashioned towers had been demolished by 1780; a new wing and a fashionable pair of flanking pavilions were now planned to improve accommodation for servants and grooms. These 'convenient additions' had not all been finished when the estate was purchased by Peter Isaac Thellusson, who in 1806 was created Lord Rendlesham.

Lord Rendlesham's schemes included robbing stonework from the ruins and the chapel at the east end of the demolished monastic church in order to create 'Gothick' lodges at his residence. Two of his four lodges survive.

By 1818 the time had come to obliterate the medieval road to Woodbridge as it inconveniently interrupted field sports. The solution was to overplant it with belts of trees. Further rectangular belts transformed the appearance of the sheepwalks, and a wide wooded demarcation was created between Tangham and the still open heaths of

Eyke and Hollesley. The sporting landscape recorded by Johnson was essentially that mapped in 1846 which survived until 20th-century plantations and airbases changed the heath out of all recognition.

Jack Kemball mirrored Isaac Johnson's transformation when he planted the belts of conifers we see on Wantisden Heath today.

Guarding a now disused avenue, the West Lodge of Rendlesham Park provides a rare glimpse of the lost world of Sandlings country houses.

The makers of Tithe maps
Tithe maps are a convenient starting-point for local historians. One of the best of the map-makers was Bland Hood Galland, a civil engineer, who worked from 1833-4 for the Ordnance Survey. However, the pay was poor and he was attracted by private work. He surveyed the parish of Chillesford in 1841. Subsequently he worked for the Tithe Commissioners up to his death in 1846.

These large-scale maps were produced for every parish in the country between 1836 and about 1850. Both the scales and, indeed, the accuracy of them vary a good deal, since they were not intended to be used for detailed measurement, but in order to number and record the shape and position of every field and enclosure as an accompaniment to an Apportionment or list. This was the necessary preamble to enabling the tithes, hitherto variably assessed, to be fairly commuted into money payments.

While all farm-houses are merely named 'Yards', the apportionments do provide every field-name, its size and its use, for instance, wood, arable, meadow or pasture. The identity of every landowner and tenant is recorded and this useful information can be collated by researchers using the age, the occupation and the household of every inhabitant of a parish in the 1841 and 1851 census records. This combination of data for the mid-19th century is enormously valuable for family historians.

Tales from the Courtroom

Chapter 9

The medieval unit of local government was the manor. Often manorial names and boundaries are the same as ecclesiastical parishes, but not always. For instance, Tangham is the name of the manor in which Capel St Andrew lies and its boundary diverged from that of the parish in several places.

A written record in Latin was kept of each manorial court on a roll of parchment – hence the documents are known as court rolls. They are often damaged and difficult to read, but hidden among the repetitive formulae in abbreviated Latin are scraps of information about ordinary people.

The court was presided over by a steward. Towards the end of the 18th century manorial courts were coming to an end. Samuel Kilderbee, an Ipswich lawyer, was employed for many years as steward of Triangle manors by the Warner Trustees, the Wrights and the Hamiltons. He befriended Gainsbrough who painted this delightful portrait now hanging in Christchurch Mansion, Ipswich.

Fascination with court rolls is an acquired taste. Not only are they difficult to lay out, being like crinkled wallpaper on the record office table, but the handwriting is hard to read, especially the garbled Latin, exacerbated by areas where purple mould has removed the ink.

Most of the content is dull and uninformative, but when long sequences of rolls survive, families can be traced through the transfer of their copyhold property. At the end of a court the 'Verdicts' dealing with fines for misdemeanours are always of interest since they provide clues to the kind of farming on the manor, and occasionally personalities are apparent.

Village democracy of a sort

There has always been a need for village government. In England its origins lie in the medieval 'courts' held in every manor several times a year. Everyone who held land there, whether as a freeholder or a copyhold tenant, was required to attend, or pay a fine. They were called the 'Jurors', as they collectively pronounced on any misdemeanours reported to the court and fixed the fines payable. They also regulated the transfer of property in accordance with the 'Customs' of individual manors.

In the manors of Rendlesham, Butley, Tangham, and Boyton the unusual 'Custom' (known as Borough English) was that the youngest, not the eldest, son inherited copyholds. In the absence of a male heir, daughters were eligible, but in that case the property would be divided equally among all of them. Of course 'fines' (charges) were levied at each of these stages and added to the lord of the manor's income from his tenants. The records his steward kept were written on parchment and sewn together end-to-end to make long rolls.

The manorial courts used set procedures to ensure an uncontested succession of land occupancy. Three copyholders could deal with a deathbed emergency. Otherwise the copyholder came to court. He brought his wife if he was married, so that she could be examined *secretly and separately* to confirm that she was content for the holding to be given up. If so, it was *surrendered into the hands of the lord of the manor* (not literally as his steward represented him on all but special occasions). It was then the lord's prerogative to re-grant the holding, or to farm it himself.

Sometimes many people had committed the same offence, usually for failing to ditch and fence their land properly. At the Tangham court held on the Eve of All Saints in 1555 the inhabitants of the village of Capel were warned they would be fined if they continued to allow their geese out during the night to graze on Wantsall Green. Court records were sometimes neatly written, but always very abbreviated as for the most part familiar formulae were repeated. Sometimes the writer would be at a loss for a Latin word and lapsed into everyday speech. Not even the largest tenant farmers could escape fines imposed by their fellow jurors. For instance, in 1553 John Stonnard was threatened with a 20 shilling fine should he not repair Mill Marsh Bridge, while William Redham had failed to repair the sluices by the Butley river, with consequent flooding.

The 'Custom' also itemised the produce and services due to the lord, such as eggs and poultry on specific dates, and work days in the field with or without the provision of food, plus 'ward' or guard duty.

The manorial courts continued regardless of plague, civil unrest and changes of ownership. When the Peasants' Revolt of 1381 reached the Sandlings in mid June, five men broke the peace and entered Butley Priory carrying arms. They were bound tenants: Richard Rook, William Coke, John Grygge, John de Cretyng and Thomas Cokeson.

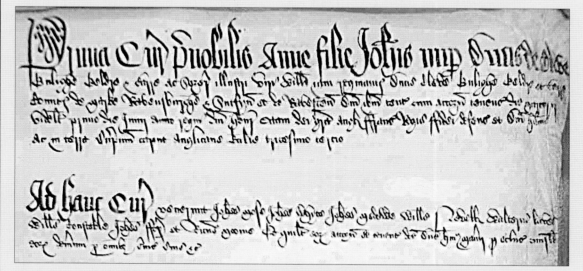

A surviving 16th-century record for Eyke and Bromeswell itemises payments for Fleeces, Cunny money, Foldage and Geese – payable at Michaelmas and Lammas. A century later during the Interregnum all records were written in English.

They knew what to seize, namely court rolls and rentals. The documents were carried out of the Priory's jurisdiction to Hollesley where they were burnt. Fortunately for us they failed to seize the court roll of Tangham, begun in 1377 (p.158). In it the incident was subsequently recorded, as was the punishment. Needless to say, all the men's lands, goods and chattels were confiscated. Five years later the canon, Walter Baa, who was Receiver of Rents for the Priory, summoned the whole 'homage' (landholders) to help him compile a new register of the services and customs of the Manor of Boyton. This, too, has survived.

In 1538 the greatest redistribution of land since the Norman Conquest occurred when all over the country monasteries were closed

The King retained Boyton Manor until he divorced Anne of Cleves, when with Chillesford it formed part of the package of lands providing her with the generous income of £4,000 until she died 'or went overseas'. Henry bestowed on her the title of The King's Sister, but the steward of the Boyton court dated 1 June in the 33rd year of his reign played for safety and used the words, *The First Court of the most noble Anne, daughter of John recently Duke of Cleve.* Usefully for local historians every landholder was required to appear at the first court of a manorial lord and on this occasion eight names are inscribed after the preamble. The third, John Medowe, had earlier received the surrender of John Egleston's land, appearing as 'John Myddow' later in the chapter.

and their manors seized. Technically Henry VIII took all the property into his own hands, but in practice many manors were immediately sold or granted to favourites. Others were quickly leased, so that agriculture should not suffer from neglect. Thus Butley Manor was granted initially to the Duke of Suffolk who rapidly leased it for a term of 21 years to his treasurer, William Naunton, apart from its woods which the King made a point of retaining.

The village greens

The manorial courts controlled the use of greens. In the three manors of Butley, Boyton and Tangham only one green has retained its identity; Capel Green is an 11-acre field, anciently known as Wantsall Green.

Old maps show there were once houses on three sides; today only a pair remain. This is where the rough precursor of football, known as Camping, used to be played. The game certainly goes back to medieval times; in 1437 there was a four-acre Camping Close on Butley Priory's estate in Bawdsey.

The Ipswich Journal of November 1785 announced the sale of Thomas Cooper's small farm of 15 acres, *'with a right of commonage upon Capel Green for 3 head of cattle. The Green carries only 18 head.'* Roy Collins, who years ago helped to demolish the cottages on the east side of Capel Green, recalled that there used to be a clump of thorn trees in the middle of the Green to provide some shade for grazing animals.

Capel Green was once surrounded by villagers' plots. On the west side two have clearly encroached by the late 18th century.

Butley's main green was Killhill Green. Its eight acres lay in front of the Priory Gatehouse and will have seen numerous village festivities. The most important of these was the Feast celebrating the birth of St John the Baptist which marked midsummer on 24 June. The green no doubt derived its name from its use as a construction site where lime was burnt for mortar during the monastery's long-drawn-out building programme. A lime-kiln is recorded in its north-east corner after the

Dissolution. When Isaac Johnson re-modelled the Gatehouse surrounds the old green was tastefully renamed Hall Green.

Only one green has been located by the authors for Boyton. A 14th-century document shows that a now-vanished hamlet lay at the east end of the ridge where there was a water mill opposite Burrow Hill. The houses lay on the Enlond [Land's End] road adjoining the two-acre Mill Green and

Looking west from Boyton Dock the site of Boyton's lost hamlet, green and water-mill lay at the end of the ridge (arrowed).

Draper's Yard. The green was still there in 1568, but had disappeared by 1594.

In contrast to the Street, High and Low Corner were Butley's early settlements and were built around greens. These were commemorated in the old names: Rielie Green and Lowsing Green.

The greens have now disappeared but clues in manorial records provide evidence for them. For instance, in 1568 Robert Mawling, George Doggett, Robert Fatter and Henry King were warned that they would be fined 3s 4d if they allowed their

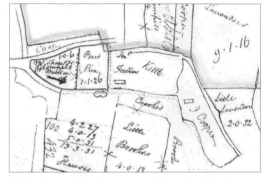

Rielie Green at High Corner can be identified on Isaac Johnson's draft survey of the Butley estate. It comprised Shoulder of Mutton and Pond Piece (outlined in red).

geese and beasts on the common called Reilie Green again.

Its two and a half acres were divided into two parts, 'Shoulder of Mutton' and 'Pond Piece'. The former was copyhold of the manors of both Butley and Kettleburgh. Subsequently this common land was used by the community in the form of allotments and the pond was filled in.

The location of Lowsing Green proved elusive; it did not feature in Butley manorial records as it belonged to Kettleburgh Manor. Fortunately the draft 18th-century survey clinched its position at the T-junction formed by the road from Chillesford Mill with that leading from the Priory. Isaac Johnson's sketch-maps enabled it to be identified as the triangular plot on which the Wesleyan Methodist chapel was later built. Not including the roadways it measured about 2,000 sq yds and was a useful public space on which was situated the hamlet's well, in common use until the 1950s.

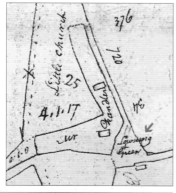

Opposite the Tiled House, now called Priory Cottage, a triangle of land was marked Lowsing Green by Isaac Johnson. Later, in 1836, Butley's Methodist Chapel was built on the site. It is now a private house.

There is no record of any common or green at Butley Street, which was a much later settlement at the junction of routes across the river. However, the small triangle of land in front of *The Oyster Inn* was larger before the roads were metalled and was shared by the villagers as the photograph on page 120 shows. The verges along the Street also constituted 'the lord's waste' and were used before they were encroached upon.

In the three manors the smallest green of all flanked the main highway from Snape to Bawdsey which ran to the west of Wantsall Green (later Capel Green). A mere 12 perches (360 sq yds), Melton Green is described in the survey of 1594, but had gone by the late 18th century. This section of the highway was known as Drieholme Way, no doubt to distinguish it from a parallel wet route, still in use, across Wantsall Green, which involved crossing the streams running down each side of it.

Capel had two other greens, both triangular. The first, known as Gospel Green, lay between the Great Wood and the bend in the road near Stonebridge. It measured 30 perches (900 sq yds) on Isaac Johnson's survey and belonged to the Manor of Kettleburgh. Today a pair of cottages stand there. On the other side of the road lay a green which took its name from Capel's former mill, superseded by the Priory mill. Mill Green's three quarters of an acre had ceased to be common land by the end of the 16th century and was farmed by John Lucock.

The man from the Shires

A few years ago men in *The Oyster Inn* would refer to folk from parts of England outside Norfolk and Suffolk as *'from the shires'*, which they pronounced *'sheers'*. This story from the court rolls of Boyton concerns members of a family from Eccleston in Lancashire, some of whom were living in the Sandlings in the first half of the 16th century. John Egleston or 'Hegylston' senior owned a freehold house and land in Boyton and had acquired the copyhold of a farm still named after its 14th-century holder, Thomas Stampard. Egleston died in 1540 leaving a nuncupative will. He left his house and lands in Boyton to his wife Mary and after her death to his son, having surrendered them in the customary way to the Lord of the Manor, by the hands of John Myddow *'to the behoof'* of his wife and child. He left his son two cows and five ewes, and also made provision for an unborn child. His widow married a local man, Robert Kempster.

For most of his career John Egleston would celebrate the Roman Catholic Mass in Shottisham like a fellow priest, Alexander Inglisshe, whose memorial brass depicts him as he would have been seen by his Campsea Ashe congregation on Easter Sunday – facing them with an elaborate chalice and the consecrated wafer. Whilst Alexander died in 1504, John survived the Reformation and had to adjust his beliefs in order to keep his living.

Manorial custom allowed a childless widow to keep the copyhold until she died. Upon her death, by the terms of her first husband's will, his freeholds in Boyton had to be sold and the proceeds given to Boyton church and to charity.

The copyhold called Stampards was not affected by the will. Shortly after Mary died in 1546 another John Egleston, the parson of Shottisham, came forward to claim that he was next-of-kin. At a court held later that year he was formally admitted to Stampards Tenement.

It was not unusual for incumbents to farm on their own account. For instance, the rector of Boyton later that century was farming more than 30 acres, a sizeable holding in those

An old photograph shows John Egleston's little cottage beside Shottisham mill, now transformed into a beautiful home (above).

days. However, the parson of Shottisham was by now an old man, having been minister there since 1509. He sold the copyhold of Stampards to a Boyton man, Matthew Armiger, for £16 3s 4d. His executors were charged with obtaining £12 16s 8d, which was outstanding. When the parson died two years later, in June 1548, he bequeathed the next instalment of £3 6s 8d to a kinsman, Edmund Haryson.

The parson's thoughts were with the poor of Shottisham and his servant Elyn Unkyl. To Elyn he bequeathed 'my featherbed that I lie on', a cow and 40s in addition to brass and pewter items. He left her his house at the mill at Shottisham, to pass after her death to Anne Unkyl. The relationship between the two was not revealed, but they were probably sisters. The corn sown on the parson's glebe was to be sold. On the day of his burial the poor people of Shottisham (the 'poverte') were to be given a seme of bread corn, a seme of drink corn, and 'every poor body' in the parish was to receive a penny. The parson's obsolete *Mannell* and *Processioner* books were bequeathed to Eccleston Church in faraway Lancashire, a part of England which retained strong Catholic beliefs.

There matters might have rested with Matthew Armiger not paying another penny for Stampards. If Lancastrian relatives had not learned of John Egleston's death before this, the arrival of his books in Eccleston will have alerted them. From what took place afterwards it is clear that Edmund Haryson had died in the meantime. The parson's closest kinsman was now Henry Egleston.

Henry rode down from Lancashire to Suffolk in early October 1553 and appeared at Boyton's manorial court to claim that he was heir to John Egleston senior's copyhold land. Matthew Armiger was present to confirm his purchase agreement. It must have been quite a dramatic scene and the court most probably took place at the *Lord's principal messuage*, the now demolished Frog's Hall down on Boyton Marshes. It seems from the mention of his name twice that the manorial lord, William Forth, was himself present and received into his own hand the formal surrender by Henry Tangham's mill stood opposite it, on the other side of the valley. However, after the Priory acquired Chillesford manor in 1411, the mills within the three manors could be rationalised.

Tangham's Carlton mill lay where the road between Butley and Capel crosses

---

The impact of sea-level rise on low-lying mills in the Triangle

After the light land was ploughed soil washed into watercourses. The gradually rising sea-level slowed the current in tidal inlets so that they became clogged with silt. Instead of being confined between their banks, brooks started to overflow farm land. People responded by building earthen banks in vulnerable places to keep their meadows from being flooded. Eventually sluices had to be constructed across streams to shut out spring tides.

A surviving register of Boyton Manor written in 1383 notes marshes which could not be measured due to their inundation by the sea. At that time the Tang was salt water as far west as the church, showing that the sluice had not yet been constructed. Boyton's mill powered by a tidal mill-pond lay downstream at Enlond, the eastern end of Boyton opposite Burrow Hill. At some time before 1568 the sluice across the mouth of the Tang was built and the mill went out of use.

Further upstream the complete remodelling of Chillesford's previously tidal mill by Prior Manning in 1530 included a sluice to permit fresh water to power its undershot wheel whenever the tide was below the bottom of the wheel. It continued to be powered in this way for the next three centuries.

Egleston of his copyhold upon receipt of the outstanding money.

Trouble at the mill
A delightful event is illuminated in Butley's court rolls for 1575. The mill known today as Butley Mills has had a number of names. Old documents call it *Butley Mill, alias Chillesford Mill alias Carlton Mill'*. The first two names are easy to understand as the mill stood on the river which divided Butley from Chillesford. Originally it is likely that it was simply Chillesford's mill, while Butley's mill was beside the Priory precinct and

Stonebridge Marsh on top of an early embankment. A meadow 'inclosed' by it used to be called Inghams, or *le Yngham*. The mill was powered by one of two streams which followed separate routes down the valley from Capel Green. At an unknown date two ditches were dug to divert all the water into Okeland Brook in order to increase the power of the Priory mill. Thus one stream lost its identity and its mill. In 1555 the mill was mentioned in the Tangham court because John Stonnard had failed to repair the bank near Melle Marsh Bridge *where the mill was recently situated*.

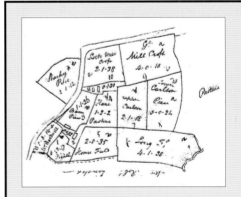

Carlton Mill
Confirmation of the mill's identity and location is provided by Carlton field-names, a Mill Croft and an Old Mill Way. These are mentioned in old records. Their position within the parish of Capel St Andrew was mapped by Isaac Johnson when he surveyed the Butley estate (far left).

It may be that when Carlton Mill was dismantled its oak beams and mill-stones were reused in the rebuilding of Chillesford's mill. This would explain why it is not until the later 16th century that we find Chillesford Mill called by three names. As riparian owner the Prior was in a position to improve the watercourses of the upper Butley river, known today as the Run. A *'Nue Brook'* was constructed which fed the water through a series of channels controlled by sluices into a large millpond.

The pond is likely to have been formed from disused peat workings. In medieval times turbaries flanked the Butley side of the river from Chillesford to Eyke. The new pond was sited on the Butley side of the valley, while Chillesford's tributary stream known as Padley Water was channelled along the north side and no longer fed the mill directly.

These improvements must have pleased Chillesford folk, since the watercourse which marked the boundary had been moved south, thus giving them an extra strip of land by the new mill. It was not acceptable to Butley villagers, especially as at one time there had been a black poplar marking the original boundary between Butley and Chillesford.

At their manorial court in September 1575 the Butley jurors testified that *a popple tree was recently growing near the water-mill of this manor… on the north side of the said mill*. The implication of their testimony was that the tree had been cut down. They stated that the parishioners of Butley and Chillesford made division signs called crosses on the boundary trees when they perambulated in procession on Rogation days.

Lastly they said they were accustomed to have half the rent and site of the mill between the poplar and the mill-house. They had measured the distance and it was 76 ft. In the space there was *one garden called a Herbe Garden, parcel of this manor for the maintenance of the house of Henry Page, Bartholomew Alleyn, Thomas Neve and Ferre of*

Butley's last working mill

The mill and old miller's house viewed from the far side of the millpond was painted by Thomas Churchyard about 1820. A mirror image of cattle, millpond and watermeadows was photographed by one of the authors in 1980 when sacks of feed awaited collection. Glyn Evans demonstrated to the authors the use of the hoist and machinery after the mill finally closed in 2002. The building has been transformed with a new lease of life as luxury holiday flats.

The black poplar by Butley church surmounts a large bank.

Reg Snowdon lamented the loss of a black poplar by Chillesford Mill. 'There was nothing wrong with it, but the Council said it was dangerous and took it down. Why , it was like that when my grandfather was alive and just as big'. The wood was particularly good for floorboards. Old Mr Kittle, the estate carpenter and wheelwright, used to say
  'Lay me up and keep me dry
  A piece of oak I will defy.'

Orford. These were the millers between 1538 and 1575, followed by Robert Bond. 'Ferre' may be identified as John Farrowe, nick-named Baker. The jurors reported that in accordance with the order of the last court they had positioned a large stone as a marker next to the roots of the poplar tree on the boundary. No doubt, like the tree, the stone has gone, but in living memory black poplars marked boundaries in Chillesford parish.

Marking the bounds

Before the arrival of the Tithe Commissioners and the Ordnance Survey few maps were concerned with parish boundaries. Beating of the bounds at Rogationtide reminded parishioners of the limits of their parishes. Wantisden parish did not have such clearly defined borders as did Butley, with its rivers and streams. Beating of the bounds took place here irregularly, but the 1820 perambulation must have been caused by a dispute with Eyke inhabitants. Three years earlier they had claimed an additional 111 acres including 30 acres of trees in Staverton Park. Isaac Johnson's annotated plan of

Wantisden Hall Farm shows only 99 acres within the Park as belonging to Eyke and this is how it has remained to this day.

A document dated 1747 was produced and authenticated by the *'chief inhabitants and ancient men of the parish'* including Gabriel Stead, who had been acquainted with the bounds for over 40 years. Those who had walked the bounds signed or marked their names in 1754, 1770, 1773, 1788, 1803 and 1805. The last perambulation, in 1832, was led by the perpetual curate, Ellis Wade, who guided the antiquarian David Elisha Davy around the county when he was an old man.

The perambulation starts at Wantisden Corner by an elm beside the house of William Pearson in Butley. Mostly they had to mark mature trees: *'an oak near where four tracks meet'*; *'ashen trees markt'*; and *'away to the nine-yard oak'*. There were few man-made features as landmarks: *'the park gate'*; *'a well'*; *'a clay pit'*; *'a stone*

There is a strong contender for the nine-yard oak. Expeditions with Jack Kemball and the Suffolk Woodland Officer, Gary Battell, were mounted to find it. Near Cumberland Mount we located a tree treated as two by English Nature, and tagged 1023 and 1024 respectively. Gary agreed that they had once formed a single tree, the centre of which has decayed. Today its circumference is some eight yards, but parts now missing may well have had the protruberances typical of very old trees.

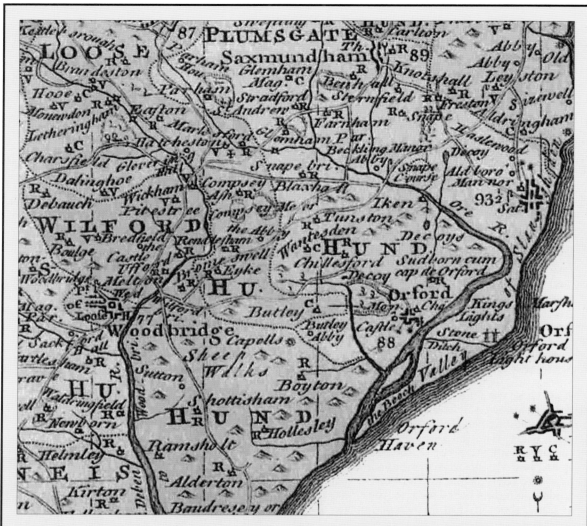

Part of a map of Suffolk published by Bowles in 1785 which depicts Hundred boundaries. Below: a de-cluttered detail. The bulge of the southern tip of Loes (red) intrudes into Plomesgate (pink) and divides Butley into three unequal parts. The church is in Loes and the Priory in Plomesgate. Capel and Boyton are shown in Wilford Hundred (green). In 1594 the Hundred boundary was used as an abutment by Radulph Agas in a few instances and the locations can be identified as: west of what is now Butley Street; the high ground at the top of Oyster Hill; and the north side of High Corner. In the 18th century the Hundred post on Oyster Hill was used as an abutment of the Poor Land. Bowles' map is consistent with these references.

cross'; Sandpit House; a shepherd's cottage; and the road from Padley Water to the starting-point. The stone cross stood by a house on the way into Drydale and it must have been still recognisable, unlike the stone cross in Butley Street.

Locating the Manor of Carlton

The *Domesday Book* did not include maps. It lists under the names of William the Conqueror's vassals the lands they held in each Hundred. The Hundred identifier is a useful aid in locating an unknown place, especially when there is more than one with the same name. However, it does not help when candidates for two places with the same name occur in the same Hundred. This seems to apply to Carlton in Plomesgate Hundred.

George Arnott in his delightful *Alde Estuary* confidently placed Carlton as a hamlet in Chillesford on the basis of the Carlton name attached to Chillesford Mill. In Domesday it follows the entry for Chillesford's 80-acre manor held by Count Alan. The Carlton entry is a long one and consists of the holding of his vassal, Hamo de Valoines – a manor of some 120 acres together with a cultivated area measuring more than a mile in length by half a mile in width. The difficulty with Arnott's theory is that Chillesford [parish] does not contain an appropriate acreage of fertile land.

The explanation offered by the authors is that the Carlton name was acquired by Chillesford Mill on the northern edge of Butley when it was rebuilt in the 16th century. At that time it was amalgamated with a mill which had formerly stood in Capel flanking Butley's southern boundary. If this identification of the original Carlton Mill is accepted, it allows the location of Hamo's rich manor and holding of Carlton in Plomesgate to be reconsidered. However, in order to be located there the Plomesgate boundary needs to be shown to have taken in that part of Capel.

There are no surviving manorial perambulations for Butley, Boyton or Capel, but Robert Forth's will drawn up in 1601 clearly drew on old perambulations to define the source of his tithable income. Most of the boundary corresponds with today's parish

---

The Hundred anomaly

Whereas Butley is listed only under the Hundred of Loes in the *Domesday Book*, in succeeding centuries it is entered under both Hundreds for some purposes, for instance, Hearth Taxes between 1663 and 1674, and the Land Tax in 1799. In other records it is either entirely omitted under Plomesgate, or Plomesgate is erased and Loes substituted. Hawes, writing his *History of the Hundred of Loes* in 1712 did not help matters, for he included the Priory in it.

However, the fact that the southern portion of Butley lay within Plomesgate seems never to have been forgotten. Agas was aware of it, although it was rarely relevant for his purposes. The 'bulge' appears on 18th-century maps, such as Kirby's 1766 *Map of Suffolk* and that of Bowles printed in 1785. As late as the 1970s one of the authors was told by William Large that he collected rents from properties in Loes and this included the north side of High Corner.

---

boundary, but there is a discrepancy between Stonebridge and Oak Wood where Butley intrudes into Capel. Starting at *'a stone bridge at the north-east end of the Horse Pasture Meadow near Old Mill Way standing in the highway south-westward unto a green called Gospel Green lying by the south-east corner of the wood called Great Wood alias Waterie Wood . . .'* Gospel Green's name may have been derived from the custom of pausing here to read from the Gospels during a perambulation.

The parish and Hundred boundaries between Butley and Capel are uncertain and seem to have changed over centuries. In Boyton's case one of its churches listed in Domesday possibly stood on Burrow Hill. The later diversion of streams to the south of the hill caused it to become physically separated from Boyton. It is certain that the largest portion of Butley parish lay within Plomesgate Hundred. Despite this, the Domesday entries for Butley relate only to the portion in Loes Hundred with no mention of Plomesgate.

It is extraordinary that all of Butley's fertile Plomesgate lands granted to the Black Canons 85 years later were apparently missed out of the survey in 1086. The obvious explanation is that they were not omitted, but formed the major part of Count Alan's holding in Butley, and that this was entered under Plomesgate Hundred as Carlton, held by Hamo de Valoines. Further support for this comes from Hamo's descendant, Theobald. He gave his daughter Bertha as her dowry the rich Butley Plomesgate lands where she and her husband founded the Priory.

The last gasp of an ancient system of manorial tenure by the youngest son. The steward's minute book for the Boyton manorial court notes that it was held in 1793 at *The Three Tuns* in Yoxford.

The book ends 120 years later with the admission of Captain the Hon. Hugh Edmund Thellusson, youngest son of the late Baron Rendlesham and therefore heir to his Boyton copyhold land in 1913.

No doubt the choice of notebook was the cause of merriment; two bottles of wine were listed as court expenses.

Orford's Turbulent Bailiff

Chapter 10

This tale concerns the only town in the Sandlings Triangle. Orford developed around a new castle, completed in 1171 to command a fine anchorage. The inhabitants were subsequently granted a charter and this encouraged an independent spirit. In the time of Henry VIII the high-handed Lord Willoughby tried to control the river and run the town as his manor. Feelings ran high in 1540 when he allowed his bailiff, Thomas Spicer, to behave outrageously. The intensive grazing of 2,000 sheep deprived the townsfolk of pasturage.

During the 16th century the mouth of the River Ore changed dramatically. Vessels on fixed moorings precipitated disputes, and information from law-suits adds to the picture of coastline-change revealed by contemporary maps.

As elsewhere in the country, fine nets were used to trap undersized fish. Acts passed in Parliament in 1488, 1491 and 1558 attempted to ameliorate the decline in fish stocks – something all too familiar today.

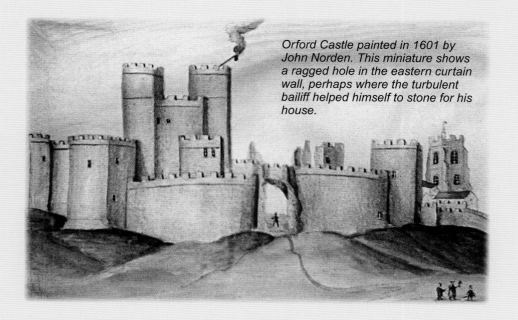

Orford Castle painted in 1601 by John Norden. This miniature shows a ragged hole in the eastern curtain wall, perhaps where the turbulent bailiff helped himself to stone for his house.

The Boyton Gull dispute of 1545

At this time Boyton Manor still formed part of the settlement made by Henry VIII on Anne of Cleves when he divorced her. In 1545 her steward granted a 30-year lease, at 20s per annum, to Edward Cleydon of Boyton for the fishing between the Gull and the Barrs at the Ferry-house in Boyton, using stall boats, weirs and nets.

However, within two months Thomas Spicer, Thomas Manning and ten others descended upon the fishery and in the usual Tudor riotous manner carried away Cleydon's *'great boat'*. Edward felt so threatened that he went in fear of his life and claimed impoverishment through loss of his fishery. He appealed to the Court of Star Chamber at Westminster to *subpoena* Spicer and his associates.

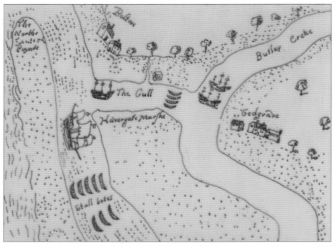

Stallboats are shown in both the Haven and Gull on Elizabethan charts. They were staked in lines across the river with nets suspended between them to catch fish swimming upstream.

Spicer and Manning counterclaimed that they were acting on the instructions of Lord Willoughby who they said held the rights belonging to the Town of Orford. They maintained that they had acted in a peaceable manner and the number of men involved was necessitated by the size of the boat. The vessel had been returned to the complainant and although they asked for reasonable costs and charges, it seems that Cleydon won the case.

Edward Cleydon himself was a formidable character and was listed as an *'able archer'* in the 1538 Wilford Muster Roll. His will made in 1551 showed that he farmed as well as fished. One of his sons was bequeathed a *'harness'* and a bill, and another son, a harness and a sheaf of his best arrows. Harnesses were worn by bowmen and billmen alike.

The Haven dispute of 1548

In the year of the Gull dispute William Forth purchased the reversion of Boyton Manor and thus ran foul of Lord Willoughby's men over fishing rights in the River Ore, known then as *'the Haven'*. Forth's stallboat was removed from Orford Haven by Lord Willoughby's bailiff, Thomas Spicer, and others. Following this Forth took the matter to Court, claiming before the Lord Chancellor that he was the owner of the site of the *'late dissolved monastery of Butley'* and thus had acquired certain fishing rights. They extended from Chillesford Mill to Orford Haven and included the Gull. He also claimed that the Priory had possessed the right to fix one stallboat in the Gull and another in the Haven. The case was settled in the High Court of Chancery; each disputant was bound by obligation for £200 to observe the findings. The Court asked arbitrators to discover the facts, and they reported in due course. Depositions, the statements of witnesses obtained by the arbitrators, give unique information about the informants' occupations, ages and more importantly, the physical changes to the river.

Thomas Manning and others involved in the removal of the stallboat gave evidence. Manning was a namesake and relative of the last Prior and had been employed as bailiff for the Manor of Butley. As usual at that time, their evidence commenced by saying the Bill of Complaint was *'invented and insufficient in Law'*; the fishing had never belonged to the priors of Butley or the dukes who succeeded them, except by permission of the burgesses of Orford. As to removing the boat, they said it was done lawfully as commanded by Lord Willoughby.

The arbitrators found that the Prior of Butley and his predecessors had for a long time been in possession of the waters from Orford Haven to Chillesford Mill, including the Gull. On these grounds William Forth now held them. However, Lord Willoughby

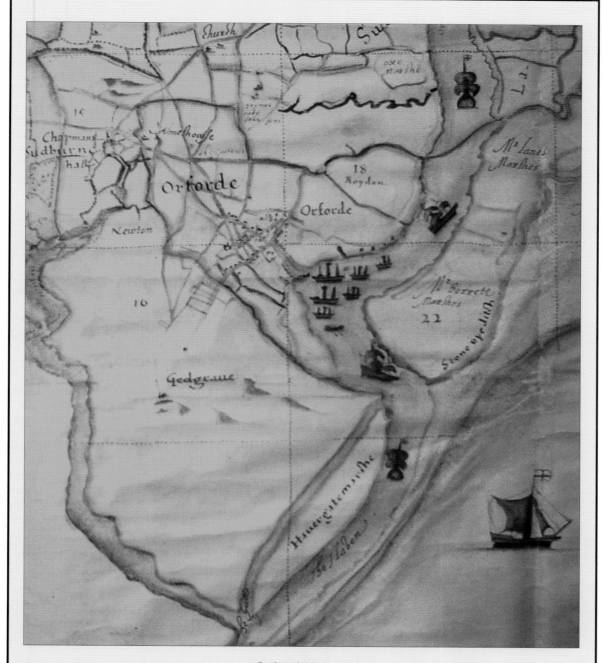

Orford Haven

John Norden's survey completed in 1602 included a small scale map of which a portion is reproduced here. A spritsailed coaster is putting to sea (right), while four ships are working their way upstream under sail. Other vessels are at anchor near Orford Quay. Marked are: the Gull and the Haven (bottom); the inned tributary of the Butley known as the 'Fleete' rising near the disputed Newton (centre left); Gedgrave Hall (lower left) and, north of it, the marsh that was disputed in 1568.

plainly owned Orford Haven and the *'standing and fixing of stallboats'* there was his right. Therefore, William Forth and his heirs were forbidden to fish in the Haven itself, or erect weirs or stake nets, without licence. The lawyers must have delighted in making plain exactly where William Forth's rights lay. They declared they extended from *'the uttermost point of Havergate Marsh to the uttermost point of Boyton Ground or Marsh as far into the seaward as any land, ooze, sand or any kind of earth which might be viewed at the half flood being neither spring flood nor neap flood'*. Norden's map makes clear that this boundary was the junction of the River Ore with the Gull and Butley Creek.

One other judgement gave Lord Willoughby fishing rights at Newineys, lying not far from Chapmans, the manor-house that antedated Sudbourne Hall. The Newineys referred to was a tributary of Butley Creek, known as the Chillesford alias Sudbourne Fleet. This was not to be successfully inned until the end of the century, as was noted on one of John Norden's large-scale maps.

William Forth lost any right he may have had to fix a stallboat in Orford Haven. A clear-cut division of other people's rights in the various waters would have made future disputes less likely.

Dispute over stallboats and shackage

The seeds of discontent may have been sown eight years before in a confrontation between Lord Willoughby and the burgesses of Orford over three matters: the number of stallboats in the Haven; shackage, that is, the right to feed sheep on stubble in the lord of the manor's fields after harvest; and the fact that in order to finance their case burgesses had sold some church valuables. The town's livelihood depended on fishing and the stallboat dispute concerned who could place them in the river now that space was reduced. Various local people gave evidence, including fishermen from Aldeburgh, Hollesley and Boyton, and Thomas Francis *'sometime mariner'* from Butley. The oldest was able to say that stallboats had been in the Haven for 30 years past; prior to that stake nets were used to catch fish. The inhabitants of Orford had four boats in the Haven, and the owners paid 10s a year to Willoughby. It was said that the cost had been increased from 2s 6d at some time in the past. Sir Thomas Rush of Sudbourne had two boats. The boats stood *'a flight's shot'* from the mouth of the Haven, said William Herbert of Hollesley. Everyone agreed that there had been 24 boats there previously, but now there was only room for nine or ten because of the *'shortening of the mouth'*.

Several deponents suggested solutions: William Herbert believed boats could be anchored nearer the town, although another said the positioning of weirs there made this impossible. John Jaye, aged 59 and formerly the Priory bailiff at Wantisden, said that stake-nets for catching fish were used before stallboats were introduced some 20 or more

The right of shackage was denied by Lord Willoughby in 1540. According to Thomas Spicer's evidence this drove Matthew Farrer, Constable of Orford, to interrupt a service in the church. During the singing of the Magnificat, the constable caused the priest to *'stay his singing'*, saying in a loud voice, *'Spicer, I command you in the King's behalf and in the name of all the town here and by virtue of the charter, that you meddle no further here in your office of bailiff under the name and title of William Willoughby esquire, and that you put away your master's sheep now being in Newton Field between this and Saturday next or else I and my fellows will drive them away.'*

Finds of post-medieval bells from Gedgrave sheep-walks.
Such one-piece 'crotal bells' were cast in numerous parts of England.
'AG' may be the initials of Andrew Gurney of Hull, operating in the 1670s.
The largest bell has a diameter of 1½ ins. Found by Alan Calver.

years previously. Another, John Weltham of Hollesley, a 40-year-old mariner, suggested they should stand in the Gull, and this idea, if acted upon, could have precipitated yet another dispute. Then the most complete explanation why the Haven was shorter was given by Weltham, and Henry Gunner from Orford. The reduction was *'due to the surges of the sea by drift of sand upon the stones.. Because the Haven's mouth coming so near, the tide doth go so sharp they [the stallboats] may not abide the violence of the storm, without they stand above a place called the Gull'.* The suggestions were ignored.

Evidence was then given that there were nearly 500 sheep in the field and 160 died as a result of their being driven out of Newton Field and Kings Field. Many others testified that the right of shackage had wrongly been removed. However, John Jaye said that ancestors of Lord Willoughby had exchanged lands with the inhabitants to extinguish the right. He, like Spicer, was employed by Lord Willoughby at this time.

The cost of the series of court cases put a strain on the Town's resources. Although not everybody approved, the 12 burgesses led by the butcher, Robert Pawling, decided to sell a chalice and silver-gilt cross for £24, and the bell to a London salt-trader at 20s per hundredweight. The length of the case and the strength of the support was such that in 1554 yet another Thomas Manning left the substantial sum of £25 to the Townsmen of Orford towards the cost of the law-suit.

Despite a Star Chamber order, treatment of the inhabitants by Lord Willoughby and his servants did not improve. The townsfolk complained to the Lord Chancellor, firstly, that Willoughby had seized certain copyholds without just cause. Secondly, Spicer had given leave to Willoughby tenants: John Sawer, to run 1,000 sheep in the town fields, and Thomas Harman to run 200 sheep there *'in the shack time'*. Sawer had leased the Chantry and other church lands, which he had ploughed, and encroached upon the highway between Sudbourne Church and Gedgrave Chapel, ploughed up a way from Orford Castle to the chapel, and the pathway leading to the chapel. Thirdly, Spicer himself was accused of ploughing part of the highway in the King's Field, and during a church service had subpoenaed John Marshall and Alexander Dame, *'for keeping of the king and queen's watch'.* He refused to pay the tithe of wool or lambs on his 800

The Sawyer and Coo families were leading Orford burghers and involved in the shackage dispute. Roger, son of John Sawer [Sawyer], was a J.P. His wife Bridget was widowed, remarried and died within the space of eight months in 1580. Her memorial in Orford church originally showed her flanked by her two husbands.

Only James Coo's brass survives, showing him in a bulky fur-trimmed gown, no doubt lined with coney to keep out North Sea winds.

The Capel St Andrew tailor, John Kerych, who died in 1508, occupied a house called Connies, a rare clue that clothing using rabbit fur may have been made locally.

James Coo, 1st mayor of the new borough of Orford.

sheep, setting a bad example for others. As a result the curate was unpaid. Finally, Spicer was behind the cutting of the cable on James Coo's boat, with the result that his anchor was lost.

During the running dispute Spicer was the target of further accusations. Twenty complaints were addressed to the Bishop of Winchester, the Lord Chancellor, ranging from *'alluring, enticing and conveying away'* William Boote's wife and Robert Cage's wife, to undermining the walls of the castle in order to build his house with the freestone, and preventing the beacon being lit to aid navigation.

The lighted beacon on Orford Castle emitted flame and smoke.

Spicer's comeuppance

These disputes preceded the 'camping time' in Norfolk and Suffolk. In 1549 the leading townsmen of Orford took the opportunity to place the pugnacious bailiff in the stocks for three days before marching him off to Melton Gaol. Whereas in Norfolk Kett's rebellion resulted in bloodshed, largely due to mishandling by the authorities, in Suffolk the 'camp men' dispersed peaceably on the intervention of Sir Anthony Wingfield. He promised that the King would pardon them if they returned home. They had assembled at Ipswich and moved on to camp in Melton that July. Later Lord Willoughby was able to turn the tables. In 1553 he had three Orford men arrested and held in the Marshalsea Prison for attacking Spicer while he was collecting rents, *'so that he was frightened of going about his master's business'*.

The making of the marshes

The opinions of the ubiquitous Spicer were still being referenced 40 years after the first dispute. They occur in depositions taken in 1568 concerning ownership of Lowdham Marsh in Gedgrave. A bundle of papers in Ipswich Record Office records yet another court case. Among these are questions relating to one dispute and answers to another, showing one of the problems faced

by researchers. The value of the documents lies in minutiae relating to a small area of marsh beside the River Ore. Included are a 1534 lease of Havergate Marsh and a small adjoining salt marsh, and a 1544 lease of Lowdham Marsh. The former was owned by George Blenerhasset; he leased it to two men who were to maintain the walls, ditches, 'cutters' and bridges.

The bundle of papers confirm the impact of sea-level rise and changes to the river and its marshes in the 16th century. The Manor of Gedgrave had belonged to Butley Priory until 1538 and subsequently passed to Robert Derehaugh. Information about Lowdham Marsh and the process of flood defence is found among the papers. The marsh was an outlier of the distant Manor of Lowdham Hall from which it acquired its name. Thomas Culpepper, the lord of the manor, married Mary, daughter of George Blenerhasset and the latter subsequently disputed its ownership. The earliest evidence in the bundle was provided by Richard

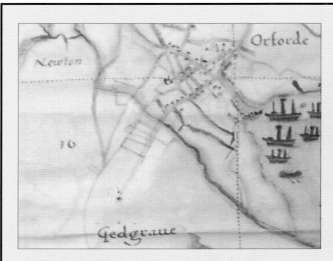 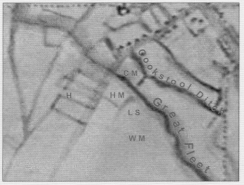

Lowdham Salt	L S	Chantry Salt Marsh	C M
Heigham Marsh	H M	Heighams	H
Wether Marsh	W M		

Lowdham Salt, as it was called in 1544, was leased by George Blenerhasset to Bishop Manning and John Haughfen, his nephew. It was identified by reference to Wether Marsh, Heigham Marsh, Orford Haven and lands 'of the late monastery of Butley.' For a term of four years the amount to be paid was 6s a year, at the mansion-house called Lowdham Hall. This fixes the location of Lowdham Salt or Marsh quite clearly. Orford Haven lies north-east of the tip of Chantry Marshes. Heigham Marsh and Wether Marsh are shown on a plan of the disputed marsh among the court papers. They lay east and south of Heighams, the present Richmond Farm, and are indicated on John Norden's map of Orford Haven (detail above; p.91).

The monastic lands described are to the west of Lowdham Salt. The names Heigham and Richmond can be connected with two people of those names. Indeed they refer to the same place. Augustine Heigham died in 1453 and Thomas Richman in 1587. Abutments are not entirely precise ways to identify property and some that were obvious to those concerned at the time cause problems to modern researchers.

Denny of Bawdsey. Aged 56 in 1579, Denny stated that when he was young the Prior came to view the marshes and told him the rent paid and the extent of the leased lands. He said that *'the Prior had occupied all the marshes except the Chantry marshes, and [for Lowdham Marshes] paid 6s to the Lord of the Manor of Lowdham'*. His statement was corroborated by two men: Walter Eadye, shoemaker of Orford, and Robert Cowper of Chillesford, who had also been a servant of the Prior when a boy.

Further statements reveal the maintenance and use of Lowdham Marsh and its adjoining small marshes, Heighams, Wether and New-inned Chantry Salt Marsh. The latter was eight acres in extent. The tide overtopped its walls and it was re-inned before 1591. Its north and north-eastern limit was the Cookstool Ditch which divided Orford from Gedgrave.

COOKSTOOL DITCH

This ditch takes its name from a chair or stool to which female scolds or dishonest tradesmen were tied and ducked in water.

Margery Bumstedde was a 'common scold' who had slandered Walter Eadye's wife, and had to be punished on the stool in 1577, or spend half a day in the stocks in Orford.

Detail of John Norden's map of Orford drawn in 1601 showing the Castle (top), and the bridge over Cookstool Ditch (arrowed). The stocks used to stand on Castle Green (top).

Sea-level rise and salt production

In 1469 Gedgrave Manor was listed as one of the two most valuable manors owned by Butley Priory. This may be attributed to its large acreage of marshes suitable both for sheep pasture and sufficiently sheltered to allow the controlled evaporation of brine. Sea salt was essential for the barrelling of gluts of fish and the salting of pork. The marsh on which John Heigham was then harvesting salt, building bridges, sluices and salt-works took on his name. The physical evidence of salt-working was still there for another hundred years when there appeared *'divers old walls or banks, at several times converted from salt to fresh'*. In Lowdham Salt John Talbas was constructing gangways and mending salt-pans in Dairy Pasture. However, a century later changes in the tidal regime resulted in Lowdham Salt *'being of little profit'*, because it was now *'at every tide overflowed and lay open to Gedgrave Walk'*.

On the marshes the main watercourse was known then as the Great Fleet. After the Dissolution it was bridged by Robert Derehaugh, *'so that his sheep could cross to where the marsh was manured by the Chantry of Orford'*, as stated in 1579. Twenty years earlier a clergyman, William Goodfellowe, living at Derehaugh's house, had been asked to drive his sheep into the marsh called Lowdham Salt, and then over the bridge to the other marsh. The 1589 statement refers back to a time prior to 1547 when all the chantries of England were closed. Robert had spent £160 on protecting Lowdham Marsh, but it seems the *'overflowing of every tide'* had reduced its value so that by 1589 *'it was not now worth 5 marks an acre'*.

It seems certain that the Blenerhassets had undertaken considerable additional work on maintaining the sea-wall and improving the marsh before 1589 and that William Derehaugh had compensated them with £304-12s-8d. The marsh retained its valuation of five marks per acre, but the maintenance and improvements were now costed at a further £1-3s-4d per acre. On the East Coast the struggle to keep out the rising sea-level was not confined to Gedgrave.

Finally, there was more information from those who were employed on improving the marshes. Edmund Oldhall worked for Thomas Culpepper and explained that there was a little ditch in the marsh next to the Wether Marsh to drain it, and when *'it lay salt'* it was a *'dry little creek of small mention until about ten years past it was made into a great ditch whereby the salt water now flows at the tides into it'*. Clearly not all attempts to keep the sea out had been successful. Robert Brande of Iken, husbandman aged 40, said *'he was a workman and wrought upon the walls'* to inn Lowdham Salt and then to work upon the Hard. Inning a marsh was a process, not a single action, as different witnesses testified. The final vignette comes from William Layton, a scavelman, who was working with his spade upon the walls of Havergate Marsh about three years previously. He told how he was going homewards from his work along a little lane next to the house where Mr Culpepper's servant lived. There he met old Thomas Spicer, still living in Orford and still opinionated, who told him that if Mr Culpepper had the right to Lowdham Hall then he also had right to the marsh. He added, in typical Suffolk fashion that *'he could have told him 20 years before'*.

Two Widows Wronged
Chapter 11

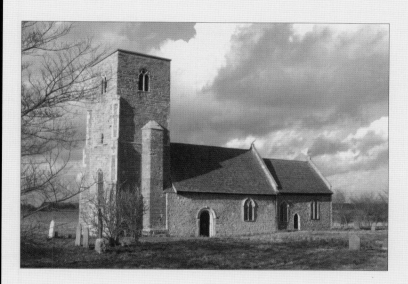

The parish of Wantisden is something of a mystery. Its lonely church by the former air-base has a huge cemetery, but there is not even a hamlet in the parish, nor has there been for hundreds of years. Yet at the time of the Domesday Survey it was extremely populous: no fewer than 63 freemen and their families lived there. The first story concerns the Sone family who built up an estate centred on Wantisden in the 16th century. Marked as 'Wantesden hall' on a map of 1601, the old manor-house lay to the north of the present hall on a site later known as *'Old Yards'* and the *'old bows and arrows place'*. Today, to the south of the church, there is a long reservoir, apparently created from its moat.

The Sones of Wantisden

The Sone family, sometimes spelt Soone, appears for the first time as tenant farmers of Butley Priory in the 14th century. In 1394 an early John Sone was fined for letting his cattle stray into the manorial lord's rye and for cutting fodder without a licence. The accounts of the bailiff, Henry Baret, show Sones holding Priory lands in Wantisden in 1509. By 1526 when the elder John Sone died the family had prospered, as is shown by his will.

> John Sone's will reveals that he had taken on various lands and two tenements called Casarde and le Heth, which he rented for 2s 7½d per annum. Additionally he was liable for rents in kind: 8 cocks and 30 hens, and had to look after 140 cattle belonging to the prior on land bordering Butley Run. One of the witnesses to the will was John Jaye, the priory bailiff for Wantisden.
>
> He left a wife, Joan, and two sons, John and Thomas. His wife was to be supported by twice-yearly payments of £3-6s-8d, made by their elder son, and she was given choice of his milch cows and his sheep in Eyke. She could keep a bedroom in his house free of rent. The younger John Sone was bequeathed his father's lands in Wantisden and Butley, and all his chattels, horses, sheep, cattle and corn. His brother was given 20s a year from the profits of the lands. Both father and son paid the 1524 Subsidy based on the value of their goods, 20 marks and £10 respectively, making them less wealthy than gentry, but of substance.

John Sone junior added considerably to the family holdings, purchasing the three manors of Alderton. He became bailiff for the Liberty of St Audrey in 1540 upon the dissolution of Ely Abbey. This was a responsible position since the Liberty comprised the five and a half hundreds of the Anglo-Saxon Wicklaw. During Elizabeth's reign its court moved to Woodbridge Shire Hall, and its gaol lay at Melton.

Henry VIII had used the income from confiscated monastic property to fund the divorce settlement of his 4th wife, Anne of Cleves. At the same time the King sold the future ownership (reversion) of this and other manors to men many of whom quickly sold them on. In 1547 the reversion of the Manor of Chillesford which had belonged to Butley Priory was purchased by John Sone

junior from the Duke of Northumberland. The Sones were unlikely to benefit until the Lady Anne died or relinquished it.

At the time of his death in 1551 John still leased the farm in Wantisden, but was also Lord of the Manor of Campsey-Haugh-and-Northlande in addition to Chillesford. He owed his brother-in-law, John Valentyne of Ipswich, the balance of £200 for the Campsey manor, and he required his son, Francis, to settle the debt. Francis was given the farm lease for its remaining years and his goods, plate, cattle and corn with which to repay the loan. The two manors were divided: two thirds to Francis and one sixth each to his brothers, William and George. It was George's death which triggered his widow's dilemma.

The will, made during the Protestant reign of Edward VI, sheds light on the family's piety; it provided for a priest, William Sone, *'to be given meat and drink, woollen and linen clothing and a chamber with a chimney and firewood to burn'*. In fact one of John's three sons, William, was to be an official at the Papal Court and Professor of Law at Louvain, while his brother, George, as we shall see, was probably a closet Catholic.

Francis Sone

Unfortunately John's eldest son, Francis, died while his children were minors and his will, written in 1561, provoked legal disputes at the Court of Star Chamber and was not proved for 14 years. The text seems straightforward, and it must be what was omitted that was the problem. He left his three daughters 200 marks each at the age of 18 or on the day of their marriage. His wife, Margaret, was left a third part of his household stuff and three of his horses. John, his eldest son, was to have all his leases and farms in Wantisden when aged 23, *'in such sort as my father by his last will did give unto me'*. There was no mention of the two manors.

An explanation for the omission of Chillesford Manor comes from one of the few manorial records to have survived. This manor would appear to have been the jointure of his wife, for we subsequently find her styled Lady of the Manor there. Her second husband was John Audley. The

Manor of Alderton was also omitted from Francis Sone's will, although a clue that the Sones held land there appears in John Sone senior's will, in which the poor of Alderton, along with Wantisden, Butley, Capel and Boyton were left 40s. George had been granted the use of Alderton manor-house for life.

Francis had an exceptional number of fine horses about which he was very specific. His wife was to have *'my white gelding, my roan gelding and my white ambling mare'*. His three brothers-in-law, Richard and Anthony Wingfield and one Warren, and his sister Naunton were given his *'young black trotting horse'*, his *'young trotting bay colt'*, his *'young bay bald colt with the white foot'* and his *'black ambling colt with a star in the forehead'*. He made his two brothers, William and George, executors along with the Wingfields. It was as executor to Francis that Richard Wingfield acted so strongly against George's widow, and this is the subject of what follows.

in Lichfield and five Midland counties were to descend to their eldest son. The couple lived at Wantisden and brought up a family of three sons and one daughter.

An abiding joy must have been the two sons who brought Richard credit. John was a soldier, knighted at Zutphen and slain at Cadiz where he was buried in 1596, while Anthony became Reader in Greek to the Queen herself. Richard adroitly married his daughter Margaret to his neighbour Francis Sone's heir and a new house was built to the south of the old Wantisden Hall, the houses providing accommodation for the two families. Richard acted as chief executor of Francis Sone's estate and took on the responsibility of bringing up his six children. This enabled him to live for some years like a manorial lord, leasing lands in Gedgrave and Iken and receiving the profits of Chillesford Manor.

Richard may have been responsible for alterations to the church: enlarging the

Some time after the Dissolution, the little church at Wantisden was 'upgraded' with bits and pieces salvaged from Butley Priory. Gargoyles and an ill-fitting door surround (left). Fragments of tracery wedged in an aperture (below).

Mary Wingfield's marble slab lies before the altar, a sad contrast with the grand tomb of her famous sister, Bess of Hardwick, in Derby Cathedral. The tiny chancel was extended, no doubt to house a vault and also to accommodate the Sone and Wingfield families at prayer.

Richard Wingfield
'Wynkefelde the Saxon held Honor and Fee Ere William the Norman came over the sea.'
As a younger son of an old Suffolk family, Richard Wingfield needed to marry well and this he did twice. His first wife was Mary, sister of Bess of Hardwick. Mary's dowry was provided by her stepfather, Ralph Leche, through whom manors and property

south doorway and creating a family vault in a lengthened chancel where gentry sat. It was here in the main position before the altar that his first wife, Mary, the mother of his children, was interred in 1582. His second marriage was to a rich widow, Joan Harbottle, with whose granddaughter he arranged a marriage with his eldest son. Joan, however, has no memorial.

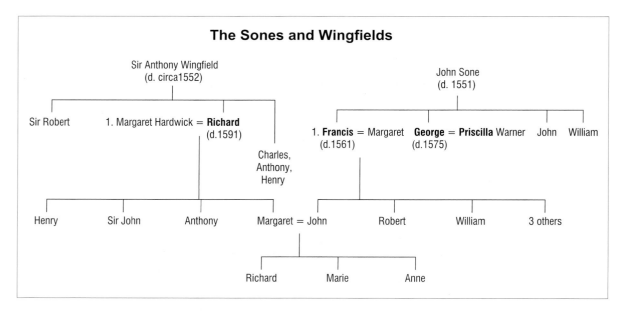

The Sones and Wingfields

Sir Anthony Wingfield (d. circa1552)
- Sir Robert
- 1. Margaret Hardwick = Richard (d.1591)
  - Charles, Anthony, Henry
  - Henry
  - Sir John
  - Anthony
  - Margaret = John

John Sone (d. 1551)
- 1. Francis = Margaret (d.1561)
- George = Priscilla Warner (d.1575)
- John
- William
  - Robert
  - William
  - 3 others

Margaret = John
- Richard
- Marie
- Anne

Priscilla Sone

Francis' younger brother, George Sone, wed Priscilla Warner and farmed Alderton Manor. George had a stock of 600 ewes and lambs, but only had occupation of the property until John Sone, the heir, was aged twenty four. In the spring of 1575 George and his wife were on a business trip to Copdock when he unexpectedly died. She believed that her husband was legally seized of the Manor and instructed her servants, chiefly Erasmus Smythe, to keep possession of the house and lands while she was away making the funeral arrangements.

Richard acts and Priscilla makes charges

Richard saw his duty was to seize control of the Alderton property as soon as possible,

The manor-house of Alderton Hall where the drama unfolded after George Sone's death in 1575. It is situated behind the church.

because he was the executor of Francis whose deathbed wishes were contained in an indenture of 8 November 1561. By this not only George, but Richard Wingfield and his brother Anthony, had a shared responsibility for the manor until John inherited.

Richard's precipitate actions while she was still grieving in Copdock angered and distressed Priscilla to such a degree that she brought an action against him in the Court of Star Chamber. The proceedings survive as large undated, unsorted and grubby bundles in The National Archives. The challenge is not only to unroll the old skins and read Tudor handwriting tightly written on lines up to two feet wide, but to make sense of the repetitive legalese. In the documents appear a cast of dozens of people living in the Sandlings Triangle in that summer of 1575. There are comings and goings at night and violence is threatened and used. The events are described so vividly by both sides that we are presenting extracts and allowing the reader to judge the rights and wrongs on each side.

Priscilla claimed that Richard arrived while she was still in Copdock and demanded the keys to the Alderton house. Although denied entry by her servants, he had forcibly entered and locked several internal doors. She did not know whether he was acting in his capacity of Justice of the Peace or of *'pretended title'*. Also, while her father Francis Warner and other gentlemen were there making an inventory of the contents, Richard sent a messenger, Simon Mawe, demanding as evidence certain documents which had been in George's custody. Being denied, Richard 'with outrage' descended and threatened to expel Priscilla 'with all riot and violence'. Out of fear the documents were surrendered. Richard was also charged with forcibly taking the key to a study at Wantisden, which George had kept at Alderton, and taking away papers.

Further intimidation

Two days before Easter Richard went again to Alderton Hall, and although Erasmus was fulfilling his duty in defending the house for his mistress, Richard attacked him and beat him with a staff or 'bastinado, being long picked'. She claimed the wounds to head and shoulders were serious and he might have died had other servants not cared for him. As it was, he lay sick for a whole month. Her next charge was that Wingfield, using his influence as a Justice of the Peace, had used a statute of Henry VI to indict Erasmus at the Blythburgh Sessions for forcible entry to the hall, and at a following Session held at Woodbridge, he obtained a warrant for Erasmus's arrest by the Melton gaoler.

The Old Gaol in Melton photographed in about 1920. There is still a village shop, but the gaol has gone.

Arbitration over the whole dispute was attempted, with Priscilla's father and William Naughton, solicitor, acting for Priscilla, but Richard 'misliked' the award and would not accept it. She quoted him as saying, 'It was a good turn I was not bound, for though I had given my word I would never stand to that award'. This was not the end of the matter, although Erasmus escaped arrest. Priscilla claimed that Richard arranged for 50 acres of rye and 20 acres of peas, oats and vetches to be taken from the manorial fields, although, while the crops were still in the ground, this had been forbidden by the Chief Justice of England himself.

On 21 July, in the night, Richard, with his son John, and son-in-law John Sone, along with 27 named accomplices, including the chief constables of various parishes, had descended on the fields and removed the crops in 14 carts. In all, she claimed seven score men had assembled, 'in warlike and riotous manner', armed with a great variety of weapons. These were swords, daggers, bucklers, long pikes, staves, pitchforks, bows and arrows and handguns. Surely she was exaggerating, although 140 men would not be an excessive number to harvest that large acreage so quickly. Perhaps she was being hysterical? It is more likely the 'riot' was fictitious as this was a common device to get a legal wrangle brought speedily before the courts. Certainly, if she lost the case she might be without either income or place of abode; she would naturally still be upset at the death of her husband. Finally, after all this 'evidence', she asked the Court to *subpoena* the principal offenders to account for their alleged actions.

Wingfield explains

Apart from Richard, nine of the principal offenders were examined at the *Greyhound* in Ipswich by three knights appointed by the Court to report on 29 November. They all denied they had acted in a riotous manner when harvesting the crops; there were not 140 men present, nor did they carry weapons. Some added details that showed how the manorial crops were harvested. Randall Smythe said he was a copyholder of Richard Wingfield's, and with other copyholders, friends and neighbours helped bring in the corn crop 'being yearly of great quantity'. The carrying away took two or three days, 'unless the weather was very contagious'. Another day, 'called the carting day', the men brought in all the wood

Richard required for his fires for a whole year. Another copyholder, William Marrett, said he helped find reapers *'to shear the rye'*, because of the goodwill he bore to Richard and the *'love he has to Sir Robert Wingfield, brother of Richard'*, to whom he was copyholder. Other witnesses said they were in Alderton on their own business, one carrying away his own rye, and another who was *'balye'* of the Hundred of Wilford, farming land granted by Thomas Seckford on behalf of the Liberty of St Etheldreda. The bailiff was Palmer, the Melton Gaoler, charged with arresting Erasmus Smythe.

Among the court papers are Richard's replies to these questions. They appear to be scribbled notes taken by his counsel, although he signed them. *'He thinketh good not to make any answer'* to the first three: the title to Alderton Manor; riot; and the fact that the Erasmus Smythe case was before another court. He then rambled on about the harvesting and carrying away of the rye and other corn. Pedantically, he claimed this was not done at night, but began at two in the morning and ended twelve hours later. *'The want of thirty persons'* came and went at various times, some at two o'clock and others *'by rising'* – presumably a few hours later. However, he thought some carts were driven to the fields the night before the reaping began. He took the opportunity to make a very involved reply. He could not recall the names of those helping, except his son-in-law, John Sone, John Dering, 'one Palmer' and Thomas Coke. Finally, he said no weapons were taken to the fields except forks to pitch corn and sickles to cut it.

Richard Wingfield's reply to the charges laid by Priscilla was extensive; another picture emerges of the circumstances behind his actions. He quickly played the religious card. William Naughton, her solicitor, was *'a very lewd bully and disordered person'*. Within the hearing of creditable witnesses Naughton had said he would proceed with the Bill of Complaint *'so long as he was worth a groat... to be revenged upon the Defendant'*. Richard explained that it was well known that Naughton was *'a very obstinate Papist'*, presented before Her Majesty's Commissioners in Suffolk for failing to receive Holy Communion in his parish church.

As executor of Francis's will, and because of the *'great love and goodwill'* he bore to his daughter's late father-in-law, he went to Alderton, knowing Priscilla was still in Copdock, to make certain no *'subtle dealings'* by some of the servants took place there. Thus in March 1575, with John Haughfen (brother-in-law to John Sone) and the lawyer Simon Mawe and others, he demanded keys to certain doors, and being denied them, sealed the doors. All this was done peaceably and not in his capacity of JP. He used a typical Tudor phrase in respect of a forceful woman, *'the Complainant, more of stout stomach than for any good or just cause'* had slanderously and unjustly alleged the contrary.

He claimed that, in Law, he could have entered the manor after George's death and removed Priscilla immediately, but he did not do so out of courtesy. However, she would not agree to continue to lease the manor, claiming that she had title as administratrix of her husband's estate.

Priscilla's father intervenes

Richard claimed that Priscilla's father, Francis Warner, had taken away various books and denied Mawe sight of them. Thus George's creditors were unable to discover the extent of his goods and chattels. When he came upon Naughton and Warner who were pricing cattle on Buckden Marsh, he asked them for certain assurances with regard to John Sone's inheritance. They prevaricated and he was forced to threaten that John, as survivor and eldest son of Francis Sone, would use the law to turn them and thus Priscilla *'out of doors'*. This threat resulted in the two men returning to the manor-house and producing the papers and books for perusal. Richard could not prevent himself from making another allusion to religion, noting that Naughton conveyed away *'a little printed book of Papistry and heresy'* which was among the papers. Thus Richard was able to take away the court rolls and evidence appertaining to John Sone's inheritance.

Francis Warner was not finished yet, though, and claimed that George owned silver plate and books kept in a locked study at Richard's house in Wantisden. Francis had the key, so at an appointed time he arrived and searched the room but found nothing belonging to George. The door was locked again and Francis wished to give the key to John Sone, now its rightful owner. As it happened, John was sick of the ague and lying abed, so the key had to be left with Richard.

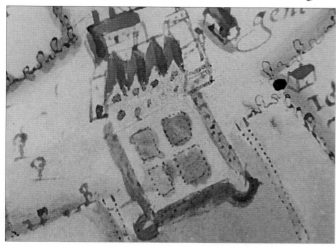

A new hall in Wantisden was occupied by Richard Wingfield during the minority of John Sone. By 1600 when Norden surveyed it John Talbot was leasing it together with Staverton Park and farm land. To the right Crooked Road led north to the old Wantisden Hall and the church.

It seems that Francis, Priscilla's father, was acting as a go-between and Richard assured him he would deal honestly with Priscilla, but it was rumoured that she was secretly conveying household stuff, cattle and corn from Alderton, leaving the ground un-manured; and thereby the profit was lost. Hence it was more difficult for Richard to perform Francis Sone's last wishes, namely, payment of his debts and the conveyance of the manor to his son.

Priscilla's anguish

Priscilla was reported as wildly saying that Richard had dealt with her as if her late husband had been a thief, by sealing up the doors at Alderton. She made no effort to be reconciled with Richard or her husband's creditors. Francis Sone also had had creditors and, *'owed great sums of money'*, whilst giving extensive legacies to his children, namely, 200 marks to each of his three daughters, entrusting their upbringing to Richard. Of Francis' six children four were still in Richard's keeping. The boys were at grammar school, paid for by Richard.

Richard's view of the fracas with Erasmus Smythe differed from Priscilla's. According to Richard it was Erasmus who attacked him, *'like one that did not know God, then like a Christian abusing the name of God in swearing an oath not to be named'*. If Erasmus suffered injury it was while Richard defended himself; Erasmus was *'an abject person of small honesty and less wealth'*, although, from Priscilla's point of view, Eramus had merely acted as a loyal servant and had properly sought to protect her property.

Judgement

Much of Richard's version of events, and especially the legal rights of John Sone, seem incontrovertible, so it is almost certain that he won the case. He made no reference to the so-called riot in the cornfields or the interim judgement at Bury Assizes, which Priscilla seems to have obtained with-out his knowledge. However, it tells against him that his charge against Erasmus Smythe was thrown out.

Priscilla defended Naughton saying that he did not have *'any zeal in religion'*. He had not offended by failing to take Communion. The sheep, which seem to have been a separate issue, and may have been taken by Richard to compensate for things taken by Priscilla, were worth between £120 and £140 a year, she said. The arbitrators then appointed were unable to agree among themselves and issued no award.

Compare Wantisden Hall's appearance today with the bird's-eye view depicted by Norden (above).

The Court-case documents do not tell us what happened afterwards, and Priscilla disappears from the record; she did not appear in the Butley manorial court to claim George's copyhold land there. Erasmus Smythe survived his ordeal at the hands of Richard Wingfield and was living at Hollesley when he made his will in 1601. He described himself as a husbandman, and left a wife, Alice, and four children. His property in Framlingham was to be sold for their upbringing until *able to shift for themselves and earn their living*.

Francis Sone's will of 1561 was finally proved. Young John Sone did recover from ague and went on to have three children. Richard Wingfield was to die in 1591 and left the Sone children the proceeds from the sale of his horses and sheep at Chillesford and Gedgrave, his corn and household stuff and plate. John Sone sold the manors of Chillesford and Wantisden to Michael Stanhope in 1592. His son, Richard, received an annuity of £6 13s 4d paid by Stanhope's bailiff until at least 1606. When Sir Michael died in 1621, he left £5 to John Sone *sometime owner of my manor of Wantisden, if he be living*. That he was still alive three years later is shown by the fact that he was left £40 by his widowed sister, Katherine Saunders.

Joan Harbottle

This story concerns the wife of a extraordinary Ipswich merchant who rose from humble origins during the reign of King Henry VIII. Remarkably, John Harbottle was able to champion the grievances of the yeoman class without incurring the wrath of the establishment. Indeed his granddaughter married the grandson of Sir Anthony Wingfield, who had acted to disperse the protesters at Melton. Even more remarkably, descendants of two gentry families proudly gave their children the Christian name, Harbottle.

The tale highlights the pressure on widows to remarry and throws another unflattering light on the man who treated George Sone's widow so unkindly. The main action takes place in Wantisden Hall.

John Harbottle, merchant and gentleman

John Harbottle had risen to be Borough Chamberlain in 1542, but must have found Ipswich duties time-consuming, for the next year he bought a discharge from holding further office there. Seven years later he became involved in a civil disturbance which erupted in the West Country and East Anglia. Around Exeter the rebels were protesting against the Protestant reforms introduced after the death of Henry VIII, but in the east their complaints were directed towards social conditions imposed by their superiors. There were bloody encounters at Exeter and Norwich, the latter known as Kett's rebellion. However, in Suffolk the camps were handled better by the authorities and ended peacefully.

Harbottle was one of the leaders of a camp set up near Ipswich, later moving to Melton. After a while this camp was dispersed by Sir Anthony Wingfield, father of Richard Wingfield, with promises that various grievances would be rectified. John Harbottle was responsible for obtaining from a Woodbridge brewer the beer needed for the camp. The thousand or more men there obtained food by stealing 120 sheep and 4,000 rabbits from Robert Browne of Leiston. He only escaped being taken hostage through absence from home. However, four local gentlemen were seized along with Thomas Spicer of Orford, who seems to have been unpopular with everyone.

Following this episode Harbottle established himself firmly in gentry circles. By the time of his death he owned the leases of the Manors of Crowfield and Bocking, owned various houses in Ipswich and properties elsewhere in Suffolk and had a share in the copyhold of Flatford Mill (made famous by Constable).

Only one child of his marriage to Joan survived to adulthood. Little Joan married the clothier, Thomas Risby of Lavenham, who was declared insane after a few years of marriage and John Harbottle became his guardian. Their only son died young, but one daughter, Elizabeth, married Henry, son of Richard Wingfield, while the other, Joan, married a lawyer, Edward Grimston of Bradfield, an Essex JP and later Master of Chancery at Gray's Inn.

Joan and John Harbottle's only child Joan, whose grim expression no doubts reflects her marriage to Thomas Risby who became insane. Brass of 1598 in Bradfield Church.

Joan Harbottle, widow

When John Harbottle died at Bradfield in 1578 , his wife, Joan was over 60. His will was witnessed by both grandsons-in-law and he made bequests to his widow and all his family with the exception of his new-born great-grandson Harbottle Grimston, *'for want of time to reform the same'*. He placed the *'government'* of poor Thomas Risby with Joan, *'if the laws will so permit'*.

Four years later Richard Wingfield's first wife Mary died and he soon began wooing the widow, Joan, now aged 67. However, his intentions were less than honourable as emerges from various depositions that came before the Court of Chancery towards the end of 1585.

The Chancery Case

Edward Grimston, acting on behalf of his son Harbottle, then aged eight, and his mother-in-law Joan Risby (because her husband *'being lunatick'* could not do so), presented the court with a request for a *subpoena* for Richard Wingfield, Joan his new wife and Robert Mawe, an attorney, to appear and answer various charges, set out in his deposition before the Lord Chancellor.

Edward related that John Harbottle had, on his deathbed, realised he had omitted some bequests from his will, and, there being no time to make a new will, entreated his wife, Joan, to make sure his intentions were honoured. An hour later he called his daughter Joan Risby to him, and asked her to persuade her mother to make a will so that the young Harbottle Grimston would receive £300. Three months later the widow did indeed make a will to that effect, adding various other bequests to her daughter and others, totalling £1,000. Shortly afterwards she paid some £700 to buy or redeem certain long leases within the Manor of

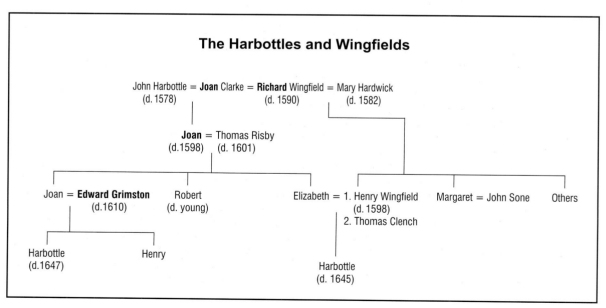

The Harbottles and Wingfields

John Harbottle = **Joan** Clarke = **Richard** Wingfield = Mary Hardwick
(d. 1578)　　　　　(d. 1590)　　　　(d. 1582)

Joan = Thomas Risby
(d.1598)　(d. 1601)

Joan = **Edward Grimston**　　Robert　　　　Elizabeth = 1. Henry Wingfield　　Margaret = John Sone　　Others
(d.1610)　　　　(d. young)　　　　　　　　　(d. 1598)
　　　　　　　　　　　　　　　　　　　　　　2. Thomas Clench

Harbottle　　　　　Henry
(d.1647)

Harbottle
(d. 1645)

Crowfield, the reversion and inheritance of which belonged to her granddaughter Elizabeth Wingfield. In addition she gave Elizabeth's husband £300 to buy copyhold lands near to Crowfield. He, along with his brother-in-law, John Sone, agreed to pay rent for these and after Joan's death distribute the sum of £1000 to those named in her will. With all this in place Joan was content that she had fulfilled her late husband's wishes.

Meanwhile she was receiving 'earnest suit' from Richard Wingfield to marry him, which for some time she resisted due to sickness and infirmity, and in consideration of her age. However, 'fine speeches' by Richard's friends and his own vows and promises to uphold her late husband's wishes, led her to yield to him. Nevertheless she was concerned that a second marriage might invalidate her will, and wished to consult a Queen's Justice who was her great friend. Unfortunately Mr Justice Clench was in London and unavailable for three weeks.

The marriage

When the widow's daughter and grand-daughter were visiting her at her house in Ipswich, Richard, it was claimed, told them it would be of 'great credit' to have the marriage solemnised immediately and that the ceremony should be the following morning at eight o'clock. The two women left, believing they had persuaded him, not only to delay the marriage, but, thinking they had received his promise, 'the faith of a gentleman', also to fulfil the terms of the widow's will. The ladies promised to return at a future date for the marriage. Poor Joan told them she hoped the marriage would not be hurtful to her child and grandchild, and that she would be known as a good grandmother.

However, the wedding did take place in Ipswich the following day at the time that Richard wished, and according to the de-position, it was consummated. It must be remembered that, should the couple not consummate the marriage, it could be de-clared invalid in law.

They moved into Richard's house in Wantisden and for a month all went well. Richard assured Edward Grimston that the marriage would not prejudice the intended legacies to little Harbottle Grimston and Joan Risby.

Doubts and fears

Joan, now Joan Wingfield, continued to worry and wondered whether she should make another will in her new name. She asked the advice of her attorney, Robert Mawe, who is said to have advised that her original will would be valid if she amended her name to Wingfield, and her husband also signed and set his seal to it in approval of the terms therein. This they both did, but Edward's counsel pointed out that the attorney should, and must, have known that she was now a *feme covert* and unable to make a will without her husband's consent. Thus Robert Mawe had to defend himself in court against complicity with Richard. Indeed, Edward claimed that Joan had loaned her attorney as much as £50 at sundry times, and it was likely that Richard had cleared the debt in return for Mawe's assistance in the matter in hand.

Some three months later Abell Clarke, a kinsman of Joan's, visited her at Wantisden, and asked to see the will. He was told it was still in her house in Ipswich. Despite the delay, he eventually saw and read it, and advised Richard that, although it was signed and sealed in both their hands, it was 'of small force to bind him'. Richard retorted that it would serve the intended purpose and took no action. Thus, according to Edward, he meant to defraud his wife and her family.

The September following the marriage, Joan fell seriously ill of a continual fever; her health further undermined by the distress caused by the situation and her fear, that through negligence, her intentions would be defeated. She called for her daughter, Joan Risby, to visit. This, Joan duly did the very next day, accompanied by Joan and Edward Grimston. She wanted them to inspect her will. However, Richard had taken the keys of her chest from her chambermaid and would not let them see it.

When Edward gave Joan Wingfield his legal opinion that her will had no force in law, she argued that her attorney had said that the altered will was valid, and that Mr Justice Clench was of the same opinion.

Distressed by the situation and fearing she would die without a clear conscience regarding her first husband's wishes, she entreated Richard to *'lovingly acknowledge'* before the two Joans and Edward, that he would honour the legacies. It was claimed that he cunningly responded by saying, *'I will confess nothing, nor deny nothing'*. Provoked by this she angrily said she might as well be married to nobody. This caused Richard to become angry too and he told the three visitors to leave his house and not return unless sent for. With other *'inhuman and violent'* words he drove them out of the chamber at an unreasonable time of the evening in a *'wild country of plain heath'*. This is an appropriate description of the sparsely populated parish of Wantisden, which was almost entirely heathland. Thereafter they were unable to visit Joan, who was in effect kept a prisoner in her chamber.

Her attorney's defence

The papers that survive do not reveal whether Richard appeared in court; only Robert Mawe's defence is attached to the deposition. He must have felt sufficiently alarmed at the accusations against him that he sought someone of the calibre of the barrister Edward Coke, later to be Attorney General, to help with his defence.

Mawe claimed that the charge against him was untrue and maliciously inserted to discredit him in the course of his profession. He had never meddled in Joan's will either before of after the marriage, but he did remember amending the draft after the marriage. Thus he changed the words *'Joan Harbottle'* to *'Joan Wingfield, the wife of Richard Wingfield, esquire'*, merely to show her change of name and with no other intention. However, he did confess that he had told Joan that the will would stand as long as her husband's consent was given. He further explained that he had acted as steward of Crowfield Manor for her, had been paid for the service, and had repaid any money borrowed from Joan or Richard.

The outcome

As with most Chancery and other Court records the verdict is not recorded, but it is probable that Richard won, despite his dis-

honourable conduct. Under the law, amendment of Joan's name would not suffice, and she would not have been able to make a new will, once re-married, unless her husband agreed. However, Edward Grimston was an able advocate and the Court of Chancery was *'an equitable jurisdiction'*, meaning that moral criteria might be taken into account rather than the strict letter of the law.

As it happens we know Joan and Richard were both alive in November 1590. It is shown by a letter written by his son Anthony to the 7th Earl of Shrewsbury. The earl's father, lastly married to Bess of Hardwick, had died the previous week and Anthony was appalled that his elder brother Henry, *'forebeareth not one whit his ordinary recreation of dice and cards'*. In Anthony's view his father's second marriage is unfortunate and *'other mischief ... may follow'*.

Richard had made his very long will in 1588 being *'in good health and sound memory'*. Rather coldly, his only bequest to his wife is in connection with the indenture that was their marriage agreement. No record of a will in the name of Joan Wingfield survives. Richard had property, leases and livestock in Chillesford, Gedgrave and Iken, and held the dowry of his first wife

Baby Harbottle Grimston, the cause of the lawsuit, sired a distinguished Harbottle who became Master of the Rolls and Speaker of the House of Commons.

Mary Hardwick, namely lands and tenements in the City of Lichfield and several Midland counties, which he enjoyed for his life and that of Henry.

He left his own properties and leases to his sons and money to John Sone, husband of his daughter, and their three children. John had stood surety to him for the sum of £680 which represented the gambling debts of Henry at that time. Six hundred pounds of this sum had to be repaid to his two brothers and to John Sone. However, in a document of 1592 his brother Anthony waived his right to his £200. The wording makes it clear there was a major family dispute and it is unlikely that the balance was ever repaid. What is certain is that the same year John Sone had to sell the manors of Chillesford and Wantisden.

Contrary to what has often been stated, there is no evidence that Richard Wingfield built or owned the present Wantisden Hall. It was probably constructed in the mid-16th century by Francis Sone. In 1575 when Richard Wingfield was resident at the hall as guardian of Francis Sone's children, Lord Burleigh in his spiky handwriting annotated his copy of Saxton's map of Suffolk with 'Soone' at Wantisden.

The west end of Wantisden Hall today. The chimney-stack with diaper brickwork indicates that this was one end of the Tudor house much changed since the bird's-eye view was painted by John Norden (page 103).

The Great Oyster, the Ferrywoman and the Landlady's Tale

Chapter 12

If you say 'Butley Oyster', people from many parts of the country will brighten at the recollection of the old inn in Butley village, or the Butley Oysterage restaurant in Orford. Both places are named after oysters from Butley Creek. The association of oysters with Butley goes back a very long way — to Anglo-Saxon times at least. In 1983, little realising how appropriate it would prove to be, one of the authors gave the *The Oyster Inn*'s licensee, Vera Sybil Noble, a giant oyster shell from an archaeological excavation on nearby Burrow Hill. The 1,200-year-old mollusc was presented in the purple satin lining of an Easter egg box. Neither of us was then aware that in James I's reign, the inn was known as the '*Great Oyster*'.

Vera's mother, Sybil Smith (in white),
and her grandmother (standing in the former doorway to the parlour).

Butley oysters

Today oysters are cultivated in Bill Pinney's baths on the Gedgrave shore of the creek. However, in the 17th century the oyster-pits were situated below Burrow Hill on the Butley shore where outlines can be detected. An oyster-bed existed there as late as World War I.

Air photograph showing Butley's former oyster-pits (arrowed).

The appearance of the oysters has changed, too. In the past they were 'natives', delicious, with smooth shells, and in the wild could grow in 14 years or so to a considerable size. However, *Ostrea edulis*, as it is known, is slow to mature, prone to disease and tastes unpleasant during the four summer months when it is breeding.

Some time after Richard Pinney took a lease on the old Ferry Cottages at Gedgrave, he decided to add oysters to his other business. He imported the spat of Portuguese oysters *(crassostrea angulata)* and laid them down for two or three years. In 1966 he sold about one and a half million, despatched, as he said in his book, *Smoked Salmon and Oysters,* to every corner of the British Isles. By the early 1970s a cousin of the Portuguese oyster, known as *crassostrea gigas*, or the Pacific oyster, was introduced from Japan and the Pinneys built a modern hatchery, consisting of large cement-lined basins, positioned to fill with the flood tide. This species has flourished here, becoming known as the Butley oyster. It has given its name to the Orford restaurant which the Pinneys own.

Before Richard Pinney arrived in Gedgrave, Orford fishermen, such as Tom Brinkley and his forebears, had dredged 'natives' in the River Ore using either an iron bar, or a rope weighted with lead strips bent round it, and fastened to a long bag of hemp netting. Richard's son, Bill, one day strode up from his fishing-boat to inspect the large oyster middens of the Anglo-Saxon settlement then being excavated on the summit of Burrow Hill.

Burrow Hill excavation of the Middle Saxon settlement. Kitchen waste of thousands of oyster shells trapped tiny artefacts and bones.
In the distance on the left is the sluice where the River Tang empties into the creek.

Since the shells varied in size, the oysters were clearly not cultivated but wild. There were nicks in their edges where they had been opened with small iron knives, and archaeologists found

Three oyster shells and two broken knives from the Burrow Hill midden.

the knives themselves and also broken-off knife tips among the shells. Bill was shown the cylindrical lead weights the team had excavated and suggested they could have been used to weight the line used to dredge the oysters.

Lead weights and iron fish hook 3¼ inches long from Burrow Hill.

The Middle Saxon people there had lived very well, discarding unbroken bones of cod, eel, cattle, sheep, goats and numerous young pigs. In contrast the rubbish pits of earlier, Iron Age, residents contained animal bones, all of which had been smashed to extract marrow – and not a single oyster shell. However, it is pretty certain that once the taste for them had been acquired, oysters became an important source of winter nourishment for Butley people, particularly the residents of the Priory, who were forbidden meat on many days of the year. They were a valuable commodity; Leiston Abbey's accounts for 1303 show that 900 oysters cost 12½d.

When a large bomb landed inside the Priory precinct in February 1944, forming a crater, 30ft deep, the explosion covered even the Priory gatehouse roof with soil, and oyster shells were widely scattered. These may have derived from a monastic rubbish-dump, or possibly from the Elizabethan mansion-house belonging to the Forth family.

The ferryman's tale

There have been several wharves and jetties on the Butley river over the centuries, with Boyton Dock and Butley Mills being the most recently used for barge freight. Old maps show two separate docks on the Butley bank between these two, and the tithe map marks Old Dock Drift leading from Butley Corner to a point on the river where the channel comes close to the river wall (Map p.123). This is where stone to build the Priory will have been landed.

The earliest recorded ferry crossed not from Butley but from Boyton, a little further downstream. Boyton's main roadway ran, as it still does, along the ridge. In the old days it was known as the Portway and at the end of the ridge made a sharp turn to run down to Boyton's 'port' and its ferry and ferry-house situated near the present brick-built dock. On the Gedgrave side the ferry met a road which ran in a straight line to Orford.

In 1365 Butley Priory acquired Boyton Manor, and some time afterwards the prior relocated the ferry more conveniently for himself at the foot of Burrow Hill on his side of the Tang tributary. The disadvantages were that, firstly, it no longer connected directly with the Gedgrave road and, secondly, Boyton folk now had to cross the Tang in order to use it. In 1512 Henry Baret paid for a new bridge *'apud Ly Ferry'*, and in 1538 five men appear on the Priory *Household List* as responsible for the fishing boats, ferry and weirs. Unfortunately we do not know which of them was in charge of the ferry boat.

Seven years after the Dissolution, which had dispersed the monastic estates, the ferry on the Boyton side seems to have been operational, because Anne of Cleve's steward granted a 30-year lease, at 20s per annum, to Edward Cleydon of Boyton for the fishing *'between the Gull and the Barrs'* at the Ferry-house in Boyton. However, with William Forth's purchases the two manors were again in the same ownership and the only ferry thereafter ran from Butley with free stowage as noted in 1594.

Revenue from oysters

Captain William Forth was the great grandson of William Forth, the purchaser of the former monastic estate in 1544. Less than a century afterwards he was forced to mortgage and later had to dispose of most of it due to financial pressure.

His sale in 1634 of the bulk of Boyton lands to Francis Warner meant that he no longer controlled both banks of the sluice by which the Tang tributary drains into Butley Creek. Therefore, the two men needed to sign an agreement to share the maintenance of the sluice, each able to distrain upon the other's goods if one of them failed to pay his portion.

The agreement took into account the fact that William's tenant, Charles Guilders, was responsible for the sluice under his 11-year lease. Guilders occupied the Butley Ferry-house, some 13 acres of marsh and the *'feeding of the wall'* from the house to Gallows Hill – in other words, he grazed sheep upon the river walls. He had the

High tide in Butley Creek in 1980, looking downstream to the sluice. In medieval times the streams which drained the low-lying marshes were diverted into the Tang or Laneburgh River. High tides were prevented from flooding the land by river walls and a sluice across the Tang.

The 1634 agreement was still in place in 1801 when Robert Benington reported that the sluice was very unsafe and repairs would cost over £100. It was resolved that it should be replaced in brick, providing the owner of the Butley estate, the Duke of Hamilton, agreed. In the event, nearly £300 was spent on the new sluice the following year.

ferriage and the use of the waters from Butley Mill to the Gull, and downstream as far as the Hope.

From what follows it is clear that the cultivation of oysters was a major business. Guilders paid a rent of £17-3s-4d yearly, plus 30,000 *'good, sweet, sound and large'* oysters, not exceeding 2,000 in one week. These are too numerous for domestic consumption and the surplus must have been despatched, alive in barrels of brine, to markets such as Billingsgate. The oysters were to be called for weekly at the Ferry-house by Captain William's servant. In addition to this, Charles Guilders will have been selling oysters on his own account.

The agreement is the only document to show how large an enterprise oyster cultivation was at Butley in the 17th century. The 1655 Devereux-Forth-Tyrell family settlement merely mentions the messuage where Carmen dwelt, the Ferry-house, ferry and oyster pits.

There is no evidence to fill the gap between the 9th and the 17th centuries, but doubtless oysters were always harvested in the creek. This is but one example of the patchy survival of information about even major activities by local people.

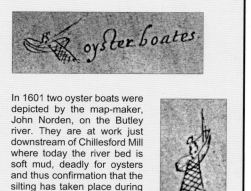

In 1601 two oyster boats were depicted by the map-maker, John Norden, on the Butley river. They are at work just downstream of Chillesford Mill where today the river bed is soft mud, deadly for oysters and thus confirmation that the silting has taken place during the last four centuries.

1881 O.S. map showing the ferryman's house. On the far side of the river a bell was rung by people wishing to cross.

Ferry men and women

The ferry across Butley Creek was always operated from the west bank. A century after Charles Guilders' lease, much of the known information about Ferry Farm derives from the 1732 will and inventory of the yeoman, Henry Swift. He left Peter Ratcliffe of Capel the residue of his lease of the house and its rights. It comprised '*a kitchen, parlour and backhouse, all with chambers above, a buttery, dairy, barn and stable*'. Sheep are not mentioned, but there were two pairs of sheep-shears in the house. He kept three cows, two pigs and a mare, grew wheat, rye and beans, made cheese and brewed beer. Fishing and wildfowling were important as shown by his two boats, two dredges, eight fishing-nets and three guns. His inventory was valued at some £75 of which £15 consisted of money owed to him and cash in the house.

Although the names of the tenants of Ferry Farm and its ferry are recorded, the only known rowers are female. In addition to Maria Smith around 1900, there was Lydia Gunnell, also a widow, who in 1791 gave evidence at an inquest on a man's body she had found in the river as she was about to '*set a man over the ferry*'. The inquest was held in *The Oyster* and 15 local men certified

from the evidence that the unknown deceased had been drowned for some while. The Burial Register reveals him to have been Philip Man of Aldeburgh, lost on Lantern Marshes '*during the Great Tide*'.

By the early 19th century the Ferry-house had either been demolished or divided into a pair of cottages in which the ferryman Smith and a shepherd lived. They were tucked below the river wall and a bell hung on the Gedgrave side used to attract the ferryman's attention. An old Capel horseman, Albie Whyard, told how villagers off to Orford by way of the ferry would set snares along the way. Returning they pocketed any rabbits and boarded the ferry before the gamekeeper could catch them.

A vivid childhood memory was published by *The Lady* in 1982. Jane Connard was aged seven when her father, Philip, rented the Ferry farmhouse in the summers of 1913 and 1914 in order to paint. She recalled that hardly anyone passed the house and the ferry rarely functioned, indeed '*the ferryman was constantly in and out of jail*'. She learned to swim in a harness, being cast by her father from a rickety wooden bridge over the Tang. An abiding memory was watching battleships of the Royal Navy steaming north to safety in Scapa Flow in August 1914.

The landlady's tale

Vera Noble's grandparents and uncle on her mother's side were Hazelwoods. Her grandfather George became the licensee of *The Oyster* in 1916, and her mother, Sybil, married William Smith around 1914.

William fought in the Battle of the Somme and a neighbour who was standing

---

The Smith family supplied the ferrymen down at Butley Creek for getting on for 100 years. George Smith, born 1857, was killed in an accident at Bromeswell Hollow in 1897, leaving Maria to row the ferryboat. His father, James, was living at the Ferry-house when censuses were taken in 1851 and 1881 and died aged 84 in 1892. It is likely that his father, also James, was the ferryman before him, as. 'Smith' is named on Isaac Johnson's 1813 map of Capel Farm as occupant of part of the Ferry-house.

'*My family were at the Oyster since 1916. My grandfather came here with my grandmother and my uncle George. My grandmother died and then my uncle died within six weeks. That left my grandfather alone, so that brought our family here to help him. I continued the family tradition.*

'*My other grandfather was killed at Melton. He was run over by a wagon in 1897. This left ten children for my grandmother, Maria Smith, to bring up, and to help make ends meet she rowed the Butley to Gedgrave ferry for a while. To stop the youngest children from getting into mischief while she was away, she would tie them to the bed post.*'

Vera Noble

Mrs Collins, Florrie's 'Butley Nana', in indoor garb; a neighbour, Mrs Wiseman, is dressed to go out.

next to him in the line was killed by German gunfire. After William got back to Butley he found that Mrs Wiseman had been told that her husband was missing and William had to go and tell her that he had seen him killed. He himself had felt a *'stinging'* and looked down to see his hand covered in blood and a finger blown clean off. He went to the dressing station. They put a bandage on and he was sent straight back to the line. After World War I he was licensee until he got arthritis badly. Then his wife took over and the licence passed from Mrs Smith to daughter, Vera, and her name alone was painted over the door.

During World War II Vera married Tom Noble, a northerner billeted at the inn. His war-work was to direct gangs building a new airbase at Bentwaters. He was said to be a quiet, intelligent man, who had an easy life, never taking a role in running the inn. The couple had no children, but Tom would sit in the Men's Kitchen out of hours educating Vera's nephew. This was George and Freda's son, Ronald, who has recently rebuilt his parents' house beside *The Oyster*.

The origin of the inn

The Oyster Inn, to give it its full title, is far older than its brick and slate exterior implies. Inside there is a 42 sq ft chimney stack and substantial beams. It may have been clad in brick and slate around the middle of the 19th century when slate became easily available, thanks to the railways. The inn was described as a 'forlorn-looking hostelry' in the *Suffolk Stud Book* in 1841, and perhaps at that time it was thatched, with dormer windows.

To trace inns in the manorial court records is problematic because these are not concerned with the status of individual buildings. A clue to identification of *The Oyster* is the 9d, payable by a 'free tenant', in a rental of 1722. This same amount was still payable in 1908. The rental recorded that the attorney, Robert Hamby, was the owner in 1722; previously it had belonged to Bickers. This wording enabled the inn to be traced in the court rolls as far back as 1612 when Robert Bickers was succeeded by his widow, Bridget, who died in 1638. Their granddaughter kept the inn for a few years.

The year 1617 is the first instance when its name, the *'Great Oyster'*, occurs, leaving no doubt of Bridget's connection with it. In 1619 she signed a recognizance agreeing not to serve meat during Lent.

Court rolls often obscure as much as they reveal, and *The Oyster* does not appear by name until the 19th century. However the

James I was always looking for ways to raise taxes, and records survive for three years from 1617 when licensed properties were taxed at 10% of their value. Bridgett Viccars [sic] paid 10 shillings.

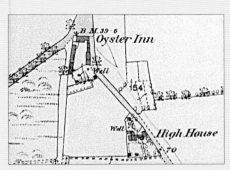

Detail of 1881 O.S. map.

In 1594 Radulph Agas recorded that Thomas Lynd senior possessed 45 acres of copyhold land, including a one-acre 'Manes Wale', and a one-acre freehold, 'White House', both at the road junction. Tenement Maynes occurs as far back as 1393 when it was described as 3 perches [48 or 54ft] long by 1 perch [16 or 18ft] wide and granted to John and Cecilia Royston for 2s 2d per annum. The dimensions suggest that it may be the site of the eastern, older portion of the inn and the cottages behind. The entry is marked with a blue silk tag and the excessive rent points to this explanation.

amount of 9d shown in the court rolls at intervals enables it to be traced farther back than 1612. In 1607 Charles Lynd was recorded as the holder of the property occupied by Samuel Wake. This is the earliest appearance of the 9d. Charles was the youngest son of Thomas Lynd senior, who had made his will in 1601. Charles' brother, William, was left a farm, but part of its land was taken and 'lately severed unto the tenement Dennes'. This was left to Charles, when aged 21, 'with the lands thereunto belonging as it is now enclosed'. He probably came of age in 1607, when this information was recorded in the court rolls.

The words 'lately severed' in Thomas Lynd senior's will suggests that the inn and its lands were created out of his farm a short while before 1601. If there was an inn on the site when the estate was surveyed by Agas in 1594, then it is not immediately evident from the documents.

The early furnishings of the inn

In 1610 Samuel Wake left his widow, Martha, the use of his house and lands in Butley for three years. He bequeathed her

the usual bedding, pots, pewter, plates and a candlestick, but his sons-in-law received, respectively, a pot of silver buttons and a piece of gold worth 15 shillings. Were the buttons snipped off the coats of gentlemen staying at the inn, either surreptitiously or as payment?

Samuel seems to have made something of his inn-keeping, but Bridget Bickers was even more successful. In 1625 she was able to purchase a property from the delightfully named Haselock Thurkittle of Aldeburgh. She bequeathed to Elizabeth Chamberlain, her granddaughter 'that tenement with all the lands thereunto belonging which I purchased lately of Thurkettell and owneth'. The will makes no mention of the inn, since her husband had left it to their son, Robert.

The description in the 1625 court rolls exactly matches an 1884 conveyance of Neutral Farmhouse: 'one hall and hall chamber with a cellar and garden at the south end of the said house… formerly of Bridget Bickers'. This was where her son-in-law, Elizabeth's father, lived. Clearly the eastern part of the timber-framed farmhouse in Mill Lane, similarly divided today, is referred to, so Bridget must have lived at the inn.

The Hearth Tax return of 1663 reveals that the inn had four hearths, and Bridget's will lists the contents of four rooms, namely, the hall and hall chamber, and the parlour and parlour chamber. In other words there were two downstairs rooms with two above, suggesting that all four rooms were heated, unlike humble cottages where only one, or possibly two, rooms had hearths.

The contents were as follows: in the hall (public area) were two buffet stools and a table, and in the parlour (private area) a bed and bedding, a cupboard, a long table, cheese press and salting trencher. In the parlour chamber were a posted bed and bedding, a large joined

Recently noticed on the main beam in the Men's Kitchen is a 'TW' incised twice. It may be a coincidence that these were the initials of Samuel Wake's brother Timothy whom he made supervisor of his will. Was Timothy involved in the inn's construction? When he died at Darsham in 1624 he was too sick to make more than a sprawling mark on his own will, but left his sons books which indicate that he was literate. For his part, Samuel used the same interlocking 'V's that are on the beam to write his name.

chest and another chest, and in the hall chamber a flock bed. In unspecified locations in the building there were a round table, a *'great chair'*, and a trundle bed with a feather mattress. Utensils, which must have been in the hall, later known as the Men's Kitchen, included a *'great'* skillet, a kettle, a pot skillet, a dripping pan, pewter dishes, a keep, a cauldron and a brass pot. Finally, she left her grey mare to her daughter, Elizabeth, married to one of the many Thomas Lynds. Travellers staying at the inn would sleep in the upstairs rooms, sharing the beds, while Bridget slept in the parlour.

Decline and revival

Not all innkeepers were as successful as Bridget. William Frent, named as *'inholder'* of the *Butley Oyster* in 1667, needed to borrow £10 from the Capel yeoman, Francis Meares.

The innholder may also have been penalised for his role in the following scandal. Local people liked to congregate at the Ferry-house. Possibly contraband liquor was available there from time to time. In 1663, it featured in the Archdeaconry Court as the location of an alleged libel by William Frent and John Draper. A number of men

The carter's accommodation at The Oyster *survives: a tiny one-up-one-down next to the stable. It was here that a World War II transmitter was recently found bricked up in the wall, no doubt a relic of Home Guard precautions.*

were witnesses, including a millwright, a butcher and the rector of Boyton. The libel was that Mrs Herbert of Cauldwell Hall had borne a child by someone named Canham. Two witnesses claimed they heard Draper say to Frent, at the Ferry-house, *'you said she was a whore and had a bastard'*. Frent's reply was *'no'*, but *'she had had a child'*, not naming any person. Frent was also alleged to have said, *'she loved one Canham'* and the millwright claimed that Frent had repeated this in *The Oyster* and, in the presence of the butcher, had said that Mrs Herbert had a child by Canham. The witnesses, including the Rector, then tried to retract.

The outcome is not recorded. It all sounds like typical village tittle-tattle, except that when her young husband, William, died shortly afterwards, he left no issue and did not name his wife in his will.

Subsequent records reveal that Frent was taxed on only two hearths in 1666 and there was no longer a four-hearth property in Butley. It shows that *The Oyster* must have been divided in two and may even have ceased to be an inn for a short time. Things got worse and Frent was excused the tax on grounds of poverty three years later. By 1674 the inn cannot be identified, but it may have been the empty and untaxed property owned by 'Mr Hastings'. Perhaps this was Thomas Hastings, an Orford gentleman, who owned a malthouse and brewhouse there. If so, Hastings must have disposed of the inn a few years later, because Playters Edgar, a member of the large Ipswich family, sold it to Thomas Hamby of Stratford St Andrew before 1701.

The Oyster stayed in the Hamby family, for when Thomas' son, Robert, died in 1732 he left the *'common inn known by the name of Butley Oyster'* to his grandson, Robert, and his heirs. The tenant was John Long who had previously been tenant of the *Cherry Tree* at Bromeswell.

His predecessor, Martha Gardiner, was another successful female innholder. She was able to bequeath money totalling £87 to her Easty relatives; she was childless herself. Her inventory, taken in 1729, lists the contents of the six-roomed inn: four contained beds, chests, tables and chairs for the use of travellers, plus the cellar and backhouse.

Jane Dowsing features in an anecdote recounted by two young botanists. In early August 1787 Charles Sutton and William Kirby, grandson of John Kirby the topographer, set out on foot from Ipswich for an excursion. They were to stay at the Orford house of the Rev. Peter Lathbury, who joined them, on horseback, at Woodbridge and together they continued, identifying plants and birds on their way and intending to dine at *The Oyster*. At Sprat Street they called at one of the two cottages and slaked their thirst with home-brewed ale. Arriving at the inn they heard the *'dismal news'* that Mrs Jane Dowsing could offer them only five eggs to be fried with bacon and the grease poured over them.

The clergyman, being curate of Butley, knew where to turn and managed to scrounge some beans from Mrs Sarah Benington at her farmhouse (Neutral Farm). The writers described the stuffed conger eel, weighing 48lbs hung up in the bar, and remarked that their hostess was a fine old woman, once handsome. There was no mention of her husband, Richard, or any of the eight sons she had borne him. It was at this point in their journal that they recorded the custom of holding frolics at the start and end of harvest which the labourers called *'whetting their tools'*, presumably in *The Oyster*. On they went, thanking Mrs Benington on the way, and partaking of a glass of wine with her and Old Nat, her servant.

Richard Dowsing was the landlord in 1760 when the inn was advertised for sale in the *Ipswich Journal*. It consisted of *'a stable, brewhouse and other conveniences'*, with about two acres. He had acquired the freehold before 1784 when he was registered to vote, and may have been instrumental in developing part of the land where, about 1780, the High House was built. He left the inn to his widow Jane in 1796. Her son was still there in 1819 when Isaac Johnson surveyed Butley. Later it passed to the Thurlow family. John the elder married Hannah, sister of the miller, Nathaniel Beedon, who left her a share in a 64-ton sloop, *Ida*. Their son John had taken over the inn by 1851.

The inn appears in the *Ipswich Journal* on a few other occasions: in August 1767 when a show of sheep and lambs was advertised, with a *'good ordinary'* offered at one o'clock; and 16 years later an auction of farm wagons, ploughs and other implements, pigs and household furniture took place. Under the Dowsing family the inn began to prosper again and play a wider role in the community. It was the venue for farmers' dinners on the occasion of the Queen's birthday towards the end of the 18th century. Later, coroners' inquests were held there, the corpse being laid out in the barn.

A death in Staverton Park

Keepers lived apart from other villagers and for this reason their houses have become desirable bijou cottages. One such is Thicks Cottage with little Gothick windows which may be glimpsed from the road beside Staverton Park. Living here in 1845 were William Tibbenham, his wife Mary and their five children. Details of a tragedy there in February were recorded at an inquest held just down the hill in *The Oyster*, and at Tibbenham's trial at Bury St Edmunds.

On the 15 February, a shepherd, James Mace, was at *The Oyster* where he saw the gamekeeper was partly stripped for fighting and quarrelling with various persons in the Men's Kitchen. About ten o'clock Mace got him to leave and helped the tipsy keeper home. His wife appeared and Mace said he hoped she was better following her confinement. Tibbenham said she was fat, and told her to get some beer. Reluctantly she went into the damp cellar after her husband had fallen while trying to do so. As Mace was leaving, Tibbenham asked him to help kill his hog, although he did not have a pig.

At the rear of a 19th-century cottage in Staverton Thicks is a pair of tiny panelled rooms. They were added to accommodate two keepers accompanying a royal guest at a shoot.

Soon after midnight Tibbenham rattled the casement of Mace's cottage and told him, *'I have shot my dear Mary Ann'*. He and his wife went and found Mary lying between the back door and the cellar. The cellar, which has been filled in since, was outside the main part of the cottage under a lean-to. Mace went to Mrs Cooper at Valley Farm for help and the policeman came shortly afterwards. The pistol was found by Tamar Gowing at the bottom of the closet. The surgeon who attended believed that the shot had been fired within one foot of Mary's head.

Tibbenham claimed the accident occurred when he was retrieving the gun from a drawer. At his trial he was charged with *'being moved and seduced by the instigation of the Devil'* and holding a loaded pistol to her head. Mace told the court that two years previously Tibbenham's wife had run away, and he said he would flog her when she was found. The jury considered the evidence for two to three minutes, and decided that Mary's death was not intended by her husband but found him guilty of manslaughter. The judge, Mr. Baron Parker, sentenced him to 12 month's imprisonment.

The inn becomes a tied house

The Oyster freehold was sold for £810 in 1886 to George Rope who had a brewery in Orford. Along with the inn were four cottages, one for the use of a carter, and stabling for eight horses. The field behind was a paddock. The tenant, George Freestone, had been there many years and his yearly rent was £70. His widow succeeded him as tenant. When the freehold was

The 'bar' in the Men's Kitchen. Regulars had their own mugs, ranging from pewter, to embossed pots, to elegant forms made in Butley's own pottery by Honor Hussey. The sink was a lead-lined trough.

The 'Ladies' shortly before its removal in the 1980s.

The hill behind the inn and a spring-line precluded cess-pits. Instead the two privies, at the top of the yard and opposite the well, had trap doors at the back so they could be emptied from the lane.

The Inn's famous landlady

To mark her 50 years as licensee, in 1988 Vera was presented by John Adnams with a decanter of 50-year-old port.

In later life Vera's complexion remained smooth and rosy, and her appearance did not vary. Her hair was always in a net, and she wore carpet slippers beneath her wrap-around floral apron.

She clearly enjoyed adding to the confusion which arose after Richard Pinney opened his Butley Oysterage restaurant. Well-dressed potential diners would sometimes pass between cloth-capped and booted drinkers arguing about the previous day's steel quoits match, to inform Vera that they had booked a table. She might delay in helping them by saying they had not booked with her (she sold only crisps and pork pies of doubtful age). '*But we telephoned you*', they might add. '*I haven't got a phone*', she would reply.

Eventually she would direct them to Orford, and they would have to run the gauntlet of the disputants again. She would leave the bar during her favourite TV programme, calling '*Serve yourself, I'll be out directly*', to anyone who entered.

sold in 1908, Mrs Freestone was paying only £50, and had been there for 22 years.

At the time Vera's grandfather became licensee in 1916, taking over from John Mitchell, the contents were valued at £83-16s-9d. The old-fashioned public areas can be pictured from their description, and some features were still evident when the authors came here in the 1970s. Her grandfather had a 'three motion beer engine', and Vera drew mild beer in this way, drawing others directly from barrels sitting on cross-trees behind the bar. In 1916 the small bar, known as the Men's Kitchen, contained a 36-inch Kitchener oven and boiler, a settle and other seats, three drinking tables (two of which remain), six iron spittoons, two gun racks, and iron rods over the windows. Bells hung in the entrance and cellar passages. The Club Room contained seven long forms and a mahogany dining table. This was the meeting room before there was a village hall.

In the Club Room the '*handsome old iron stove*', was lit on only three occasions between 1972 and 1988, so fearful was Vera

of the pub burning down. The meagreness of the fire in the small bar was legendary, and she was quoted in the *East Anglian Daily Times* as saying, '*I can't stand it when people start poking around my fire.*' Between the wars Vera bought an ex-airfield hut for £50 and erected it in the yard for dances and other entertainment. Villagers no doubt counted as entertainment having their hair cut in the hut by an itinerant barber.

Postscript

The Oyster Inn is owned by Adnams, the Southwold brewery. A recent landlord has moved the bar into the former Club Room. Since Vera retired in 1988, there has been a succession of tenants. The ferry has been revived by local volunteers and in the summer months can be booked to take walkers across the Creek. Vera's airfield hut has been demolished and a modern village hall, shared with adjacent parishes, has been built on the former Stable Field.

The triangular piece of common land in front of 'The Oyster' was once much used by villagers. Horses were tethered with nosebags tied to the white rail round the inn sign. When the carter was coming through folk gathered with produce to load and goods to await. This photograph of c. 1914 was taken from the old doorway of the inn. The wagon is drawn by two horses and has a cover like those used in the Wild West.

Trade and Extraction: the Coprolite Rush

Chapter 13

Before metalled roads and railways came, East Anglian estuaries were used for communication and transport. In addition to its ports there existed small docks. One lay at Boyton, well positioned at the junction of Butley Creek and the River Ore.

Throughout the 19th century the export of corn from Butley Mills to London and the North-East continued and sailing barges returned with horse manure from London or coal from the Tyne. For short periods clay and coprolite were shipped from Boyton Dock.

Within communities craftsmen and small traders provided most daily requirements. Prior to the 18th century few can be identified as craftsmen from their wills. They usually described themselves as yeomen or husbandmen, because they were also farming on a small scale. After 1840 the ground is firm: censuses and trade directories name tradesmen.

A collier unloading downstream from Orford, painted by Emmeline Rope in 1888.

The now roofless brick warehouse. Before World War II it was still used by Winch's barges, including the Bluebell, *to store: hay and straw awaiting shipment; and offloaded coal.*

there. The owners were Deressham and John Saverssham from Skilling, Holland, who paid £4, and a further £5 was received from Clement Draper and Jeremy Beckes of London. The following month a similar boat the *'Poppen Jaye'* from Aucusan [Haugesund in Norway] anchored loaded with timber and £6 13s 4d was charged for groundage.

White clay

When William Forth sold the Manor of Boyton and other lands to Francis Warner in 1634 he probably didn't know about the seam of *'white earth'*. This fine clay, sought-after as a slip for earthenware, appears in a document dated 1675 from which it can be deduced that 300 tons were being extracted annually.

An opportunity to export clay to the Netherlands occurred after the end of war with the Dutch and the 'Glorious Revolution' which placed William of Orange on the throne of England. However, Edmund Warner fell foul of the authorities in 1693 because he was suspected of

Boyton Dock

The high ridge of Boyton carried an old east-west route, once called the Portway, which terminated at a ferry-crossing and a landing-place on Butley Creek still known as Boyton Dock.

Further upstream at Burrow Hill there was another ferry, while at the end of Dock Drift lay the Priory's own dock, convenient for the import of building materials and wine, and the despatch of wool and grain from its barns. At the head of the creek barges could turn and load grain and flour from the dock which served Chillesford and its Mill.

Robert Forth's estate included the Manor of Boyton and he will also have used the dock there for his own produce. However, the court rolls record two occasions in 1576 on which he obtained income from the use of the Dock. In October a 'fleebote' named the *'Free Butter'* (Freebooter) was anchored

Benjamin Furly was Warner's agent in Rotterdam. As a young man he was converted when he heard a Quaker preach in his father's hayloft in Colchester. He resided in Rotterdam for 55 years until his death in 1714. There he built a library worth over £7,500 and was a noted linguist and scholar. A possible descendant of Benjamin twice scratched his name on a window-pane at Butley's Oyster Inn where he presumably lodged in the 1770s.

exporting fuller's earth, then a prohibited substance due to its rarity in Europe. Depositions were taken from various witnesses, including Warner's agent.

The deponents said that in times of peace in Europe clay would be obtained from Flanders, Germany or *'Sweedland'*, but in times of war from England. Conclusive evidence that Boyton clay was not suitable for fulling lay in the price obtained. The

A vellum document records the sale of Boyton Manor by William Forth to Francis Warner of Parham in 1634. Francis' son Edmund Warner did not prosper financially and in 1689 he had to mortgage the estate in order to raise £1,500. After his death his widow was forced to sell a portion to pay his debts. Enough remained, however, for his granddaughter Mary to set up a charitable trust with Pryce Devereux and other Suffolk gentry. She died before her almshouses were completed in 1746 and six poor men and the same number of poor women were admitted. The building was enlarged in 1828 and 1860 and is still in use. Trustees continue to administer the estate to provide an income to support it.

Butley Creek, its former dock, ferries and mills

'Harold Smy was skipper of the last barge to come up to the quay below Butley Mill. He delivered shingle for the building of Watson's stables at Chillesford Lodge in the 1920s and 30s. It took him so long due to low tides that he refused to go up any more. William Watson's father had turned up on horseback and hoped Harold would be faster with the next cargo. Harold explained that he would, because he was going to deliver it to Rope's Quay at Orford!'

Dutch potters paid between 25 and 30 guilders a 'last', whereas fuller's clay was worth at the highest 6 or 7 guilders a last. The clay was being exported in quantity; one potter had bought 1,000 lasts the previous month; another had 900 lasts on his books *'because so many ships had arrived together'*, although two ships had recently been lost at sea. The clay was used to make white or painted earthenware.

London potters also needed fine clay and in 1744 trustees of the charity created by Mary Warner and led by Viscount Hereford of Sudbourne signed a contract for seven

---

The quantity of pottery made in London in imitation of colourful Dutch delftware is shown by the an inventory of Nathaniel Oade's pottery in Gravel Lane, Southwark. It included no fewer than 109,661 pots and tiles when his son, Thomas, inherited the business in 1726. The father and three sons made public their tempestuous relationship. Thomas was a potter at Luke Talbot's Lambeth pottery until the business collapsed in 1723 when he, no doubt reluctantly, joined his father's business. He made annual business trips to eastern England. Joseph Groves was less successful and was insolvent in the debtor's prison in 1770, owing £5 10s to the Warner Trustees.

---

years with Joseph Pierce, Henry Grace, Thomas Oade, Thomas Bodle and George Groves. The trustees arranged for the yearly digging, removal and delivery on board a ship or hoy to be sent by the potters, of 150 tons of clay at the rate of 5s 6d a ton.

From the charity's accounts it appears that one of their tenants, Robert Barber [father of Robert Barber in Chapter 19], was paid 2s 6d a ton to load the clay on to the ships. All hazards from this point onwards were to lie with the potters. They were restricted to two periods in the year when the ships were required to be loaded. These were the month of May, and between 20 September and 20 October.

The trustees' account book shows that the clay seam was becoming exhausted. In 1775 only 57 tons were extracted and the entries end abruptly in June 1785. Davy, writing in the early part of the next century noted that the two pits, in a field, called Claypits Field, had been disused for *'some years'* and were believed to be exhausted. The trade had lasted for little over a century.

Small lead seals from Packard sacks have been found near Orford by Alan Calver.

Coprolites

Around the time Boyton clay was exhausted another useful substance was found beneath the ground at Levington, although its value was not realised for another fifty years. This was coprolite which was exploited for an even shorter period than the white clay. Professor John Henslow found these lumps of phosphatic rock, once thought to be the dung of dinosaurs, in cliffs at Bawdsey. He knew that Edward Packard of Saxmundham was working with others in 1843, dissolving bones in acid hoping to produce a fertiliser, and contacted him. As a result Packard built a small works in Snape for grinding the nodules and eleven years later he erected a factory at Bramford for producing super-phosphates and sulphuric acid.

By 1850 the coprolite rush was on throughout the area. Coprolites were first found on Valley Farm belonging to the Almshouse Trustees, occupied by William Miller. The financial arrangement was for the farmer to dig, sift and cart the coprolites to Boyton Dock for which he was paid £1 a ton by Edward Packard, the Trustees receiving 10s a ton. Seventy-one tons were sold in the first year. The following year, in November, 100 tons lay in John May's barn and 60 tons at the dock, plus 40 tons already sold. The dock and Dock Farm had been leased by members of the Benington family for several generations and Benington was paid 7d a ton dock charges. Two barges were named, usually the *'Lady of the Waves'*, but Captain Saxby's *'Industry'* was also involved. John May was able to sell coprolites at around 60s a ton to Packard and Edward Rausby of Bawdsey in 1855. He claimed it now cost 30s a ton to raise, and cartage cost 3s a ton. May's best year was 1856 when he sold 223 tons for £639 15s, making a profit of £384, less the cost of cartage and raising the mineral and levelling the ground afterwards. However, the pit on his farm was now worked out.

Alfred Chambers was a carter and in the business of digging for coprolites on his own behalf in a cottage garden abutting Capel Green. Five tons came from this source and another five belonged to his sister. A *'dipper'*, like a giant corkscrew, which shuddered in the foreman's hands when it struck a seam, was used to search for the mineral. It is said, however, that a bribe of 6d by a tied tenant, who did not want his garden to be dug up, was enough to persuade the foreman of a digging gang to report 'no coprolite'.

In 1857 Chambers signed an agreement with the widow Elizabeth Cooper and her son William for the right to excavate, raise and sell coprolite from a meadow behind a cottage on Capel Green. Chambers paid £15 for the right and he agreed 'to remove the Flag or Turf and the topsoil to the depth of One foot and a half' and level it afterwards. He would leave two tons of coprolite on the premises as a guarantee. Chambers was illiterate and merely made his mark on the document, but he must have been able to use figures to some extent.

The account book of the Boyton black-smith, William Clouting, gives some idea of how such coprolite diggers operated. Entries for Mr Ling and Ealey Sutton show that they had a wheelbarrow, and a horse and a pony to draw their carts. Their 'sivs' required frequent repair and sometimes they needed a replacement pick or shovel. A pump was required to deal with flooded workings. Their poverty is shown by the fact an annual bill of little over £4 took three instalments over ten months to clear.

There was a coprolite works at Butley Low Corner, where the mineral was washed in long tanks of water by means of sieves positioned just beneath the surface of the water. The washer manoeuvred the sieve by the use of a pole. Then it was the turn of boys with keen eyesight to pick out every-thing that was not coprolite. In this manner fossils and the teeth and bones of extinct animals came to light and could be sold for a few pence to local collectors.

The trade was short-lived and ended abruptly in the 1890s due to cheap imports of phosphates from South America and else-where. It seems to have come to an end in Boyton a decade earlier. The price had dropped to 34s a ton by 1870 and to 14s by 1879.

Crag and brick earth
The area is pockmarked with pits of all sizes. Once worked out, the larger ones were 'waste' and frequently were thought fit for

Pit near Butley Priory, 40ft deep. In the absence of local stone, blocks of red crag from lower strata were used for the foundations of the monastery.

labourers' cottages. On Tunstall Common a cottage roof can be glimpsed way below the level of the road. Red crag was extracted for spreading on fields to improve the soils.

Clay for bricks was more abundant than potters' clay. Bricks were made on the site of the later Chillesford works before 1600 when John Norden mapped them and recorded that the lessee lived where the *Froize Inn* is today. Around Chillesford church the Tithe Map shows three Brick Kiln fields. *Kiln Walks* near Staverton Park relates to the pit later known as *Gypsy Hole* where Romanies once camped. *Brickles* is the modern name for a Butley field near Stonebridge where there were brick kilns in the 18th century.

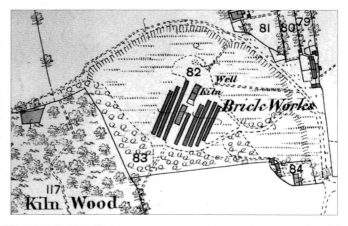

Brick-kiln and drying sheds from the Chillesford O.S. map of 1881.

Paddy O'Beirnes explores the overgrown kiln at Chillesford brick works.

Village craftsmen

Building and roofing

Henry Mome of Capel died in November 1624, leaving his wife *'certain million flags'*. At this time 'million' was not a usual expression and probably meant a huge quantity. Flags or 'flakkes', were turves cut from the heath and were not used for burning but for insulating roofs and wall construction. A further clue to Henry's trade may lie in the bequest of his *'daudes'*, that is his working clothes, trowel, handsaw and bag of tools to Richard Careman. Careman may well be the source of the surviving name Carman's Wood in Butley. The game-keeper's cottage, transformed since Florrie Warne's day, probably stands on the site of an earlier tenement.

It is unfortunate that tradesmen seldom identified their craft when making their wills. The Victorian guide to Orford Church reprinted in 1935 mentions that Philip Capon of *'Capel next Butley'* re-roofed Orford church in 1563. The agreement, made on 14th May 1562, was for him to replace the roof by the Feast of All Saints. After 333 years it had to be again replaced. Carpentry could be lucrative. In the early 17th century Richard Bradie was regularly employed at Sudbourne by Sir Michael Stanhope. In Butley he was in a position to enter into a penal bond of £100 with Sir William Forth and left this sum to be recovered for his four children in 1612.

Shoemakers, tailors, butchers and smiths

The few tradesmen identified from their wills include the following men. The Boyton shoemaker or cordwainer Thomas Cook probably hailed from Marks Tey in Essex since in 1584 he asked to be buried there. The twenty one lines of religious preamble to his will shows he was of Robert Forth's persuasion. He set up in Boyton before 1568, when he had more than four acres of copyhold land and a cottage on Ferry Way. While Forth had a live-in tailor, he did not have his own shoemaker and probably employed Cook. Much earlier in the century when the extravagant costume of some Priory canons caused comment, there were well-to-do tailors in the locality: John Kerych of Capel had three properties, while Richard Blanchflower who died after the

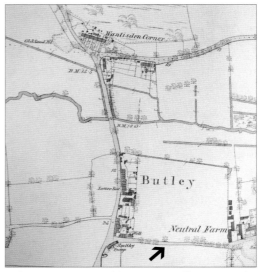

Butley Street in 1881. Haughfen Street, now Mill Lane, arrowed.

Dissolution farmed in Capel and Boyton. From his will it is clear that he was also a barber-surgeon.

Before 1667 there was a butcher in Butley named Nathan Harvy and another, Stephen Long, died there in 1709 leaving each of his five sons and three daughters only the sum of one shilling. Nathan had borrowed £5 from a Capel farmer, so clearly neither butcher prospered.

The earliest houses on Butley Street lay at the junction with the present Mill Lane, the western part of which was known as

The first development in the Street was White Row, the terrace of five three-storey houses on the left. They were built in 1830 on 'croached' land where much earlier a cottage had stood. Rent was paid for the gardens separately. At the rear there are no windows and this is thought to be because the houses 'encroached' (overlooked) manorial land. The cottages, grocery shop (left of centre) and tradesmen's premises were built later in the 19th century.

Haughfen Street alias Butley Street. At the end of the 16th century the nucleus of a new settlement was formed at the junction of several roads by two stopping-places for refreshment and repair: an inn and a forge. Both facilities were provided by the Lynd family. As it grew in importance this part of the main road acquired the name of Butley Street while Haughfen Street with its older settlement lost its identity, becoming Mill Lane.

At the junction, the farmer William Lynd owned a house called Puntings. Before he died it had burnt down along with its adjoining forge, although the four-poster bed and other furniture were saved. In 1638 William left his son £6 and the timber towards the building of another tenement. The lessee was a master smith named John Fisk, who had taken as apprentice in 1625 a poor orphan from Orford named Thomas Symley. The lad was to learn the *mystery* of the blacksmith's craft and stay until aged twenty four. During those years he was not permitted to marry, play at cards or dice, nor frequent taverns or ale-houses except on his master's business. At the end of the term Fisk had to supply his apprentice with a suit of clothes for *holy days* and another for work. Blacksmiths working from the same smithy identify themselves in the records 150 years later. They are William Easty, Isaac Clarke and Robert Last. The latter two lived in another cottage. Malkins flanked the forge, and was also once a Lynd

Malkins, Isaac Clarke's tiny cottage (right) still exists and his monogram can be seen under the virginia creeper.

The history of Malkins can be traced in the Staverton manorial records:

1515 one acre enclosed, recently built upon, occupied by Andrew Otherly.
1530-1630 members of the Blanchflower family occupy its successor.
1630-1738 members of the Lynd family are the copyholders.
1738-1739 Thomas Mulliner gent. transfers it to William Easty.
1777 William Easty transfers it to Isaac Clarke.

The junction of Butley Street and Mill Lane in the early 1930s. William Burch and his son pose outside the later forge built on the 'waste'. Much altered, it survives today as a house. Its yard and garden are still a rented portion of the former Town Land. The site of the earlier forge is the lean-to to the left of Malkins in the background.

property. When Clarke's properties were surveyed by Isaac Johnson in 1826, his successor was Robert Last and the old forge had become a cottage occupied by a widow.

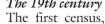

A new smithy had been constructed on the opposite side of the road just prior to 1739. It encroached on the verge ('Lord's waste') and resulted in a manorial court summons. The upshot was incorporation into the copyhold. The present brick and rubble cottage backs on to the Poor's Land of which its garden, rented from the Trustees, forms part.

At the end of the row of cottages which he built for his son near Wantisden Corner, William Large constructed a blacksmith's forge and trav'us. Around 1875 it was dismantled on the orders of Lord Rendlesham and an extension added to the smithy at the junction with Mill Lane. This extension consisted of a trav'us, the annexe to the forge where young horses were confined when they were shod for the first time.

Pair of minute cottages in Mill Lane before demolition in 2007. The sunflowers provide a scale. Malkins is on the left.

The 19th century

The first census, giving the names of the inhabitants, was taken in 1841. On the highway were the wheelwright, William Hunt, the blacksmith, John Crosby, Samuel Clark,

Towards the rear of the plot lay his house and around it 'wheelwrights, smiths and other shops, stables, outhouses, yards and gardens' as a scrap of paper pinned to the purchase shows. William Large used a horse to power his drive-shaft. The workshops have now been converted into cottages.

the bootmaker and Hannah Till, the shopkeeper. Round the corner next to Malkins the tailor, Thomas Jackson, occupied the site of the cottage which had recently been demolished.

At the far end of the Street, on Wantisden Corner, there lived the carpenter John Read. The Tithe Map made five years later shows that several of the inhabitants were owner-occupiers.

The 'first' William Large, builder and wheelwright, came to live in Butley from Sutton after his marriage to Eliza Cooper in 1852. She was the granddaughter of Abraham Cooper of Valley Farm, and the family still farmed there when William acquired the premises which William Hunt had developed on the Street directly opposite the farm. They comprised the north part of the Lynd land on which the five cottages had been built 30 years earlier.

William Cooper Large gave one of the authors an insight into the tradesmen of the village before World War I. Undertaking had been added to the family business. On the site of the double-fronted house his father built in 1912 were also the blacksmith

On Wantisden Corner there was another shoemaker, Charles Mann, and a tailor. Charlie had a stutter and his wife was blind. They lived in an old run-down cottage now beautifully restored and extended.

and William Richardson, a shoemaker. He made a shoe known as a *'straight'*, and old Mr Large did not think much of it as the foot had to adapt to the shape of the shoe.

Clothes made by all

Villagers made their own homespun cloth. The daily chore was part of everyday life for men, women and children. Fibres such as flax are seldom mentioned in local documents, but were essential for linen under-garments and bedding. It was woven commercially for sailcloth in the Ipswich and Woodbridge area. Hemp, vital for sacking and cordage, and also clothing and bedding for the poor, was grown adjacent to most cottages. Hempland appears regularly in all kinds of records. The *Inquisition of the Ninth* reveals that flax and hemp were taxed in Butley as far back as 1341.

John Huggins of Capel, a singleman, left his eldest brother in 1631 his wearing apparel and *'a pair of twill slays to weave withal'*. He is unlikely to have owned his own loom.

Robert Woolfe of Wantisden died in 1616, leaving his son Owen money and a bedstead along with half of his looms and slays with 'implements of weaving'. The other half he left to another son Robert. With more than one loom, and money available for bequests he was clearly engaged in manufacture on a larger scale.

A few cottages are recorded with hemp-land adjoining. The growing, heckling, spinning and bleaching of hemp was in the hands of numerous smallholders and cottagers. In Butley and Capel the crop was grown in small plots, and retting pits feature in manorial records.

Hemp was especially useful as it could be grown on the same land year after year. Seed was usually sown at the end of April, so Robert Clarke of Capel was behind with his husbandry when he left his wife his *'hemp which is to sow'* as he lay sick in May 1617. Women and children did most of the work, looking after the crop and its subsequent treatment.

Hemp seed and hemp *'pilked or unpilked'* appear in wills and inventories in the Butley area especially from around 1580. There were two kinds of hemp: carl and

Cottage weaver, after a Flemish manuscript.

Village shop-keepers

Well into the last century clothes continued to be home-made from material bought in the village shop.

Reg Snowdon (born 1921) reminisced: *'In Butley each hamlet had a shop. The shop at Low Corner was where Dr Ball lives. It sold loose sweets, tobacco and tea. People were so poor they could only buy very small quantities at a time. The shops were invaluable because there was no transport and only youngsters had bikes. People had to walk; many never even went into Woodbridge from one year to the next. Buses did not come until after World War II. The Kittle's shop in High Corner never amounted to very much and just sold bacon, sweets, tobacco, tea and so on. The Hazelwoods' shop in the Street could supply everything – boots, clothes... If you wanted something they did not have, you only had to ask and it would be there in a day or so. The Oyster used to sell sherry and port from the cask – you just took your bottle. Adnam's sherry was excellent...'*

Wesley Hazelwood (born 1898), son of the shopkeeper in Butley Street.

femble. Henry Mome left his wife 18 sheeves of carl hemp, all his femble hemp and a hog *'ready killed'*. Carl hemp produced the seed and femble or fimble hemp was spun. To pull or pill ('pilk') hemp is to separate the fibre from the core.

The process required that the hemp be soaked in retting pits, so that the fibres, now stinking, could be peeled off leaving the core to be discarded. Although soaking hemp in running water is said to have been prohibited, because it fouled streams, our local records show that there were retting pits on the Run (page 143) and on Oakeland Brook.

After soaking the hemp had to be dried, either in the open air or in special kilns or drying sheds. In 1606, William Fould of Capel directed that his son should *'build up a chimney'* in the hemphouse, and then his wife should have it during her lifetime.

Wills and inventories left by widows in the 16th century, such as Elizabeth Lyttell and Anne Capon refer to *'my pashell and my tow combe'*. The hemp had to be beaten, and to pash is to smash. The long-toothed comb was used to straighten the fibres.

The goods belonging to two Capel husbandmen, Thomas Drane and William Blanchflower, were priced by their neighbours. Six bushels of hempseed were valued at 12s in 1583 and 10s in 1590. Quantities of hemp were measured in rimbles, worth 6s a rimble and 6s 4d, unpilked, in those years. Although references to hempland and retting pits occur regularly in wills they end in 1638 in the core parishes. Doubtless people too poor to leave wills continued to engage in this activity, since hempland continues to feature in the records and on maps for the next two centuries.

Postscript

Today people live here, but work elsewhere. There are neither working pits nor tradesmen in our three core villages and all but one of the pubs has closed. However, the Finlay brothers have a garage workshop in Boyton, Honor Hussey has a pottery and studio at Butley Barns in Mill Lane, and Butley Mill's old agricultural buildings have been converted by Lawrence Edwards into workshops for sculptors and painters.

Farmers of the Manor

Chapter 14

The rhythm of the farming year was paralleled by larger cycles of plenty and dearth. Absent and resident owners of estates affected the amount of land retained as demesne or farmed by tenants. Whatever the disadvantages for yeomen and husbandmen, the priors of Butley created stability with their continuous on-site management from the 12th to the 16th century. Thereafter, most of their successors lived elsewhere, leasing land to large tenant farmers. Some of these were innovators, at the forefront of the Agricultural Revolution which began in the 18th century.

In the 19th century the Suffolk Punches bred by large tenant farmers in the Sandlings became world-renowned. Their numbers are today much reduced. but some are still trained as working horses and are put through their paces at rural events, such as this one at Easton Farm Park.

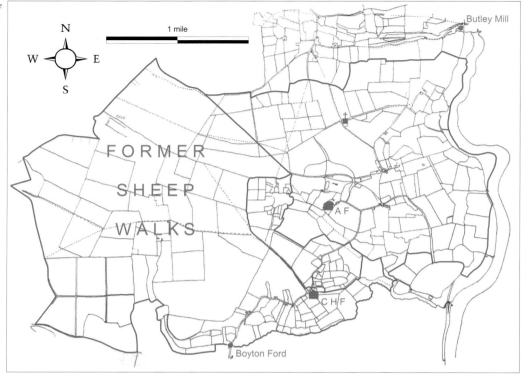

Outline map of the manors of Butley and Tangham c. 1818, showing the two large farms into which they were divided: Abbey Farm (AF) and Capel Home Farm (CHF).

Introduction

The Priory's *Household List* shows that there were plenty of qualified staff in the spring of 1538 to maintain farming on the demesne until Henry VIII granted it to a new owner. Familiar with the Butley and Tangham estate from his lengthy visits to the Priory, the Duke of Suffolk was anxious to add it to his Suffolk landholdings and arranged for it to be farmed by his Treasurer, William Naunton, who resided at Alderton. However, the King foresaw a potential conflict between the Dukes of Suffolk and Norfolk. The latter was a major landowner in East Anglia, and in July 1539 the King decided to sell the ex-monastic estate to him for the sum of £1,329-0s-10d. Suffolk's power-base was moved to another county, but Norfolk had to respect the 21-year lease already granted to William Naunton for £51-3s-4d per annum.

The lease describes the estate as it was farmed at the very end of the monastic period and can be used for comparison with the way farming was carried out subsequently. It consisted of the site of the Priory and the demesne lands in the parishes of Butley and Capel St Andrew, some 3,500 acres, the greater part of which was heath. The Boyton component was retained in the King's hands until the following year when it was settled on his fourth queen, Anne of Cleves, as part of her divorce settlement. The reversion was bought by William Forth, and the three monastic manors were reunited after an interval of seven years.

William Naunton and William Redham

William Naunton's 1539 lease provides a snapshot of the Priory demesne immediately before it closed. It lists the commons, arable, marshes, pastures and meadows by name and acreage, and also the underwoods (coppice) and monastic gardens. The 'Common Fields' of Butley, Tangham and Capel comprised some 3,000 acres. Clearly this was an estimate, but they represented more than 80% of the land in the two parishes. These were the sheep-walks where Naunton, small farmers and villagers could run their sheep and from time to time cultivate small clearings with crops such as rye.

There were approaching 200 acres of marsh and a similar amount of pasture. Meadow extended to about 40 acres, while arable was less than 100 acres with the largest field containing 30 acres. As much as 250 acres of arable and pasture were enclosed. The marshes were also enclosed – by the 'wet fences' formed by drainage ditches. Many names were used for centuries to come: Broom Close, Cow Marsh, Haws, Capel Hill, Staverton Park, Parks, Horse Marsh, Great and Little Stevensons and Inghams, but the Frith, a causeway leading to Burrow Hill, used to be known as the Old Drift. It borrowed its later name from the marshes flanking it which lost theirs.

William Naunton held the lease for only six years, but during that time he increased the demesne from 534 acres to 628 acres of mixed arable, meadow, pasture and under-wood. A much greater percentage of it was ploughed, but the heath commons had not yet been touched. In 1545 the Duke of Norfolk disposed of the estate and the King sold it to William Forth of Hadleigh for £910-2s-3d. Clearly Naunton relinquished his lease, whether willingly or not, and Forth, who the next year also acquired the former monastic estate of Boyton, looked for a new tenant farmer.

The man Forth chose, William Redham, was a wealthy man in his own right. He owned property in three parishes in the north of the county and the *Swan Inn* in Ipswich. Having agreed to take the lease, Redham reneged upon it. Forth had to take him to court because the estate had suffered as a consequence.

Forth's *'supplication'* to the court gives some interesting information about the farm. The rent was to be £100 a year. The dereliction of the farmer meant than 500 sheep were *'not thoroughly shorn'*, *'great cattle were wasted'* and the rent and profit of the manor lost. His tenant farmer clearly had a multiple role. He could sub-let to others, and could farm on his own account, but he must also farm cattle and sheep for his master. Redham's rent was actually £100 a year plus the upkeep of Forth's sheep and cattle. William Forth also owned sheep in Boyton. Since he remained resident in Hadleigh, it is likely that he continued to be a clothier for the rest of his life, dealing in wool from his Tangham and Boyton flocks. Years earlier, his Hadleigh grandfather, also William, probably obtained wool from the Priory, since the monastery featured in his bequests.

In the event Redham took the lease for 14 years and was referred to in the manor court rolls as *'the Farmer of the Manor of Butley'*. He sublet to John Stonard and John Pyke who were paying £20 per annum to him and were known as *'the farmers of Butley Abbey'*. In addition to farming the demesne lands Redham had the use of *'a stall boat, two cock boats, anchors and ropes'* once the right of the Prior. He also had the use of a copyhold tenement in Butley, *'late Shepherdes'*.

Redham's farm management revealed

When Redham died in 1552 he left his properties in three north Suffolk parishes to his son, William, who with his mother was given all his *'cattle, sheep, lambs, milch beasts, dry cattle and oxen, steers, bullocks, buds, calves, horses, mares, geldings and colts'* and the whole

Butley Abbey farmhouse was probably created out of the Prior's Lodging soon after the Dissolution to house the first farmers of the manor. Their yards later housed the famous stud. Lady Greenwell recalled the sight of 38 horses galloping down the lane to Low Corner in a cloud of golden dust to spend the night on the marshes, returning of their own volition the following day.

profit of his Sandlings farms until the following Michaelmas. The farm animals were to be sold and the money and the profits of the farm were to be used to pay his debts to *'my good master Master Forth without any fraud or guile'*.

He left his wife and son the proceeds from the sale of his corn, timber and farm implements. He made further provision for them by ordering that 500 sheep and his best milch cows, to the value of £100, were to remain in the hands of Stonard and Pyke for a period of eight years. At the end of that time, William was to receive £60 and Alice £40.

Thus Stonard and Pyke were, in effect, mirroring the arrangement between Forth and Redham in that they were looking after Redham's animals in addition to paying rent, but taking their profit from the increase. The annuity or rent received from the two sub-tenants was also divided between wife and son. In a complex paragraph, in which the copyist seems to have transcribed *'viij years'* as *'my years'*, it seems Redham left the £20 income in the proportions of two-thirds to his son, and one-third to his wife.

Continuity with the previous regime can be deduced from names mentioned in his will. A Robert Pyke was a horse-keeper at the Priory and two witnesses were Robert Smythe and John Leche, both names of

Capel Home Farm is today a private house, but the adjacent yards and barns still belong to the Greenwell estate.

carters in 1538. Others who appear soon afterwards in other contexts were beneficiaries: he left his fox-furred gown to *'Goodman Lynne, my very friend of Butley'* and his long gown faced with fox to *'my gosseppe Hawes'*, probably another friend, its old meaning being intimate friend or crony.

Even the largest tenant farmers could not flout manorial rules. The Redhams and their sub-tenants appear in Butley and Tangham court rolls. The earliest entry concerns Matthew Stonard and John Pyke who were accused of taking faggots from the Lord's wood using wagons. Redham himself was in trouble, too, having insufficiently repaired Melle Marsh Bridge. This is the present Stonebridge, and remains of the original bridge lie below the road from Butley to Capel. As *'farmer of Tangham'* he was charged with making waste upon the manor in 1556, by building a kiln there, and as *'farmer of the Manor of Butley'* he was in greater trouble for not repairing *'le selives'*, probably the sluices, causing flooding on pastures occupied by others. John Stonard was fined the following year for allowing his geese to feed on the green. Then his *'great beast'* had escaped because his land was insufficiently fenced, and he had failed to repair the bank near Melle Marsh Bridge.

Not until the end of the 18th century did individuals again lease large portions of the former monastic estate. In the intervening years stewards and bailiffs operated on behalf of owners who either farmed on their own account or let it in smaller portions.

Later tenant farmers

When William Forth of Hadleigh died in 1558 he left his eldest son, Robert, his Sandlings estate. Robert moved to Butley, extended the Gatehouse accommodation by building a mansion on the east side, and farmed the demesne himself. His terrier of Boyton made in 1568 shows that he only farmed the marshes there: 608 acres between the Gull and Caldwell Hall where his dairy herds were pastured and 30 acres of salt marsh beyond the sea wall on which he had built fishermen's houses for yearly letting. A 1594 survey of the three manors shows that he built up a farm of 3,223 acres, half of which was arable. Subsequently most of the

Boyton part was sold to the Warners and the Butley and Tangham/Capel parts were gradually split up between different owners. As a result Butley Abbey Farm, as it came to be called, was not leased again as an entity until the last quarter of the 18th century. By this time aristocratic landlords were creating huge sporting estates, and planting the stands of trees that were to become a feature of the Sandlings Triangle throughout the following century.

Arthur Young was the first to use the name 'Sandling'. An agricultural writer, he was particularly interested in the cultivation of carrots in the area between Woodbridge, Saxmundham and Orford. He mentioned that carrots had been sent by sea to London for as long as 200 years, but due to competition from areas closer to the capital they were now being used to feed horses. Since he regarded the Suffolk horse to be an outstanding farm animal, he reckoned the substitution of carrots for corn and hay to be to the benefit of the breed. Before recommending this in his reports he wanted to visit the area in person. In 1797 he began at Sutton, and continued to Shottisham, Ramsholt, Alderton and Hollesley, and confirmed his earlier opinion. However, when he came the *'great farm of 2700 acres'* of Samuel Gross at Capel and Thomas Chandler's of a similar size at Butley Abbey he found carrots were no longer grown; they were consumed by the innumerable number of hares preserved as game by the aristocratic landowner, Lord Archibald Hamilton.

Thomas Catlin

At the turn of the century Thomas Ablitt farmed there. He was succeeded by two outstanding agriculturalists: Thomas Catlin farmed from 1808 for 47 years, followed by Thomas Crisp who farmed for 14 years. Although Catlin gained the highest accolades from his fellow farmers and at horse shows around the country, it was said that his son, also Thomas, who farmed at Chillesford Lodge, was the inspiration for the improvements made at Butley Abbey Farm. When he died in 1841, aged only 29, his father took the Chillesford farm too.

There is a pen-portrait of the elder Catlin in volume I of *The Suffolk Horse Stud Book*,

Archibald Hamilton painted by Francis Cotes when he was 25 years old and a keen sportsman. His mother inherited Butley and Tangham lands in addition to her Rendlesham estate. After her death in 1771 and aided by his brother-in-law, Archibald set about creating a sporting landscape to the detriment of his tenant farmers.

where he is described as *'a jovial old man who rose early, drove about in a four wheeler, farmed all day and never troubled his head about matters beyond an easygoing routine of a not very eventful life'.* However, excitement and satisfaction were gained at the county and national shows and he believed nothing was superior to what could be found at the Abbey Farm. His outstanding success was at the Royal Windsor Show in 1851 when, in front of the Queen herself, two of his horses, Duke and Captain, were first and second in their class. Captain was given the nickname Ripshawe, since his temper was not dissimilar to that of Ripshawe, the governor of Ipswich Gaol. Duke on the other hand *'could be led by a boy'.* He won more prizes than any horse of his day and sired 42 colts. Captain's line quickly became extinct, but the strain was carried on by a colt bred by a widow, Mrs Garrod, who lived at Neutral Farm, Mill Lane.

Catlin had long leases from Lord Rendlesham. Such leases encouraged farmers to make costly improvements and he farmed in the 'golden age'. Following his death the stud was sold on 24 September 1855, and a note in the diary of Samuel Gross records that 116 carthorses and 16 nags realized £6,000.

The tiny church at Chillesford where Thomas Crisp, breeder of the 'Ufford' horse lies, along with many of his descendants.

Thomas Crisp

Thomas Crisp was born at the Red House, Rendlesham. The first Suffolk Punch, 'Crisp's horse of Ufford' belonged to his grandfather who had moved his family and the stud to Gedgrave Hall, an 800-acre stock farm, when Thomas was about nineteen. His grandfather died in 1823 aged 86 and is buried in Chillesford churchyard.

The young man then farmed Gedgrave for his mother and family for 45 years. In 1855 he was able to take on Butley Abbey farm in addition. With his tenancy of Hill Farm at Chillesford he was farming at least 4,000 acres. Later he gave up Hill Farm and took Tangham Farm in its place; his energy was exceptional.

Crisp is recorded in the *Stud Book* in even more glowing terms than his predecessor at Butley Abbey. '*The marvellous stories of his shipments for abroad are amply testified by the porters at the railway stations*'. Horses were

James Lewis was Thomas Crisp's head horseman for many years and when the Butley Abbey stud was broken up in 1870 he devotedly followed old Cup-bearer 416 to his new home in Carlton, near Saxmundham.

Brass plate from the stockman's box which accompanied Cup-bearer to shows.

Beribboned punches at Sudbourne used to be paraded before the estate-owner on Sunday mornings to be fed extra strong mints which made them sneeze, his son, Kenneth Clark, recalled. He thought their form more perfectly proportioned than when they were later bred two and a half hands taller.

exported to the colonies and Prussia. His sheep yielded '*incredible clips of wool*', and his crops included '*curious grasses of rapid growth, and an enormous yield would be raised from seed direct from some unknown region in the Wallacian Provinces*'. In dry summers, walks on the Tangham farm were knee deep in sheep feed when other farms were suffering from drought. He had as many as 3,000 sheep away from the home farm at times. Yet only a few years later Frederick Clifford, the *Times* correspondent, was told it was virtually impossible to obtain a living from these lands.

Greater yields from 'high farming' came about through much-improved drainage, machinery, chemicals and seeds. Better transport meant that produce and cattle could be moved from rural areas to the major centres of commerce and industry with their teeming populations.

At the time of the 1861 census, Thomas Crisp employed two millers, ten shepherds, 58 labourers, 28 women and 31 boys. In January 1869, whilst riding with Lord Rendlesham's foxhounds at Parham, he suffered a fatal heart attack. He left a widow who had previously been the widow of Thomas Catlin, junior. Crisp's obituary in the *Ipswich Journal* described him as '*perhaps the foremost of the little band of agriculturalists who have made the name of the county of Suffolk famous in England and on the Continent*'. In

Butley church there is a stained glass window to his memory.

Samuel Wolton

Crisp's successor was another noted horse breeder. Samuel Wolton had to cope with the farming depression which began around 1870, the rise of agricultural unions and the subsequent Lock-out of 1874. This story is told in Chapter 17. Wolton farmed for 20 years at the Abbey, and these included the notorious Black '79 which followed a succession of poor seasons. That year began with one of the coldest winters of the century and cold weather continued into May. Then it was wet throughout the next three months and the following winter began early. In England and Wales three million sheep died or were killed because of rot, and many farmers were ruined. The depression continued for the rest of the century, culminating in the crash of 1896.

Conclusion

Since the Dissolution there have been only two periods when the Butley estate has been managed by a resident landowner; Robert Forth built an Elizabethan mansion on the site of the Priory and lived there for nearly 40 years, farming on his own account, and the Greenwell family made Butley Abbey their home in the 1930s and are farming the estate to this day.

The challenges have been the same for whoever managed the land: the sea has had to be kept out; the marshes drained; and recurrent poor harvests, stock mortality and fluctuating farm prices endured. The three types of soil were traditionally divided between arable, dairy and sheep farming, but economic pressures, particularly in wartime, led to increasing reliance on arable. Consequent diminution of permanent pasture and heath was made possible by improved irrigation and artificial fertilizers. While the superlative heavy horse bred by large tenant farmers has been replaced by enormous machinery, water management continues to be the key to farming success in the Sandlings.

Horseman's lore

The ability of horsemen to manage the intact stallions in their care was proverbial and they guarded their 'secrets' carefully. Reg Snowdon, was born in Chillesford and while still a child, was taught to plough by his father. In old age he finally allowed one of the authors to transcribe the tattered notebook handed down from his grandfather William, saying '*It has been all over Suffolk.*'

The instructions make horrific reading, for example:

To make a horse draw

Put him in a long trace. Chain him to a tree take a stick and hit him withinside of his knees till you bring him down. Then whip him over the wallows till he will draw down on his knees then coax him and give him comfort then whip him so until he will draw kindly.

For a horse with a cough or cold

Take 1 dram of powdered opium 1/4lb of powdered aniseed 1/4lb of powdered liquorice 1/4lb carraway 1/4lb of powdered squills. Mix the above well together with syrup into 20 balls and give one every night in a bran mash.

To jade or draw a horse

Get some grey toads and hang them upon a whitethorn bush till they are dead then lay them into an ant hill then take them out then put them into a small stream take that which separate from other dry them into powder. Touch a horse on the pit of the shoulder to jade him and on the rump to draw him.

The horseman's skill was greatly valued by his employer; there was competition between large farmers and landowners to have prize-winning Punches and the finest fetched large sums of money.

At Bawdsey Manor the Quilters had a fine stud and surely paid for the exquisite roundel on groom John Lankester's gravestone which faces their enclosure in Bawdsey churchyard.

Mrs Youngman and Other Tenant Farmers

Chapter 15

Clearly those farming on a small scale were always more numerous than the larger tenant farmers. Manorial records describe their holdings over hundreds of years. A feature of the landscape from early times were small enclosed arable fields in which sheep could be folded on the stubble. Their scattered droppings did not have to be spread like cow manure and they made the sandy soil fertile. No evidence for the Midland type of three-field system has been found here, although the use of tenants' clumsy ox-teams made more practical the cultivation of the largest demesne fields in strips separated by baulks.

The Domesday Book lists only two horses in the whole of the Triangle; oxen ploughed the land. They were still harnessed here as late as the 19th century, although rarely recorded in documents. Mrs Ogilvie's team at Thorpeness was photographed in 1906.

The extent of early enclosure in the Triangle is reflected by the near total absence of enclosure awards: in Sudbourne 150 acres were enclosed in 1807; in Gedgrave and Orford about 46 acres in 1878; and in Hollesley 44 acres of heath in 1844. In the 20th century 1,134 acres of heath were enclosed at Shottisham and 148 acres in Bromeswell.

Typical small fields with tree-lined hedges surveyed by Norden in 1601. Hedgerow oaks reduced the need for woodland.

Chillesford hedgers at work: a seasonal labour now done by machine.

The old enclosures were mostly small; one acre took a day to plough and was a convenient size for one man to cultivate. All the hedges were carefully maintained to protect crops, as well as to provide faggots for firing, since woodland was the preserve of the manorial lord. Oak trees in the hedges were a valuable resource for house and barn construction. In places they can be seen marking the line of ploughed-down hedges within today's larger fields.

Cultivating the land

Robert Forth's estate was surveyed in 1594. It consisted of the three manors of Butley, Boyton and Tangham (Capel St Andrew) and was calculated as 5,301 acres. He farmed 3,223 acres of this himself. The home farm comprised the manor-house and Home Park, 22 acres of gardens, orchards, yards and ponds, while he kept all 129 acres of woodland. There were 50 tenements, 8 cottages, 2 water-mills, 2 separate barns, a ferry and a ferry-house. During the previous 40 years, reflecting a decline in sheep-farming, Forth had reduced the heath commons by a third, while his arable in the three manors had all but tripled to 1,600 acres. None of his tenants had large farms and the majority held their land 'at his will'. Only five of these had farms of more than 100 acres and they were rented on an annual basis only. In the three manors little more than 386 acres were either free, leased or copyhold and they were divided among 34 small farmers and cottagers. He let land on

an annual basis to 42 men. They included men who also had freehold and/or copyhold land of their own to farm, and also purely tenant farmers such as: Edward Ablett with his 208-acre Dairy House Farm in Boyton; and John Gilders who rented 335 acres including Edwardes Farm in Boyton and all the salt marsh on the estate. The latter flanked the Haven on the east shore of Boyton and amounted to 120 acres. John Herbert of Hollesley supplemented his 6-acre copyhold arable with 232 acres rented from Robert Forth along with 27 acres of pasture. His cultivated land was in the western part of Boyton, but his pasture lay down by the sea wall. In the Triangle mixed farms needed to comprise fields on marsh, sand and the better soil; the small farms tended to be sited where they occur close together.

There were ten freeholds, but these totalled only 47 acres or less than 1% of the estate, and most were cottage plots. The largest freeholders were: Robert Bourne with a 31-acre farm called Creetings in Boyton; Robert Brooke with a 6-acre farm called Tones at Butley High Corner; and Thomas Lynd junior with 6¼ acres near Butley Street.

Contemporary church records have not survived except in the case of Boyton, and we lack supplementary information for the size of the population in this period. Although 57 men and 3 widows were listed as landholders, small pieces of land and cottages in the three parishes actually

The last remaining unmodernised farmhouse in Butley. Low Farm incorporates carved limestone blocks from the Priory in its walls which mask a timber-frame construction. No doubt the farm once exported its produce from a dock on the adjacent creek .

belonged to other manors and were not included, while some tenants had their homes outside the three manors. The use of the 'Domesday formula' of about five per household for the 60 known landholders provides a very rough estimate of 300 for the total population in the three parishes. This may be an under-estimate as it takes no account of casually employed, landless families in crowded cottages. As late as the 19th century farming was still essentially unchanged with all able-bodied women and children required to help with labour in the fields at certain seasons of the year.

Tudor small farmers

Some Butley families can be traced in records over three centuries and others come and go within a lifetime. The Blanchflowers and Haughfens can be found at least as early

as 1350 and were tillers of the soil. The former never rose above the status of husbandmen, various members of the family owning or renting small farms in Butley, Capel and Boyton, where their name disappears around 1670 with the death of Robert. John Haughfen was fortunate to be bequeathed by his uncle, the last prior, the manor of Russells in Chillesford, and his descendants were prominent manorial lords in Tunstall in the 17th century, owning Justices (Church Farm). They are commemorated by brasses in the floor of the church opposite.

Two other names, of the Francis and Brooke families, belonged to well-to-do devout men, Robert Francis and John Brooke. Unusually, they asked to be buried in the chancel of Butley church. Their families were recorded in the parish for only a century, but two of them left their mark. In 1531 Robert Francis left 13s-4d for a stone cross to be erected in Butley Street close to where he lived. It was subsequently damaged and later described as *'the stumped cross'*, mis-transcribed *'stamped crouch'* in other documents. His grandson Augustine was living there in 1594 when he built a new cottage on the half acre of copyhold and held a five-acre field. This suggests that the Francis family's income did not derive principally from farming but from a related trade.

John Brooke's son Augustine, who had been educated at the Priory school, carved his name underneath the original lock of the church door, most probably because he had constructed it himself. The Brooke family lived at High Corner where they owned one

Was this old timber-framed farmhouse at High Corner built by Augustine Brooke?
In 1980 it was still known as Brooks, since when it has been modernised and much enlarged.

of the few freeholds, namely a six-acre farm. In addition they held the copyhold of two other farms, one in Butley Street and the other in Capel Street, comprising 36 acres of mixed arable and pasture. In 1534 John's will shows that he owned 80 sheep, four mares and four neat.

The northern part of Butley Manor had embedded in it numerous plots of land belonging to other manors, and it was on these that smallholdings and cottages were erected. They formed the basis of farms created from assorted fields and strips along the valley. The Lynds can be traced for 200 years by way of entries in numerous Butley documents after the 1550s. In the later 16th century William and Thomas senior each had freeholds there in addition to copyholds. William had two half-acre freeholds at the cross-roads on Butley Street and was likely to have been involved in trade. He, or possibly a namesake, is recorded as the holder of some copyholds in Rendlesham including the mill, so this may have been the source of his income. There was a mill situated on the Run opposite the north-east corner of Staverton Park. It had fallen into disuse by the time that John Norden came to annotate his map of Staverton Park in 1600.

A farmhouse built on the western portion of Mill Lane was called Reppes after John Rippes, a 15th-century occupier. It became copyhold of the Lynd family and was inherited by Thomas Lynd junior in 1573 and then sold by him to his brother, Thomas senior for £35.

The stretch of lane which ran between the house and the main roadway was known as

How did Neutral Farm, Butley, get its name? It used to be called Street Farm because it lay on Haughfen Street. Then in 1803 its owner, Perry Nursey, put the 170 acres on the market and the two neighbouring landowners, the Marquess of Hertford at Sudbourne Hall and Peter Isaac Thellusson at Rendlesham Hall, colluded in a London coffee house and agreed to share the property. They acquired it for £4,170, each paying Perry Nursey half that sum. Because it belonged to neither of them, it became known as *'Neutral Farm'*. The sale documents survive in Ipswich Record Office. The farmhouse is described as a *'Hall and Hall Chamber'*, repeating the description used in 1638 when Bridget Bickers had owned it.

Haughfen Street. A post-medieval settlement in the north of the parish lay at the junction. The *Oyster* site seems to have been developed at the end of the 16th century when Thomas Lynd senior built a house on a one-acre freehold by the cross roads. In addition to his 45-acre copyhold of Reppes and two cottages he rented 57 acres from Robert Forth. The 102 acres subsequently evolved into Street Farm, known as Neutral Farm after its purchase in 1804. While the Lynd family had copyholds along the east side of what is now Butley Street, there is no evidence that they built on them. The only house recorded there in the 1594 survey was a cottage on the verge, or waste (today the site of three-storey White Row), occupied by Widow Bruton.

Meanwhile Thomas Lynd junior was active in the north-west part of the manor, acquiring 12 parcels of freehold land belonging to five manors. He farmed the high ground there known as Flegbury Hill and rented some 64 acres, cottages called Snowes and a turbary known as Grubs Leighton. In the mid-18th century his surname disappears because there were only female heirs. His

Thomas Lynd's farm. Flegbury Hill lies on the left, his messuage Poll (now Valley Farm, Butley) was in the centre and his turbary in the valley on the right.

In 1583 William Warren's farmhouse in Boyton contained a Hall, Chamber and Soler, with a Buttery, Dairy and Barn. There was unharvested corn worth £7 and in the Barn were hay, malt, barley and rye along with 'unrett' and retted hemp worth about £2. The Dairy contained two firkins of butter worth £1, a small amount of whey and equipment for making cheese. His cart, plough, harrows, traces and rollers were worth 12s, and the other tools a mere 3s. In the yard were:

9 milch neat and a bull	£16
4 shotts, 2 gilts & a sow	£1-18s
9 ewes & 7 lambs	£2-5s
3 mares, with 2 sucking & a horse	£4
7 geese	2s-6d
8 hens with chickens & cocks	4s

Finally, he was owed £24-8s and the total value of his inventory was £74-6s-1d.

The Warrens ceased to farm in Boyton, but the rooms show that theirs must have been one of the principal farmhouses, such as Frogs Hall or Boyton Hall.

messuage 'Poll' was the precursor of Valley Farm.

Some husbandmen's livestock

Several of the numerous small farmers left wills, but only a few inventories survive. Wills give information about the farms and the houses, such as their names, and furniture and goods which provide indications of numbers of rooms and standards of living. However, they are less useful as regards the number of animals kept and the quantities of crops grown. Manorial rolls are mainly concerned with the transfer of copyhold land and this rarely equates with the total extent of the farm, which might include freeholds and land rented on a yearly basis.

Probate inventories provide comprehensive lists and we are fortunate that seven early ones survive, spanning the years 1571 to 1590. The deceased were: Margery Fattur of Butley; Richard Tyler of Boyton; Thomas Drane of Capel; Peter Gardener of Chillesford; William Warren of Boyton; William Blancheflower of Capel; and Anne Capon of Butley. An inventory required three men to make a list of the goods and agree on their valuation.

Some farmers, appearing in court rolls as copyholders, were actually holding land or were resident in nearby parishes. Such were the Herberts of Hollesley. In 1594 John Herbert, the second-largest farmer in the three manors with 259 acres, was living in nearby Cauldwell Hall, Hollesley, while Robert Gaiton's home was what is now Dale Farm in Wantisden. Conversely, in addition to his mainly arable farm and home in Butley, Thomas Lynd senior ran his sheep within the manors of Staverton and Bavents in Rendlesham.

Decline of sheep-farming

At the end of the 16th century sheep-farming on the Sandlings was still important, but was giving way to arable and dairy-farming. The 3,000-acre expanse of heath commons had been parcelled into sheep walks on the poorest land interspersed with cultivated fields. Staverton Park had lacked deer for at least 200 years, and was divided into areas of arable, pollarded timber and wood pasture.

Jeffrey Cookson kept a heifer and sheep in Staverton Park, and five and a half wethers on his 61-acre farm in Capel Street. The 'half wether' kept at home must indicate a shared arrangement. This and other wills show that the manorial flocks contained small numbers of sheep belonging to various owners. His executors were to sell 80 of his lambs and his four houses for the benefit of his three daughters. He left them, in addition, two cows each and his hogs, geese, bees, corn and hemp. Examination of local non-gentry

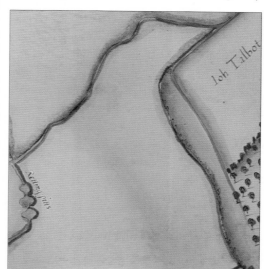

The west corner of Staverton Park in 1600 showing an area of cultivation within it. Note the three retting pits upstream (left) flowing directly into the Run.

wills of the 17th century reveals only one reference to sheep, compared with scattered references to cattle. The explanation seems to lie in the reduction of wool prices after 1620 and the greater profitability of dairy-farming.

A contemporary writer, Robert Reyce commented in 1618:

'Large dairies of most goodly milch cattle... are kept... especially in the cheife ports of this shire tending to the East, more naturally given to meddow, pasture and feeding than the rest of the shire... Great profit doth arise from these dairies, both for butter and cheese... a great quantity spent here in victualling many ships here at home for long voyages'.

The extensive areas of marsh pasture in Boyton adjacent to its dock promoted successful dairy farming, and cheese will have been taken from there to Woolwich and London. Sadly, no local records of this activity appear to have survived.

On a national scale the 1600s were in the main a dire century for agriculture. Apart from high taxation, the Civil War, poor harvests and a deteriorating climate, the gradual fragmentation of the Butley estate combined with landowner absenteeism exacerbated its decline. The Boyton portion, sold as a unit to the Warner family and administered by trustees, escaped some of these ill effects.

Although incomplete, the court rolls from about 1600 to the 1780s provide names of many tenant farmers, but there is a dearth of detail from other sources. In the two centuries intervening between Radulph Agas' one-off survey of 1594 and Isaac Johnson's detailed maps from 1780 onwards nothing comparable survives. A main reason is likely to be changes of ownership of the Spencer's former seat of Rendlesham Hall, together with the fact that it was consumed by fire on more than one occasion.

Despite this loss, at the beginning of the 18th century a slow recovery in Butley and Capel can be ascribed to the arrival of Edward Spencer on the scene. For a number of years he was an energetic steward of the estate and his family purchased farms when they became available. For instance, in 1704 his uncle purchased for £3,500 nine farms totalling 351 acres in Butley.

Three comprised between 70 and 100 acres; four between 20 and 63 acres; while two were smaller than 15 acres. Tiny farms, in which husbandry was combined with other activities, including hemp production, turf-cutting, reed-gathering and livestock-grazing on commons, are a constant feature of the late- and post-medieval periods in the Triangle. For this reason they should not be dismissed as necessarily uneconomic by modern researchers.

The Cooper family

In 1755 Lord Hertford purchased the Sudbourne estate from Viscount Hereford and became the owner of the 117-acre Valley Farm and 28-acre Mill Farm in Butley. Meanwhile the late Edward Spencer's daughter, followed by his grandson, were leasing Butley Abbey Farm and Capel Home Farm to the leading agriculturalists described in the previous chapter. At the beginning of the next century Peter Isaac Thellusson purchased the Butley and Tangham estate of 4,050 acres. It included four farms of, respectively, 180, 33, 32 and 25 acres let on an annual basis. The rents were approximately £1 per acre. Other farms were leased.

John Cooper's branch of the family were farming down at Capel Green in the 18th and 19th centuries. Isaac Johnson recorded the acreages of the farms there in 1796:

John Cooper	32 . 1 . 38
John Stebbing	23 . 3 . 30
John Knight	13 . 1 . 31
John Cable	5 . 2 . 30

It shows that the size-range had changed little, if at all, from that recorded by Radulph Agas 200 years earlier

Valley Farm

Lord Hertford's tenant at Valley Farm was Abraham Cooper in the late 18th century and one of his descendants married into the Large family. William Large (1881-1981) was a builder and wheelwright in Butley as was his father and grandfather. Two of his brothers, Arthur and Herbert, emigrated to Australia before 1914. Before he died, William sent many documents, including two leases of Valley Farm, to Herbert's descendants in Queensland. It was their interest in the family's history which led to correspondence and a realisation that the Cooper papers survived.

Chillesford reed-beds and reeds drying out. It is said that reed will last for a century and straw a generation. Reed thatch is always ridged in straw which of course needs to be replaced more frequently.

Valley Farm: Christian Youngman

A vignette of what was involved for an 18th-century tenant leasing a 117-acre farm is preserved in one of the documents copied in Australia. The Michaelmas following her husband's death in 1774, Christian Youngman, née Cooper, signed a 21-year lease with Lord Hertford. The conditions were attached to what will have been a standard lease on the estate. They were designed to ensure that a tenant maintained a farm in good order. Mrs Youngman was obliged to keep up the house and barns, along with fences, gates and stiles. Thatching was required to be with wheat or rye straw, '*if done with reed then . . . [she] shall pay the cost of cutting such reed*'.

The farm will have been improved as a result of her duty to '*yearly make 40 rods of hedging, ditching and banking*' and to plant 20 oak, ash and elm saplings taken from Scudgrave Wood or elsewhere on the Manor of Sudbourne. Clauses in the agreement relate specifically to her responsibilities with respect to preserving the landowner's game and preventing poaching.

Prohibitions included removing manure or turnip crops from the premises, breaking up the meadows and borders of fields, cutting or lopping any of the timber trees, or successive sowing of corn. Within the lease were ancient rights pertaining to manorial lords which were soon to disappear.

Hertford required her to do two day's work yearly with '*an able team carriage and servants in carrying stone piles or other materials to some part of the marsh walls belonging to the said Earl*'. She was not to take any '*plough boot or cart boot from off the premises.*' These old manorial rights, usually spelt 'bote', refer to using wood for repairing – in this case, ploughs or carts.

Valley Farm: Abraham Cooper

Christian's brother, Abraham, took the lease following her death in 1792. He was obliged to plant yearly 20 willow stands, white- or blackthorn, plus oak, ash or elm trees. Trees were automatically the property of the landowner. Buck-heading of the 'fences', that is, closely planted trees making a tall hedge, was not allowed. Ditches were to be kept clean, and the '*first peat*' from them was to be spread on the fields as manure. Forty rods of dry ditching were to be done yearly, making the ditches four and a half feet wide at the top and three and a half feet wide at the bottom. The house and buildings were to be kept in good repair, and even the

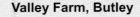
Valley Farm, Butley

The derelict thatched farmhouse in the mid-20th century.

Today the tiny house and its former dairy are engulfed in modern extensions.

number of times chimneys had to be swept was stated. If any thatching was required, reed rather than straw must be used. The rent was £50 a year in 1775 and £63 a year for the duration of the lease taken out in 1796.

Cultivation was now more carefully controlled. In 1792 on Valley Farm there were 19 acres which were not to be ploughed, and the remaining 98 acres were to be farmed according to *'five shift husbandry'*, that is, one part summerland (fallow), one summer corn, a one-year layer, a two-years' layer and one winter corn. The five-shift husbandry was a variation of the classic Norfolk four-course rotation. The average field measured five and a half acres.

The only evidence from the lease that cattle were kept comes from the requirement that no turnips were to be sold off the land but must be fed to the farm animals. Turnips were grown in the Sandlings as early as the

1680s and eaten in the fields by cattle in order to manure the land. The layers were for sheep, and the lease stipulated that the marsh walls should be *'fed with sheep'*. This was the time-honoured way of keeping marsh and river walls in repair. The 19 acres of permanent pasture would not have supported more than the farm horses and a few cows.

Valley Farm: Robert Hazelwood

A later farmer at Valley Farm during an agricultural depression was Robert Hazelwood. Following his death in 1896, his farm stock was sold. There were 126 Suffolk ewes, 35 lambs, 2 rams and 50 pigs. The horses consisted of 6 carthorses and 4 hackney colts or fillies. The carthorses were named in the catalogue and bore the names of Brag, Smiler, Boxer, Captain, Depper and (another) Boxer. Smiler, a four-year-old chestnut gelding, sold for £26-15s-6d, and was the most expensive. The ewes sold for between 26 and 45 shillings a score, and a breeding sow and ten pigs for about two guineas. The stock realized £537-17s-6d, and the house furniture a further £83-2s-3d. It is clear that cows were not kept at this time, although originally the dairy formed a separate part of the farm-house.

The Tithe Map and after

When the Tithe Map for Butley was drawn up in 1846, the parish was still dominated by Abbey Farm. The smaller farms covered the whole of the northern edge of the parish, and its south-eastern corner. Smaller farms ran to less than 250 acres, and most were much smaller than this. However, Thomas Whitmore, who farmed 220 acres around the ferry, including 45 acres of saltings, also farmed in Capel. In the north part of the parish, in addition to Valley Farm and Neutral Farm's now 158 acres, there were fields attached to Butley Mill and, north of the Run, 25 acres of Butley land were farmed at Church Farm, Chillesford.

In 1867 Lord Rendlesham was able to mop up the only remaining independently-owned farm in Butley. He purchased for £1,025 the 19-acre High Corner Farm from David Webb. The farm was in another part of the parish where manorial ownership was

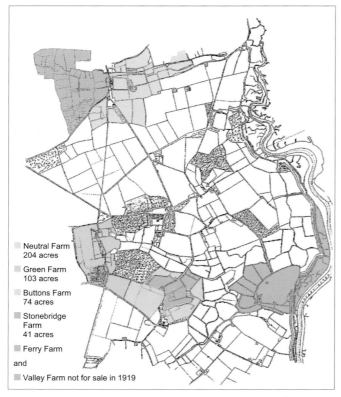

Neutral Farm 204 acres

Green Farm 103 acres

Buttons Farm 74 acres

Stonebridge Farm 41 acres

Ferry Farm

and

Valley Farm not for sale in 1919

The low point for Butley's tenant farmers. Walter Boynton used his wife's railway fortune to buy up portions of the Rendlesham and Sudbourne estates after World War I and was later bankrupt. Neutral Farm and Ferry Farm were sold by the Loan Commissioners for £2,400 in 1928, representing £6 per acre. More than a century earlier Neutral Farm alone had realised £4,170.

Claude Read with an old friend (he actually uses a Ford New Holland). He is the last independent farmer in the area. His farm is an historic one, on the site of the moated manor-house of Russells inherited by John Haughfen in 1544. In the later 19th century it was rebuilt as part of an enlightened programme of improving housing on the Sudbourne Estate. It has changed little since.

Church Farm, Chillesford

THE BRICK-BUILT AND TILED FARM RESIDENCE stands near the road, opposite to the Parish Church of St. Peter, and contains on the Ground Floor, Entrance Porch, two Sitting Rooms, Kitchen, Scullery with Copper and Bake Oven, Coal and Milk House. In the Basement, Cellar; on the First Floor, six Bedrooms and three Attic Bedrooms. A Store Room and Privy adjoin the House. There is a capital Garden on the east side.

THE WELL-PLANNED BUILDINGS are ranged round Yards, Brick and Weatherboarded with Tiled and Thatched Roofs, and comprise Trap-house, Wood-shed, Carpenter's Shop, two Loose Boxes, Cowshed for ten and two Calf-boxes, Barn and Loose Box, Chaff-house, open Cattle-shed, seven-bay open Shed and one-bay closed ditto, Cart-horse Stable for twelve, Chaff-house and Harness-room and Range of seven Loose Boxes.

On the opposite side of the road is a three-bay open Cart-shed, Store-shed and Granary over, three-bay open Cart-shed and Lean-to Implement-shed.

In Enclosure No. 184 on the Plan is a detached Brick-built and Tiled four-roomed Cottage with Shed, Pigsty and Garden, and two Brick, Lath and Plaster and Rough-cast Cottages, with Outhouse, Pigsty and Gardens.

Particulars of the 446-acre mixed farm (left) when it was bought by the Forestry Commission in 1919. Much was planted, but Claude was able to purchase the house with the remaining 200 acres in the 1950s. He and his wife Grace brought up seven children there. He never kept sheep, though he had previously learned sheep-farming. As dairy was too much of a tie, he raised suckler cattle on the marsh pasture.

Now aged 84, Claude is still farming. Every year he says he is giving up, but he keeps on going.

complex and the manors of Butley, Staverton and Kettleburgh were involved. The several valuations were: freehold lands £700, Staverton lands, including tenements, £225; Kettleburgh lands £75; and those of Butley Manor £25. The price paid by Lord Rendlesham was about double what his predecessor and the then Lord Hertford had paid per acre for Neutral Farm at the turn of the century. As a tenant, Harry Stollery was the last farmer at High Corner, giving up in 1980.

The small farmers were least able to bear the agricultural depressions which followed the end of World War I. Tenancies failed to attract occupants and land lay uncultivated with labourers and craftsmen out of work. In the thirties Sir Bernard Greenwell had the capital to purchase land as it came on the market and was determined to find work for the unemployed. He recreated a huge managed estate, not unlike the monastic one. The difference lay in the virtual absence of small tenant farmers. Nowadays neither tenant farmers nor farm-workers are needed to work the land. Stock is all but absent, while the arable is cultivated and irrigated by high-tech machines and contracted to outside firms. Sheep no longer graze the sandy heaths; the new 'gold' is top-quality turf destined for urban made-over gardens.

The coming of the forests

Afforestation transformed the Sandlings landscape and marked the end of the heath commons. Forestry Commission plantations based on Tangham were created on parcels of the poorest land purchased from landowners and small farmers at knock-down prices in the decade following 1920. Scots and Corsican pine were the main species chosen, but also maritime pine, Douglas fir and larch. By 1930 more than 3,500 acres had been planted.

The part which young women played in the work is little known. Louie Reeve (born 1898 at Wantisden Corner) was the daughter of a horseman on Dale Farm. With others she was employed to plant by hand thousands of saplings after the soil had been harrowed. Their uniform included gaiters, boots and a hat complete with badge.

The hurricane of 1987 transformed the landscape once again. It toppled vast stands of mature conifers, cutting off some villages until American air-base machinery cleared the roads. Since then, replanting has created stands of deciduous trees with glades and wide verges, so that the forests today have a gentler appearance.

In places, on the edge of the plantations, a few giant conifers survived the hurricane.

Pastimes for the Men

Chapter 16

Villagers of all ages created their own entertainment in the few free hours available to them. Landowners responded by allocating pitches and playing-fields, occasionally taking part themselves.

Some games may appear unsophisticated to those with telephones, let alone to the iPod generation, but they were crucial to social cohesion and well-being, especially for women. Annual excursions were red-letter-days, allowing a peep at the world outside. As late as the 1980s in these scattered settlements the 'outing' for pensioners was the highlight of their year and an opportunity to meet friends.

A Sunday outing in Alderton circa 1900.

Chillesford's quoits team circa 1898.

Steel quoits

We seem to like difficult games in this area, and one is steel quoits. Most probably it originated hundreds of years ago when someone perceived the possibility of making competitive sport from hurling horseshoes at a peg or stake in the ground. Indeed, this form of the game is played in America today. An early record of quoit-playing comes from a parish in Wiltshire. In 1409 a miracle was attributed to St Osmund of Salisbury. A carelessly thrown quoit struck a girl on the head. She recovered and brought the quoit to the shrine as an offering. Reading this, one of the authors uncomfortably recalled a similar incident at Butley in the 1980s when an onlooker asked to try pitching a quoit which flew dangerously wide.

Old quoit forged from a horseshoe.

Quoits was the favourite game in the Sandlings, where men would often practice in their gardens, using the clothes-line as a guide for the height to throw them. The game has a basic quality that is rooted in the timeless earthy activities of the village – its elements are steel, clay, sand and water. The quoits are pitched on to a bed of clay kept soft by water, and the sticky clay is removed by rubbing on a cloth with the aid of sharp sand. To keep his pair of quoits bright during the close season, a horseman would drag them through the sandy soil tied to his plough.

Quoit beds are set 18 yards apart, and the quoits, weighing 7¼ lbs a pair, are thrown from each end in turn. In the centre of the bed is buried a steel pin, and its position is marked by a piece of paper, called a light. It does not matter whether a quoit lands flat or remains at an angle in the clay, but on no account must it 'turn a woman', or it is eliminated and removed from the bed. A 'woman' is a quoit that alights with its outer curved side nearer the clay. A quoit encircling the pin scores two points and is removed immediately, otherwise the scoring is like bowls. It can be played as singles, pairs, triples or teams of six.

Sixty years ago boys began playing quoits using old horseshoes made into a ring by a blacksmith. They were passed down in families. Reg Snowdon of Chillesford started playing when he was aged about 12 with light quoits made for his grandfather as a boy by the Chillesford blacksmith, Mr Green. Boys were passionate about quoits and would even play in the dark, throwing a quoit to extinguish a lighted match on the quoit-bed. As a result they became extremely skilled. Around 1900 the Chillesford team included Jack, Ephraim, William and Walter, members of the Chittleborough family who were employed at the brickworks. A little later the Snowden and Walsh families in Chillesford could muster a dozen good players. It was Reg Snowdon's prejudice that nobody who had not played quoits all his life could possibly be any good. Several surviving quoits were made commercially by Wynn and Timmins.

The earliest cup, the Suffolk Challenge, was presented by Charles Cullingham in 1888. The first tournament was held at Stoke rectory and the winners were Ipswich's Waterside Works, who won the cup outright in 1913. Currently the County of Suffolk Steel Quoits Association organises the competition for the present cup.

Reg Snowdon, a champion player, preparing to throw a quoit.

The Challenge Cup was played for at about the same time as the Lord Rendlesham Cup. Few men entered both because *'working men cannot afford to lose two days so close to one another, even though they love the sport'*. The war caused a gap until 1922 before the cup was contested again, and about this time various leagues came into being. When Reg Snowdon moved to Butley in 1950 he restarted the team. The Butley and District League comprised Orford, Tunstall, Sudbourne, Chillesford, Alderton, Bawdsey, Shottisham, Boyton, Hollesley, and Sutton. Most quoit beds were attached to the local pub.

After World War II Butley hosted a tournament on the Flower Show and Fete day. This was for a singles cup presented by Sir Peter Greenwell, and for a while many county tournaments were played there on the playing field. Reg was delighted when the Butley team won the Lord Rendlesham Cup in both '73 and '79. There was little money in the game and funds were raised by asking patrons of *The Oyster* to guess the number of pips in a marrow, placed on the Men's Kitchen mantlepiece, alongside the odd misshapen potato and mandrake-like carrot. The messy business of counting the pips took place just before Christmas. In the 1980s, some of the younger players formed a new Butley club, and the following decade, joined with Kelsale, as both clubs had too few players to form a team to compete in the Stoke-by-Nayland League. This was successful for a few seasons, during which the league and cup titles were won.

Lord Rendlesham was keen to promote the game in villages, and he personally presented the magnificent silver cup in 1914 which is still played for. That first year at Saxmundham, it attracted 100 players, although only one team came from Ipswich.

Other pub games

In an inventory taken at *The Oyster* in 1916 there is a three-pin board and triangle which is still brought out for the village fete. The iron-shod wooden bowl used to be kept behind the bar, in water to stop it shrinking. The idea is to bowl it along a wooden board aiming at the front pin, so that it demolishes another, while the bowl ricochets on to the remaining one - even more difficult than it sounds. When played in *The Oyster* yard, boys would be paid a penny a session to place the skittles back in position, and winners would sometimes win a copper kettle. A form of indoor table-quoits was played at *The Oyster* and the game of darts was popular there as elsewhere. Sometimes an unusual form of darts was played on a 'fives board'. All segments were multiples of five and the appropriate scores were recorded on a cribbage board. Cards were played and sometimes money changed hands. Quite illegally, bookmaking operated from one of the cottages in the Street.

Camping

In 1644 the Eyke parish priest, Nicholas Stoneham, was accused of having been present at Camping on the Lord's Day,

The authors made an unexpected discovery – the earliest-known reference to camping in the county. The Manor-house at Bawdsey had a four-acre Camping Close *'le campyngclos'* on its east side and Walter Fulbourn's description in 1438 locates it on the west side of the cemetery.

showing that men used to play it on the only day of the week when they did not have to work.

The antiquary Davy mentioned, when writing about Boyton around 1820, that quoits and ninepin bowls were played regularly by working people on summer evenings. He noted that the primitive game of football, called *Camping* had been played on Capel Green. However, this had died out not long before, due probably, he reckoned,

St John the Baptist Day

During the Reverend Charles Luther Wanstall's 24-year ministry in Butley from 1899 the patronal festival was marked by what the *Woodbridge Reporter* called 'more or less a holiday' in Butley and Capel. Every 24 June there was a church service followed by a procession to his parsonage, at that time the Gatehouse, where he provided teas, children's sports, concerts including the school violin band, book prizes and a tug-of-war between Butley and Capel. Above: the girls' tug-of-war teams.

to the fact that so many men were drafted for the Napoleonic Wars. Camping involved many more players that the present game of football, and was often violent. As at Bawdsey it may have been played on the Green as much as four centuries earlier.

Thomas Tusser reckoned the activity improved the land, perhaps by treading down molehills or land that had 'heaved' in winter frosts. In 1573 he advised,
'In meadow or pasture – (to grow the more fine)
Let campers be camping in any of thine,
Which if you do suffer when low in the spring
You gain to yourself a commodious thing'.
'Camping' derives from the same root as

'Kampf', as in Hitler's *Mein Kampf,* and refers to the struggle involved. To score a snotch the ball had to be carried between improvised goal posts. Injuries and even death occurred, and for this reason it was eventually banned.

Folk-singing
There has been a tradition of folk-singing at *The Oyster* for many years, and George Ewart Evans, in *Ask the Fellows who Cut the Hay*, gives a flavour of singarounds and step-dancing to the melodeon in the *Blaxhall Ship*. Singing and 'tune-ups', that is, instrumental music, took place at irregular

Tennis and football fostered

It was mainly due to the enthusiasm of Dr Montague Rendall, a previous owner of the Gatehouse, that Sir Peter Greenwell provided the land for football, tennis, bowls and quoits where the present village hall stands. Before this the games had to be played on waste land.

The Butley football team of 1947-48. Dr Rendall stands on the right.

Rendall, the retired headmaster of Winchester, had bought the Priory Gatehouse in 1925 where he made his home. He had been a keen footballer at Harrow and Cambridge. His large frame and ungainly manner were suited to goal-keeping and this was his position in the University team. He boasted that in a match against the Old Etonians *'the game was memorable for a terrific encounter between the Etonian Macaulay and myself: he was a famous quarter-miler and got clean away, moving straight for the goal at heroic speed. I ran out to meet him and we clashed with a jar and impact I can still feel after 60 years. We both fell in a heap, but the goal was saved'.* His considerable talents and energies hardly abated up to his death at the age of eighty eight.

Girls did not feature much in village games, but played tennis, as Florrie Warne recalled: *'We thought the world of Dr Rendall. He organised the football team for the boys and we girls used to play tennis down in front of the Gatehouse – there were two tennis courts as well as his bowling green – most evenings during the summer. There'd be scores of people... the women used to come there, the men just to sit and watch. I used to play regularly, and was quite good at it!*

'There was a tennis court on the heath near Butley Mills and a tin shed and that for all the equipment. We children used to go and sit on the grass and watch them and when the village hall got going they had the tennis courts down at Butley Street, but I never did play there. I used to play at the Priory. The bowls, I believe they were Dr Rendall's thing, just for visitors.'

intervals at *The Oyster* until, in 1973, one of the authors took on the role of chairman and began a series of Sunday night singarounds that continued for more than 20 years. Soon the Men's Kitchen was bursting at the seams with listeners, and the following year the music moved into what was the old Club Room. The chairman wished to continue the tradition of the Blaxhall singarounds. His objective was to let everyone sing or play two or three pieces, with variety as a major criterion. The last half-hour, though, was chorus time, so everyone left in good humour at closing time, having sung lustily to the end.

Old singers, like Percy Webb, Bob Hart and Percy Ling, came regularly and they were the strictest in observing the courtesy of not singing other men's songs. Bob Hart told of a ruse to get everyone to participate when requested:

'A man who will not sing, according to his call,
Will have to stand a quart, or be bumped
against the wall'.

In due course *The Oyster* became a focus for folk-singing, known across the whole country. As an innovation, special evenings were introduced when songs on a particular subject might be sung, or perhaps poems read, for example, on Armistice Day. The old singers made no distinction between folk, World War and music hall songs. Hallowe'en enabled ghost stories to be told, and Oak Apple Day, when Charles II was restored to the throne, was observed. When Vera was a child, it was the custom for anyone not wearing oak apples on 29 May to be chased with nettles. Later, Brian Foster, the head of Bawdsey School, brandished them and light-heartedly threatened reluctant performers, who were able to escape by merely reciting a verse from a nursery rhyme.

Percy Webb died in 1976 and was buried in the cemetery of Tunstall Baptist Church. His friends from *The Oyster* bought a tree to plant near his grave, and also a pewter mug, suitably inscribed, to be sung for each year. After Bob Hart's death, a rowan tree was planted in his memory on the green opposite the Snape *Crown*.

In 1976, Taffy Thomas brought his Magic Lantern Show to the area. He specialized in street theatre, using circus skills, but also folk traditions. Other activities took place in and around Butley. *The Shepherds' Play*, a mystery play, was performed in *The Oyster* yard, one year in the snow. It was a magical experience, taking place the Sunday before Christmas, and was followed by carols in the Big Room. Taffy wrote *The Butley Autumn Play* that was performed by the Butley Guizers for many years thereafter. This integrated the Guy Fawkes story and Hallowe'en with a Mummers' Play.

After he had moved away, his ideas were taken up. One year, for St George's Day a play featured the saint and the dragon in the shape of a cockatrice made from paper stretched on withies. It was paraded around Oyster Field, and afterwards burned.

Another memorable night occurred in 1985, the year the replica of the *Godspeed* sailed to the USA. Four hundred years earlier the first voyages began with the intention of establishing a colony in the New World. In 1607, the *Godspeed* and two other ships had sailed from England and made landfall in what became Jamestown, Virginia. The replica was built in America and brought over to Ipswich, to recreate the original voyage. George Salley, who was also

Village children, dressed to represent the countries of the British Empire, standing on Wantisden Corner on a sunny 24 May. Empire Day, the birthday of Queen Victoria, used to be kept as a school holiday. Florrie is Britannia.

a shanty singer, captained the American crew. They sang at Eyke *Castle* and also came to *The Oyster*, one Sunday in April 1985, for an evening devoted to shanties and songs of the sea. Ten years later, in July 1995, there was a free festival to celebrate 'Twenty One Years in the Big Room'.

Skills for the young

It was A.J. Swinburne, the school inspector, who had a profound effect on schools in East Suffolk. He introduced a unique prize scheme in East Suffolk in 1881. This promoted practical skills, such as swimming, needlework and drawing. He also encouraged recitation and poetry, embracing a wider spectrum of work. He believed it made a significant contribution to the progress of local children. Some of the children's poetry was published by their schoolmaster, C. F. Miles-Cadman, in a slim volume. Photographs of three of them *'wooing the muse'* later appeared in the *Daily Mirror*.

Singing was an integral part of school, church and chapel. Swinburne thought the prize scheme provided the magic touch to

improve immeasurably the singing in Suffolk schools. Although the county has been well-known for folk-singing and music-making for a century or more, there was no tradition of part-singing as in some other counties.

Perhaps the inspector did not appreciate or experience the solo voice heard in the village pub. He tells the amusing story of a master who said, *'We don't take part-singing. The fact is, we kind of Holloa together'*. Another said, *'We teach it here on Howler's system'*. He meant Hullah's System.

Butley School founded in 1842, photographed in the 1940s, and now a private house.

Butley School staff and pupils in 1901. The vicar is on the left and Miles Cadnam, third from the left.

Originally a gentleman's game

While most of the old games are too unsophisticated for modern folk, cricket has prospered. It was originally centred on country houses such as High House, Campsea Ashe (page 66).

At Sudbourne Hall's ground, cricket was played enthusiastically. The team was boosted in the 1920s by the occasional presence of Beverly and Malcolm Lyon, sons of a new owner and both county players. By May 1930 the ground had been improved *'almost beyond recognition by the generosity of Mr Lyon who has engaged the services of a large number of the unemployed'*. The reporter remembered the old cart ruts and the long grass from previous years.

A game that has prospered locally; the Sudbourne XI in front of their new pavilion.

The Harvest ...
a Quarter less than Needed
Chapter 17

The condition of the poor was very largely dependant upon a good harvest, and two successive bad ones would result in destitution and even starvation. Over the centuries many paupers in England died from cold, hunger and need. The recurring agricultural depressions, which led to widespread unemployment and destitution, also affected both tenant farmers unable to pay their rent, and village tradesmen with outstanding bills.

Out-of-work, a shepherd, wheelwright, mole-catcher and labourer took part in the Priory excavations.

As late as 1932, villagers were glad of temporary employment in the excavation of Butley Priory ruins. In the Depression the stone pit by the roundabout at Bromeswell provided work digging gravel in exchange for food tickets. It was only the creation of the Welfare State that put an end to the recurrence of this kind of poverty after the Second World War.

In the beginning

'*The poor are among you always*', Jesus said, and usually they are anonymous. In the Sandlings Triangle villagers were better off, although owing services to their manorial lord. In this area there was an exceptional number of freemen and only three slaves were listed in the *Domesday Book*.

From time to time the stability of the feudal system was upset by royal taxes which fell on rich and poor alike. For instance, in 1380, in order to sustain the army in Brittany, every person in the realm over 15, both male and female, was required to pay three groats, although beggars were exempt. Landholders, including abbots and priors, were taxed on the value of their estates.

Despite its broad support, the popular rising which started the following year has always been called the Peasants' Revolt. It began in Essex and moved elsewhere, reaching Suffolk. There a priest, John Wraw, and 10,000 men robbed and destroyed houses indiscriminately. In Bury they even beheaded the Abbot and the Chief Justice of the King's Bench.

Among the targets of the insurgents were manorial court rolls, which contained the record of the rights of the lord over his tenants. Public burnings of these records took place. Staverton manor-house was destroyed by fire and there were other incidents in the Triangle.

Butley Priory's titular head, the Bishop of Norwich, Hugh Despenser, eventually intervened to quell the uprising. He raised an army and many of the rebels were captured and beheaded.

Vulnerability of the rural poor

The *Chronicle* of Butley Priory records the pitiful state of the local poor during the famine of 1528. They were also afflicted by sweating sickness. It notes that corn rose from 16s a quarter to 20s and thereafter to 26s 8d, and barley from 10s to 13s 4d a quarter. Many paupers in England died due to cold, hunger and need. There had been

The last rites administered to a dying man on a 15th-century font at Great Glemham. The priest holds a chrismatory from which he anoints the ears, eyes, nose and mouth of the dying man.

plague throughout 'Anglia' in 1525, and Chillesford, Capel and Boyton were singled out for mention, along with Woodbridge and Orford. An earlier plague known as the Black Death was the most severe of numerous plagues which affected the whole country. It entered the county near Sudbury at the end of March 1349, and records show an extremely high mortality among clergy that June and July. Locally, Woodbridge and Snape priories were affected and new priors instituted. There is no record that Butley suffered, although a document from its archive noted that Sir Nicholas Kyryell, the

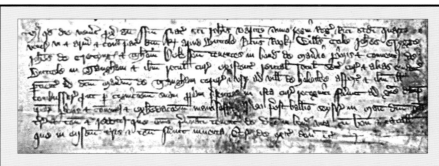

Peasants' Revolt

The proof that rural unrest disturbed the Triangle in 1381.

The court roll of Tangham recorded the seizure and burning of documents by the Priory's bound tenants in Butley.

last heir of the Founder's daughter, had died in the first outbreak. In four monasteries in the diocese it seems that everyone died. No doubt the clergy were particularly at risk when they performed the last rites for victims. Diocesan archives showed that they worked tirelessly.

Throughout the Elizabethan period various Acts of Parliament attempted to deal with the poor, many of whom were living as vagrants. The latter were treated harshly and driven from place to place, whilst the 'deserving poor' were placed where work could be found for them. Town-houses were built in villages to either accommodate them, or provide a work-place, or rental income for distribution to them. Later, in the mid 18th century, Union work-houses started to be built solely to house the poor of a district, rendering parish accommodation redundant.

Following the end of the Napoleonic wars many men returned to their villages to find there was no work. Violence broke out mainly in the extreme west of Suffolk and in Cambridgeshire. In 1830 the so-called Revolt of the Field was centred on 'open' villages all over southern and eastern England. Then in the 1840s Suffolk was at the centre of a spate of arson attacks on barns and stacks. 'Open' villages were those where there was a large proportion of independently-minded men, often with Non-conformist beliefs, and where living conditions were at their worst. 'Closed' villages were owned by the local squire who was able to control who lived in his cottages. The latter were where trade unionism flourished in the 1870s. Butley was one of the centres of this unrest which led to a bitter strike.

The care of the poor

When William Forth purchased the dissolved Priory he was acutely aware of the need to continue to provide for the poor. In his will he gave £20 to be distributed in weekly portions in Hadleigh, and a further £20 to *'the poor people of Butley and Capel .... especially to the poor people which do dwell in the late parish called Capel, now united to Butley'*. His executors were charged with distributing the money through four honest

Almshouses were set up by wealthy Elizabethan benefactors, such as Henry Tooley in Ipswich and Thomas Seckford in Woodbridge, to provide individual homes and care for the inmates. The Warner family's Boyton land was left in trust by Mary Warner in 1736. The Trust's ownership of land effectively protected the parish from being swallowed up subsequently in the shooting estate of an absentee landowner.

men in Butley. One was John Malling, a former member of the Priory staff and as usher had probably distributed left-overs from monastic meals to the poor at the gate. They were required to buy land or stock, the profits and rents to be distributed to the poor thereafter. The will is referred to some 30 years later in the Butley court rolls when the trustees were Thomas Lynd senior and junior, Jeffrey Cookson and William Spinke, two from each parish. Four parcels of arable and pasture had been purchased, three called 'Haughes' and a furlong strip called 'Moyses'. There was also a cottage, *recently of Stephen Moyse and previously of Richard Hunte*. They all lay at or near High Corner. In 1594, the *Inhabitants of Butley* were described as holding six acres in the parish, that is Haws, Moises and an empty tenement called Bronnes. A remnant of these six acres survives today as allotments known as the Shoulder of Mutton (p.80).

Butley and Capel also had separate Town Houses. Provision for the poor of Capel was made before 1596. Capel Town House, which survives today as a timber-framed thatched cottage at Low Corner in Butley, stands on land which belonged to Staverton

Capel Town-House, Butley. In 1983 it still had an outside pump, earthen floor and ladder access to the bedroom. It has been transformed into a fully equipped bijou cottage.

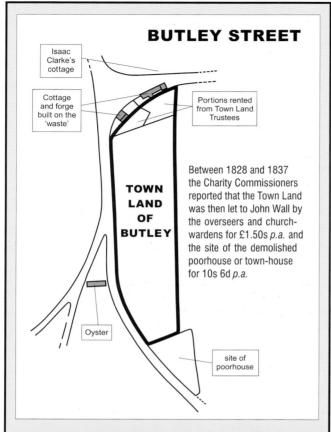

BUTLEY STREET

Isaac Clarke's cottage

Cottage and forge built on the 'waste'

Portions rented from Town Land Trustees

TOWN LAND OF BUTLEY

Between 1828 and 1837 the Charity Commissioners reported that the Town Land was then let to John Wall by the overseers and church-wardens for £1.50s *p.a.* and the site of the demolished poorhouse or town-house for 10s 6d *p.a.*

Oyster

site of poorhouse

Unlike the other parish hamlets Butley Street had no village green, apart from the triangle of land in front of *The Oyster Inn* and the once wide verges of the narrow roadways then called the manorial 'Waste'.

However, in 1731 a leading villager, Thomas Lynd, gave an acre of his land to the inhabitants, to be administered by trustees. Known as the Town Land of Butley, it lay between the poorhouse and Mill Lane, on the verge ('waste') of which a cottage and a forge was built.

A century later when the blacksmith, Isaac Clarke, died the land was mapped and showed the precise site of the poorhouse on Oyster Hill. Isaac lived in the cottage opposite his forge where he scratched his initials and Mr Miller occupied the tiny cottage.

They both rented part of the Town Land as 'yards' and Isaac grew potatoes on the remainder of it. Today the 'yards' are the garden of the house built in the space between the earlier buildings, and the rest of the parish land is allotments.

The very poor might have small plots on which to grow food. James Crosby rented one here in March 1856. His was one of the then 42 needy families in the parish who received coal and blankets funded out of rents from the Town Land.

the cottage was kept in good repair. Although all the trustees were dead, the accounts had been kept and were available from 1768, while the rents had been properly applied *'for the general relief of the poor'*.

There is no record of Butley Town House except in the manorial court roll of 1587, when the 'farmer', John Fosdike, was told to repair the fence around it. Fosdike was probably responsible for the inmates and the job was farmed out to him. Robert Forth's minister, Thomas Reddrich, died in Ipswich in 1616 and left £4 to the poor of Butley and Capel, *'being now as one parish'* to be used as a *'town stock there to set the poor to work and to have continuance forever'*.

The location of the building was fixed by the statement that it stood by the Hundred-boundary post, between Plomesgate and Loes. A more precise location was provided by Thomas Lynd's bequest *(see box to left)*. Later all this land and the site of the house became the allotments beside Oyster Hill (see page 166). It is still known as the *'Poor's Land'*.

Thomas Lynd appointed his son, William, with Joseph Benington as trustees of the Poor's Land. Although the Lynds sold up in Butley soon afterwards, the Beningtons continued to farm there. The Poor's Land was let as one piece for £1-15s-6d to John Wall around 1830, when reports were made by the Commissioners of Charities. The occupation of the land was auctioned in *The Oyster* for a number of years before it was converted into allotments. By 1885 the rent was distributed through the Coal Club, to which the poorer parishioners contributed eight shillings a year. Before Christmas each of its members, numbering about 60, received half a ton of coal delivered free by the farmers.

Until recently, a pair of cottages in Chillesford was known as the Workhouse Cottages. Isaac Johnson marks it as 'work-house' on one of his maps made in 1797 and the division of the present building, its lower level laundry and large well, which survived until the 1980s, confirm his identification. A house is shown, set back from the road, on Norden's map of 1601. It appears to be the site of the present cottages, now 33 and 34

Manor. In the earlier 19th century the Town House, with nearly two acres of hempland, was let by the overseers, for £6 yearly. However, by the middle of the century the rent had declined to £3-12-0. A well had been sunk at the expense of the parish, and

Padley Water, which are likely to have replaced an earlier Town House, but few records for Chillesford have survived.

> In the *Ipswich Journal* for 19 January 1805 the Chillesford overseers advertised for a man and his wife to undertake the management of the workhouse, *'Wanted directly, a man and wife to undertake the management of the Poorhouse at Chillesford. For particulars enquire of the Overseer.'*
>
> Two years earlier the Tunstall overseers had elected to provide out-relief for the poor in their own homes and the poorhouse was put up for sale:
>
> *'Household furniture, beds, bedding, washing and brewing utensils, 6 beds and bedding, 4 pots and stump bedsteads, 9 pairs of sheets, 6 pairs of blankets, a 36-gallon copper, a 12-gallon copper, brewing tubs and washing keelers, bowls, dishes, and beer casks. All new 18 months.'*
>
> These are two workhouses which do not appear in the national records from 1776 onwards.

A House of Industry was provided at Wickham Market in 1837. At Chillesford the little building was divided into Workhouse Cottages for four agricultural labourers, wives and 14 children when the Tithe Map was drawn up in 1839.

Some of the poor identified

Peregrine Styles lived in Hollesley in 1671 and was accused of being the father of a child born to Mary Pinkney of Marlesford. He was ordered to pay the overseer of the latter parish 2s a week for the upkeep of the child until aged eight, and then £5 towards his apprenticeship. He appealed and the amount was reduced to 1s a week.

Later he moved to Butley, and either shame or the cost of the child's upkeep resulted in his being one of the few men who never married. He died in 1679 and his sister was appointed administrator of his possessions.

James Houseson from 'Capel by Hollesley' was also a trouble to the authorities. The JP, Devereux Edgar, the son of Thomas Edgar, in his *Commonplace Book* records in 1705 that Houseson, described as being *'a tall, black man, aged about 40, his own hair black'* was *'a notorious bastard getter'*.

Men were not only pressed into the Navy but, if found to be able-bodied and with no visible means of livelihood, could be forced to serve in the Army. Constables were required to identify such men. We know from the *Commonplace Book* that the recruiting captain appointed by Colonel Peyton received 20s for enlisting Houseson, while Constable Marsh received 10s to escort him to the barracks. Two years later, records of the Woodbridge Quarter Sessions show he was back in Capel, having been wounded in Flanders, and was unable to work. He was allowed 20s from the Mariners and Maimed Soldiers Fund and not heard of again.

At the same time that Houseson was pressed, John Allen of Sutton, aged 18, was handed over by the Justices. His father thereupon voluntarily enlisted *'resolving not to leave him.'*

Richard Lettice was discharged from a poor house in 1756, because he had been *'behaving himself in a disorderly way and refusing to comply with the orders of the house'*. The house named was the *'Poor House in the parish of Butley'*. The house near the *Oyster Inn* was gone by this time and thus Lettice must have lodged in Capel Town House at Butley Low Corner. It is likely that Richard, his wife Margaret and their children were all in the Poor House at this time. Two of their

Fanny Reeve with her daughter Elizabeth, when they lived in the old (windmill) cottage, now demolished near Butley's watermill. They worked for the Hewitt family, milking the cows as well as baking the bread on Fridays and washing the clothes on Mondays, fitting everything else in on the intervening days. They also brewed the beer from malt and hops in quantities to satisfy the thirst of all who came to the watermill on business as well as the workmen.

children died in infancy and were buried in Butley churchyard, and Margaret herself died in 1763.

Men and women were moved from place to place by the overseers who were keen to avoid the cost of paupers falling on the inhabitants. The Quarter Session records are full of arguments about where the poor should be 'settled'. They do not give the reasons, although Devereux Edgar gives details occasionally. For example, Edward Long testified on oath in 1712 why he should be settled in Butley. He explained that he had occupied a farm in Bawdsey, paying £50 a year and rates. The previous Michaelmas he went with his family to Butley to live in a tenement paying £4 a year, one-third being his by right of copyhold.

Justices often commanded the parish officers to house the destitute. In 1643 the overseers and churchwardens of Butley were ordered to provide a house for John Barker, a poor, aged and blind man, along with his wife. Six years later Helen Stannard, spinster, very poor and with child was settled in Butley with orders to provide for her according to the law. On the other hand Elizabeth Hawes of Capel was sent to the House of Correction at Melton for refusing to maintain herself and her children. In 1663, Elizabeth Valentine of Butley appealed to the court because her house had blown down in a recent gale, and she was utterly destitute. The parish was ordered to provide the necessary house for her or be in contempt of court. Another sad case was that of George Curtis of Capel, who was on his sick bed in 1686 and *having nobody near him that would write*' expressed himself verbally in a nuncupative will. He left his cousin his goods and a shilling to his sister.

The poor's view of the world and the daily grind

In general the poor fared well or ill according to the price of food relative to their wages. Both of these rose considerably during the wars with the French, which continued, on and off, for the thirty years to 1815. Any hardship felt by the poor at this time was as likely to be blamed on trades-men as employers, as a folk song from the Napoleonic Wars illustrates:

Now here's to the butcher, I must bring
him in,
Charges four pence a pound and yet thinks
it no sin,
Slaps his thumb on the scales, and makes
'em go down,
He declares it's full weight, yet it lacks half
a pound.

The baker provides a loaf *no bigger than your fist* and the landlord's *measure is short*. The tailor *skimps with our clothes* and the cobbler *pinches our toes*. The chorus echoes the theme of malpractices with the words, *These are the rigs of the times, me boys, these are the rigs of the time.*

The Suffolk historian, Robert Reyce, noted in 1618 that the poor, especially the women in whole villages and towns, without other means of subsistence '*do live and maintain themselves by spinning*'. One means of employment for paupers either in home or workhouse was *kembling*. This was the skilled sorting and preparation of fleeces to produce a variety of threads which were not woven locally, but carried weekly to London or Norwich to be made into luxury fringes and fabrics. Children could be employed in spinning, as well as women. Two of the latter, Sarah Crosby and Frances Thurkittel, of Butley, were convicted of reeling *'false and short'* yarn in 1784, and paid a penalty of 5s.

In Union workhouses permission had to be obtained to vary the diet specified by the Commissioners. Women and children between 9 and 13 years of age had a lesser quantity of bread, meat and bacon than the men. There were 3 meals a day: breakfast and supper never changed; the former consisted of 6oz of bread and 1½ pints of gruel (sweetened porridge) and the latter, 7oz bread and 1½ oz cheese. Bread and cheese were served for the midday meal on 4 days, on the 5th day there was 8oz meat and ¾ lb vegetable, on the 6th day 5oz bacon and ¾ lb vegetable and on the 7th the ration was 1½ pints soup with 8oz bread. The sick fared a little better, having rations of milk, rice, butter and porter.

The food has to be set in the context of the monotonous diet of farm workers at this period. If the quantities seem good, we have to remember that the quality would have been poor: fatty unflavoured stew, cabbage, root vegetables and Suffolk bang, a cheese so hard that it gained a national reputation.

This was a considerable sum when it was estimated that women earned only 3d a day.

Spinning hemp was a daily chore for the poor cottager. It was *'so unclean, so laboursome, and with so small earnings'*, as was the processing of hemp, for rope, sackcloth and textiles. In the days before polythene there was a continuing demand for sacking needed to contain all kinds of produce, whether stored or exported. John Kirby in 1735 recorded that nearby Woodbridge *'has formerly traded considerably in Sackcloth'*. The trade was not subject to depressions unlike other manufactures.

Sarah Crosby

Sarah Crosby is an example of the way that the older Poor Laws dealt with misdemeanours. In June 1771 the Overseers of the Poor in Butley were instructed to provide her with *'such sums from time to time as they shall think convenient, not exceeding thirty shillings, for and towards her lying in'*. By August her illegitimate child had been born and she was allowed one shilling each week until the next quarter. Weekly payments continued until in February 1772 the father, Harman Howell, was traced and ordered to pay £6 on account of his bastard child. In June 1774 Sarah was still receiving her weekly shilling, unlike those who were forced to live in the House of Industry, in Melton, later the County Lunatic Asylum and known as St Audrys. Between 1768 and 1774 as many as three quarters of the poor were receiving support in their own homes. They included those unable to work due to sickness or injury. The overseers also funded the burial of paupers.

Children raised inside the Union houses were placed with employers where suitable: Samuel Woolnough of Butley was sent to a Hacheston farmer for a year, supplied with two shirts, a coat and waistcoat, a pair of shoes, two pairs of stockings and a hat; and James Easty of Butley was sent to a Wickham Market surgeon similarly equipped. When Lord Archibald Hamilton accepted Rebecca Woolner as a servant, the Governors expended 16 shillings on her clothing. Following an outbreak of smallpox everybody was inoculated, although for children parental consent was required.

The Lock-out of 1874

The National Agricultural Labourers' Union, led by Joseph Arch, a Warwickshire man, was formed soon after they were legalised in 1871. Places such as Butley, where as many as 70 men, to say nothing of women and boys, were employed on one farm, were ideal places to look for the trust and solidarity necessary for combination

Enamelled badge worn by members depicts a plough.

against those employers who were not inclined to pay more than the minimum wage.

Trouble began in the village of Exning, near the border with Cambridgeshire, in September 1872, when 17 labourers requested a rise of a shilling a week. The farmers formed an association in response, agreeing to act together on matters of pay and to ignore the letter. Then, in February 1874, the men threatened to go on strike if their request was not met. The farmers responded by locking them out, and the following month the trouble spread to Wilford Hundred, which included Boyton and Capel. About 170 men on 12 farms went on strike. The farmers affected appealed to their neighbours to ask their men to help on the strike-bound farms. The men refused, either because they were Union members themselves, or else through fear. Thus the men of Butley were drawn into the struggle, since the farmers locked out all the men who would not give up their Union cards.

The lock-out continued throughout the Spring. One week in the month of May, about £56 was paid out in strike pay to Butley men, the largest amount paid in the area. The rate of pay was a flat 9 shillings a week, so about 120 men were on strike. This number probably includes men from Capel, since the total number of males of all ages in Butley alone was around 190 at the census of 1871. It indicates just how strongly the Union was supported in these villages.

Pay had improved only slowly after 1850, but large farmers and landowners were faring very well during the 'golden years'. However, Samuel Wolton, who began farming at Abbey Farm in 1869, was faced with falling prices for his corn and stock, as competition, especially from the United States, was increasing. The lock-out began when work was slack and most of the sowing had been completed. The crops could be left to grow during the spring and summer months with little attention. Of course, cattle and other animals had to be attended to, but farmers banded together. With their families and bailiffs, and a few strike-breakers, they kept their farms ticking over.

One farmer in Wilford Hundred wrote a pamphlet referred to by *The Times* correspondent, Frederick Clifford. The farmers' fear was that the men would use the strike weapon at short notice at key times in the farming calendar, led on by Union delegates from other parts of the country, who *'did not know the men'* as they, the farmers, did. From Clifford's observations, the farmers treated the delegates wrongly, refusing them recognition and then exchanging invective with them. The charge against the delegates from the 'Sheers', is sustained by the language they used, which derived from 'enclosure country' inapplicable to the Sandlings Triangle. Men were told they had been robbed of their land, their birthright, they were mere 'wage slaves', and there were often references to Biblical verses, dear to the hearts of the Primitive Methodists and other non-conformists.

The lock-out continued through the summer months, with only a few men giving up their union cards. On the strike pay they were receiving, much being provided by Unions from outside the area, life was very hard, and many must have succumbed to the temptation of poaching. Whereas game was poached surreptitiously at night, on Lord Rendlesham's estate, stealing eggs was carried out openly. His agent came upon 40 or 50 labourers in one of his lordship's coverts collecting eggs, and claiming they *'had as much right to wild animals as anybody else'*. Another old complaint was out in the open.

The former Cock and Pye Inn at the top of New Street, Woodbridge.

Woodbridge was the centre for Union demonstrations in the east, and the men would march provocatively in twos down the Thoroughfare to the *Cock and Pye Inn* at the top of New Street, whereas the farmers met at *The Bull*. The men wore a blue favour, the recognised badge of the Union, and some were carrying banners saying, *'No Surrender'*, *'God is our Strength'*, and *'No Tyranny'*. One of them accurately described such occasions for all time using the words, *'We cum marchin' in like sogers, but we goo hoom like a flock a sheep'*.

Various songs, distributed by means of broadsheets, were sung at the demonstrations and elsewhere, and one, which was sung a hundred years after the strike in *The Oyster* is, *'We're all jolly fellows that follow the plough'*. According to the *Times* correspondent, it was a common complaint by farmers that the average labourer was slow, if not

Pen and ink sketch by Emmeline Rope, April 1889.

lazy, and it is instructive that, in the song, the labourers, with their new-found confidence, challenge the farmer, who had declared them idle. It says, *'We've all plough-ed an acre, so you tell a damned lie'*. Only one song, noted by Clifford, contained any direct reference to the lock-out, but the chorus of another song has been handed down by oral transmission:

> *'Oh, the Lock-out wor the cry,*
> *The labourer will be wanten bye and bye,*
> *Du wat tha wool, du wat tha can,*
> *Tha can't du without the labourin' man'.*

On 4 June, Joseph Arch himself came to Woodbridge to address the labourers. A huge crowd assembled on a meadow opposite Beaumont Chapel, but from this high point the fortunes of the men declined. As the harvest ripened, men returned to work, making as good a deal for themselves as they could. It had been the Union's policy to encourage emigration to the colonies, or migration to other parts of the country, but it was Arch's complaint that few men were prepared to do either. In Butley the population actually increased in the decade 1871 to 1881 from 369 to 383. However, farmers who had struggled from February to June with very little help, found they could manage with fewer employees all the year round, and this, coupled with the farming depression which followed, led to a major drift from the land. The population had fallen to 270 by 1901, before climbing again, but never reached the peak of 1861, when it stood at 385.

The National Union retained its members in the immediate aftermath of the return to work, but arguments broke out, as usually happens after a defeat. To hold the line Joseph Arch visited many villages at the centre of the lock-out, coming to Butley on 21 October 1876, where *'a largely attended meeting of agricultural labourers was held at the Oyster Inn'*. At four o'clock tea was provided, Arch being teatotal like all Methodists, and the meeting began at seven. Something of this meeting was recalled over one hundred years later, when Wesley Hazelwood (born 1898) remarked that Butley had a large number of allotments because *'a man called Archer'* had told the landowners they should provide allotments for the poor.

Although low wages were the main bone of contention, it was said that, where unions appeared in the 1870s, there had often been complaints over local charities. One such complaint was that a single tenant was preferred, when land was let, rather than making small plots available to the poor to cultivate themselves. In Butley the subject of the Poor's Land came under consideration at the Vestry meeting in 1856. It was resolved that tenders be sought for a period of three years. The whole was let to Frederick Moss, the innkeeper, for £6 a year and the poor received between 1s and 2s 6d each.

Subsequently, Thomas Crisp was asked to produce the 1731 deed relating to the Poor's Land and as a result for some reason, it was

Farm workers Bun and Jimmy Clarke, for many years occupied the corner of the Mens' Kitchen in the Oyster Inn, where their portrait by Honor Hussey now hangs.

decided the rents would not be distributed. It was not until seven years later, in 1866, that the Vestry distributed the rents again. They were now handed out through coal and clothing clubs, but the money not paid out for seven years would have left a strong sense of injustice in the village.

Two views of Butley's Town Land today, looking down the hill with *The Oyster Inn* on the left. Leeks are growing on the site of the Poorhouse. The allotments on Oyster Hill produce prize-winning vegetables. They provide gardens for cottages with little land.

Baptism in the Pond
Marriage in the Porch
Burial in the Orchard

Chapter 18

During the Interregnum and about five years before Charles II ascended the throne, the Quaker preacher, George Whitehead, introduced the Society of Friends into Suffolk.

The Baptists built their first chapel in England in 1612. The movement grew in popularity in the 19th century when chapels were built in Sudbourne, Sutton and Tunstall.

The Quaker meeting-house built in Turn Lane, Woodbridge in 1683. The burial ground is now a nature reserve and the building a private house.

Methodism was founded by John Wesley in 1738 at a time when the Church of England was largely moribund. Chapels were built in the 19th century in Butley, Hollesley, Bawdsey and Orford in addition to Woodbridge.

While every parish had its Anglican church, non-conformists might have to walk several miles to their nearest place of worship, setting off with a basket containing a bible and food to spend most of Sunday at chapel with their friends. In the Triangle many villages consisted of scattered settlements and people took walking to their place of worship in their stride.

George Snowdon in the Sunday best he wore when he walked from Chillesford to Tunstall Baptist chapel.

Butley parish church in 1992 when the thatched nave had a new straw ridge.

and Gedgrave. The two latter have been demolished, but the interior of Wantisden church preserves a tiny chancel arch and very early pews which once held rush lights.

The interior of Butley church will have looked very different in the past. It will have been extremely dark, lit only by its slit windows and the gleam of candles kept burning day and night on the rood beam, also called the candle-beam. Candles were made of beeswax, but poor people had for light a smelly taper made of reed dipped in animal fat. From the 13th century onwards larger windows were inserted – only the chancel and porch windows match. No doubt the rest were 'cast-offs' from the Priory during rebuilding works. Large wooden images of the Crucified Christ flanked by the Virgin Mary and St John on the rood beam separated the congregation from the chancel where the priest performed the Mass. Parish churches had colourful interiors showing saints, angels and prophets on walls, screen and windows. For villagers lacking a single book or picture, it was an amazing, awe-inspiring place, full of hope for a better life and warnings of damnation.

The parish church

In the Sandlings there are parishes with isolated churches. Examples are Butley, Blaxhall, Iken, Sudbourne, Wantisden, Rendlesham and Ramsholt. Invariably local tradition has it that houses once clustered round the church, only to be abandoned after the Black Death. This is certainly not true of Butley which has always consisted of scattered settlements. No church is mentioned in Domesday, but within 100 years of 1086 there were two churches in this tiny village. The first was the parish church with a nave 43ft long endowed with land by the Norman knight, Theobald de Valoines. Its priest was Ernald. Of that first church four tiny windows and two doorways survive. Soon afterwards the church and its glebe were granted by Theobald's daughter, Bertha, and her husband, Ranuph de Glanville, to a college of priests, known as Augustinian or Black Canons.

This little church was inadequate for their needs and they constructed a huge church a short distance away. Every day for the next 369 years a priest, dressed in his black habit, will have walked from the Priory and up the sandy track to say mass in Butley church. He was the villagers' comforter, tending the sick, walking in procession with a chalice and the host, and carrying it to anyone on the point of death. He will have stooped to enter the little chancel door, having checked the sun's shadow on the Mass dial. Other Priory priests served the nearby small churches of Wantisden, Capel

A sundial by which the priest knew the time of day was scratched beside the little doorway through which he entered the chancel. There is also a faint trace of another, much cruder, dial.

Only by chance are the names of any of Butley or Capel's priests recorded, for instance, Alexander *capellano de Buttel* witnessed a charter a few years after the Priory was founded. In 1485 William Potoke, parish priest of Butley, witnessed a will, while John Nedham, parish priest of Capel, received payment to intercede for the soul of the deceased in 1501.

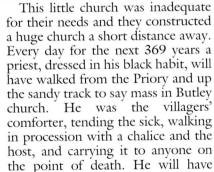

One of the original slit Norman windows, now blocked up.

The Protestant Forths decided that Capel church was no longer needed and amalgamated the parish with Butley.

Many modifications to Butley church date from their time:

- to hold the extra parishioners a gallery was built at the back of the nave. Blocks of crag from the foundations of the dismantled Priory were used to build a projecting staircase wall in the south-west corner. Today it is a 'mystery staircase-to-nowhere' to the left of the tower. Perhaps the gallery also served to replace the Priory's schoolroom. Cawston church in Norfolk has a medieval 'plough gallery' reached by just such a vice, as the stairs were called.

- buttresses of crag reinforced the tower.

- images, wall paintings and even the altar were removed.

- a communion table in the nave replaced the altar in the chancel.

- a pulpit was placed on the south side of the nave.

- clear glass replaced stained glass – except for the family's coats of arms in the east window. If you dared to pray in the old way you would be praying to the Forths.

- the rood beam was taken away, together with its large effigies. As in many other churches, removal of this tie beam weakened the eastern end of the nave.

- the low screen was allowed to remain but its painted pictures of saints were stripped to the bare wood.

St John the Baptist

An image of the church's name-saint had a prominent place. His birthday came exactly midway through a year reckoned by saints' 'feasts' – and not by months and days. Thus his feast on 24 June was the time for mid-summer processions, bonfires and junketing, finally stopped by reformers. With his rough clothes and his lamb, their patron saint was a comfortable person to whom to turn in time of trouble. The drama of the Passion was emphasised at certain times of year by lowering a curtain in front of the rood screen. At the same time the Easter sepulchre against the north wall of the chancel was a centre for devotion. This was a timber framework shaped like a hearse. Butley's sepulchre was saved from religious vandals by the parishioner John Loues who left it in 1550 to his daughter Joan, clearly hoping it would be restored to the church, as no doubt it was when Catholic Mary came to the throne three years later. It will have been permanently removed under her successor.

Two gilds, of St John the Baptist and the Holy Trinity, functioned as do friendly societies as clubs for the mutual support of both men and women. The provision and maintenance of lights to burn before images became one of their chief activities. The wayfarer will have always seen the church windows twinkling in the dark. Wills mention bequests for 'torches', flaring lights with thick plaited wicks coated in a mixture of resin and wax. John Stryk's will of 1453 left 13s-4d between the two Butley gilds 'of ancient foundation', but the last bequest was in 1473.

Not long after Henry VIII closed the Priory and confiscated its lands, William Forth, the Hadleigh cloth merchant, purchased the manors of Butley, Tangham (Capel St Andrew) and Boyton, together with responsibility for their churches (p. 23).

The font

The carved limestone font would originally have been brightly coloured. Money for colouring Snape's font is recorded in 1523. Unfortunately any traces were removed when the Butley font was restored. However, since the angels supporting it have six wings, they must be seraphim whose wings were always blue: a pair stick out like butterfly headdresses; two cover their bodies

Framlingham church (above) has a tall font similar to that at Butley Priory. The Priory font, reduced in height, was placed in the parish church.

behind their shields; and two more are used for flying. Their four shields represent: the Trinity, the Passion, the Church and the donor. The font is late 15th century and was probably carved in a Norwich workshop. It is incomplete and since the missing portion was found in the Priory ruins it shows that it originally stood in the Priory church.

The door
In 1538 there were 67 lay men and women serving in the Priory complex. Seven local

boys were educated free of charge in the Priory school. One of these, Augustine Brook, now middle-aged, carved his name and '1571' on the back of the porch door, a date which happened to be 400 years after the priory had been founded. By means of his ability to write he served many Butley parishioners and wrote their wills for 25 years until his death in 1575.

Two views of Butley church
The antiquary Davy recorded the interior of Butley church in 1810. In place of the rood there hung *'two tablets of the Decalogue with the effigy of Moses behind them'*. On each side were printed paper sheets of the Lord's Prayer and Creed, for such parishioners as could read. High above this was suspended a decayed cloth painted with the arms of

Charles II. The oak roof was hidden by *'Plaister camerating whereon is represented a starry firmament in painting very indifferently performed'*. The old gallery must have been demolished, for in 1843 a balcony was constructed for the Sunday school.

Nearly two centuries after Davy a devout 80-year-old reminisced about the church when she was a child. First, Florrie Warne talked about the Victorian gallery, now removed like the medieval one. *'The wooden stairs were at the back and the side was enclosed but had no door – not like Snape. We sang every Sunday always up there with choir practice every Wednesday night and anthems every Christmas and Easter, young as well as old. The balcony was pulled down when Sir Bernard bought the organ that's there now. It had pipes and could not fit on the balcony.'*

'About 50 yards from the church by the lane that's where the stable was. It was only made of tin. The Reverend Wanstall, he had a horse and cart and he put it there. Old and young Mr Abbot used to live at the top of Oyster Hill and they were churchwardens for all their lives and I can see them lighting the lamps. They always wore black shiny shoes which used to squeak as they walked down the aisle. We wore hats – you never went into church without a hat. My sisters and I used to pick about 60 little bunches of primroses with three leaves tied up with wool to decorate Butley Church. We gathered daffodils in Water Wood, bluebells in Staverton and primroses in Carman's followed by bluebells. Ever since my mother died I have done flowers on that pedestal, every week for 27 years, never missed, except for the seven weeks in Lent, that's all.'

Marriage in the porch
Evidence that Wantisden church once had a porch is recorded in a visitation of 1686 when it was *'cracked and needing tiling'*, showing that it was of brick and tile.

The 15th century seems to have been a period of intense tower and porch construction. Wantisden's tower can be dated from two mid-15th century wills. It was built of coralline crag and construction was in stages, to allow the foundations and mortar to settle. Alexander Blok in 1445 left goods *'to pay out of my goods for the work of the new tower 2 yards in height'*. Six years later

Medieval marriage scene from an East Anglian font at Seething, Norfolk. The priest is joining the hands of the bride and groom. Behind him a clerk holds open the service book. The bride wears an elegant dress with a looped train. The groom's bulky unbelted gown has long open sleeves.

The earliest local porches were doubtless built of timber and have not survived. Butley's later porch was built of brick. There were clay pits close by and also brick-kilns. Parishioners contributed to the cost, leaving money in their wills: John Kenton in 1465 left 3s-4d for this purpose and in 1473 John Cooke left the same amount

The porch (above) after the Puritan makeover when it was rendered and the niche for its patron saint was filled in. The rendering has recently been removed (picture page168).

Like Wantisden, the churches of Hollesley and Boyton no longer have the porches mentioned in old documents.

John Thorn bequeathed *'to the reparation of the tower to be newly made 17s at three separate work-stages'.*

It is interesting to look at the tweed-like texture of the Sandlings' flint towers to see how many stages of construction can be made out. Before metal scaffolding, alder poles were used. The square holes, known as putlogs, where the poles were inserted are sometimes hard to spot, too.

Weddings took place in church porches, with a Mass in the church afterwards. By chance Butley's 14th-century marriage vows survive. The bride concluded:

*'I take thee . . . to my weddid husband . . .
in sekenes and in helth to be boner
and buxom att bord and in bed
tyll deth us depart.'*

Butley's existing porch will have replaced a wooden one It incorporated a 13th-century hood-mould and traceried windows, doubtless architectural salvage and a by-product of modernisation of some Priory buildings.

A few years ago the old door had to be repositioned at the entrance to the nave in order to protect it from the weather.

Non-conformist places of worship

In the early days Quakers were prone to violent verbal outbursts against the established church, interrupting church services and dismissively calling the buildings *'steeple houses'*. Their refusal to say more than 'yea' or 'nay' whenever they had to take an oath may also have played a part in their being persecuted during more than three decades. Later they were better known for gentleness and pacifism, taking a lead in various reforms in connexion with prison conditions and the abolition of slavery.

The Baptists believed in baptism for adults and not children, and by total immersion for individuals who confessed their faith and sinfulness.

John Wesley, who founded Methodism, considered himself to be a member of the Anglican Church until his death. It was only later that Methodists counted themselves among Non-conformists. They were organised in circuits under a minister and they met annually for a conference. The ministers, who moved between circuits, were supported by lay preachers, who maintained interest in their localities.

Burial in the orchard

The suffering of people called Quakers was diligently recorded in the 30 years after 1655. They were hounded because they avoided all contact with the church for baptism, marriage or burial. Action was taken against them when they refused to pay tithes.

For example, in 1676 Nathaniel Keeble of Tunstall had rye, barley and peas removed by bailiffs acting on behalf of the local vicar. Subsequently two bulls, 17 cows and seven calves were seized from this prosperous farmer. However, the writer noted somewhat gleefully that *'the calves run away from the balys so that they could not get them out of the grounds no more.'* Seven years later he was to be held in Melton Gaol with other Quakers, because they refused to pay fines imposed for *'a riot'*.

Their meetings were also targeted. Thomas and William Lynd, blacksmith and bladesmith respectively, were Quakers. Thomas' forge was in Melton before he moved to Butley. He had fallen foul of the Conventicle Acts which forbade meetings of more than five people who were not of the same family. In 1678 hay and steel were seized from his property, so he must have held meetings at his house. Thomas and his wife had only one child, a daughter, Katherine. Quaker records state that she died in 1682 and was buried *'in her father's orchard in Melton'*. This orchard was behind Thomas' forge which stood in Melton Street.

Robert Blake, whose father was the blacksmith at the other forge opposite Melton's Victorian church from 1946 until his death in 1990, recalled the demolition of a pair of cottages in Saddlers Lane. He was told that a grave had been found in the garden. Perhaps the grave contained the bones of young Katherine. Whether they were reburied in consecrated ground is not known, but it would be ironic if she found a final resting place in a churchyard of the established church.

Thomas' move to the remoter village of Butley in the 1680s may have been prompted by the persecution he had suffered. However, the Lynd family had a 100-year connexion with the parish, interrupted by a dearth of male heirs.

Thomas set up a smithy in Butley Street, on the site of the house and forge known as Puntings which an ancestor, Thomas Lynd, had inherited in 1638.

Thomas was less likely to be hounded in Butley because there was no resident clergyman and the perpetual curate usually lived elsewhere. In any case the great tithes were

> Confusingly every Thomas Lynd named sons, Thomas and William, whilst every William Lynd named sons, William and Thomas. One William Lynd even named two of his sons Thomas. They were an extreme example of a practice widespread in these villages. As a result nicknames were very widely used.

due to be paid to the landowner not to the curate. Indeed a long-drawn-out dispute between John Clyatt and Walter Devereux over the Butley estate in the 1680s may have led to a period when not all tithes were collected. Fifty years later George Wright was forced to go to law to establish his right to the great tithes.

Thomas' brother William lived at Tunstall where he prospered as a bladesmith. At a Quaker meeting in Woodbridge in 1697 Nathaniel Keeble suggested that some future meetings be held at Tunstall. This may have been at Nathaniel's own house or that of William.

An inventory of William's goods was made in 1703 and the large amount of seating shows that meetings could have been held there. Among the furniture in the hall were two tables, six joined stools and twelve chairs, three with cushions. There were also a clock and some books and glasses. Although the later Methodists were tee-

Watercolour by Laura Churchyard records the forge which the Quaker, Thomas Lynd, occupied. In the orchard behind it he buried his daughter.

total, Quakers were not, and William Lynd brewed beer at home and had barrels standing on ale-stools in the buttery and the cellar. Like many tradesmen at this time, he also farmed, keeping pigs and cows and growing barley and peas.

Some time after the bladesmith died, his widow, Alice, went to live in Butley, presumably with her sons, Thomas and William. There she died in 1721, being buried in the Friends' Burial Ground at Bredfield. Her death seems to have ended the family connexion with the Quakers, but not with Butley. Whereas the Quaker, Thomas, left £10 to 'poor friends' at the Woodbridge meeting, Alice's son, Thomas, gave the Poors' Land to Butley parish in 1731.

The Lynds do not appear in the Quaker records thereafter and the family disappears from manorial records in 1737. They had been borrowing money, £700 to be repaid in 1733 and £1,000 in 1736, both with interest of five per cent. By 1739 the blacksmith's shop in Butley Street was now held by William Easty, *'William Lynd being the last freehold tenant thereof.'*

Encroachment on the Green

Wesleyan Methodists built a chapel in the hamlet of Butley Low Corner. In medieval times the settlement was known as Lowsing Green. At the intersection of three tracks there lay a small triangle of common land which did not belong to the Manor of Butley. The plot was left to be sold in the will of John Day, a tailor of Orford, in 1830. There were no bids at the auction. It was offered again in 1836 and a bid of £12 was accepted from *'people called Methodists'*.

An indenture was drawn up between various people in Halifax, Yorkshire *'for the use of people called Methodists in the connexion established by the late Rev. John Wesley for the use only for the building of a chapel'*. John Day's executors signed as did the following: The Reverend William Griffiths, Superintendent of the Circuit, John Fowler, furrier, John Hayward, farmer, both of Woodbridge, George Dowling, brickmaker of Melton, Thomas Whitby millwright of Ipswich, Edward Sawyer, shoemaker of Hollesley, William Newson, and John Markham, labourers of Butley and Francis Ashkittle, labourer of Boyton.

Butley's Wesleyan Chapel attracted people from nearby villages. Built in 1836, enlarged in 1863, the chapel is today a private house.

Baptism in the pond

Before the present Sudbourne Baptist chapel was erected, the faithful held their services in the old workhouse, made redundant after the construction of the Union workhouse at Wickham Market in the 1830s. They were 'Particular' Baptists, later called 'Strict'. Their leaders were Mr Brand of Aldringham and William Large, a prominent member of the Sutton and District Strict Baptist Church. The first service was held at Sudbourne on 30th May 1860; baptisms were public, in the pond near the old workhouse.

When the first pastor, John Brett from Leiston, died in 1863, the congregation asked William Large to be pastor. He agreed to a trial period of three months. This was extended to nine, and then continued until the end of his long life.

The workhouse was too small, so for a while they used the village wheelwright and blacksmith's shop, which had to be cleaned the day before. It was *'littered down with straw with a very old table to lay the bible on'*. The rent was a shilling a week and the first monthly collection was 5s-7½d and the minister was given 1s-7½d for his month's ministry. This he gave to the building fund. A site in School Road was purchased for £40, and the chapel was built by the pastor who was now a builder and wheelwright in Butley.

Sudbourne Baptist Chapel built by William Large. His memorial can be seen on the other side of the porch.

He married Eliza, eldest daughter of Elizabeth Cooper who farmed Valley Farm opposite his premises. In 1860 when the chapel opened £203 was still owed to various people for materials and labour. After an anxious time for the pastor and his wife the last instalment was paid off within four years.

The building measured only 30 by 20ft; the present porch, gallery and Sunday School hall were added later. A baptistry was constructed when the chapel was enlarged. Music was provided by violins until 1871 when a harmonium was purchased.

William Large died in 1898 and was buried in Butley churchyard where the Cooper family were interred. He never lived at Sudbourne; every visit from Butley was by horse and trap. He must have travelled

The Large Family

The Larges were long-lived: George had lived to be 94; William to 84; William Josiah (Wiggy) to 81. His son, William Cooper (Young Wiggy to all) was also a builder and carpenter and lived to be 99. Beside his workshop he built the only double-fronted house in the Street, today known as Havergate House. The story goes that he wished to set the new house further back, but his wife insisted that it was built by the road so that she could hear the gossip!

The old workshop has been converted into houses and a modern house has been built in the yard.

Two Larges died during the First World War. Young Wiggy's brother, Herbert, emigrated to Australia where his descendants are living today.

William Large and his wife, Eliza, née Cooper.

Wiggy in 1870 with his bicycle when he was aged fourteen.

Tunstall Chapel drawn on 1 July 1848

The asymmetrical roof of Tunstall Chapel puzzles passers by. It results from extending the north wall 32 years after its foundation in 1805. The original burial ground was in the pit to the right; the headstones have now been moved to the perimeter. The chapel thrived and a much larger graveyard was opened on Tunstall Common in 1868 when there were more than 200 members.

Eight roads converge on Tunstall, making it a natural hub. As a result the chapel attracted its adherents from a wide area, becoming a centre of devotion for at least 21 villages.

Even today, not everyone chooses indoor baptism. A current member recalled that his father elected to be immersed in the River Ore.

Burial in the pit

Sudbourne chapel was on land with a water-table too high to be used for burials which took place in the disused pit beside Tunstall Baptist Church. Today the gravestones flank the wall or are concealed under the far hedge.

A rare early photograph of adult baptism in a Suffolk pond, in this case at Office Farm, Dennington.

more than 33,600 miles in those years. His son, William Josiah Large, described his father as *'not an educated man, but one who preached from the heart'*. He said that his grandfather, George, who was a Norfolk shepherd, born in 1773, was *'a walking Bible concordance.'* At some time, William Josiah switched his denomination and became treasurer for the Methodist chapel, built on the former green at Butley Low Corner, and now a private house (page 173).

Conclusion

In the Triangle there are still active Baptist congregations in Tunstall, Sudbourne and Bromeswell, while the Methodists have consolidated their chapels in the larger settlements of Orford, Melton and Woodbridge. As the smaller chapels became redundant, their good quality brick construction made them highly desirable for conversion into private houses.

Where the Church of England is concerned, not all parish churches in the benefice known as the Wilford Peninsula have survived into recent times. Capel St Andrew and Gedgrave were demolished in the 16th-century, when Capel was combined with Butley and Gedgrave with Orford. Ramsholt and Wantisden are tiny communities of a farm or two and a row of cottages, and their churches, although lovingly cared for, are today used intermittently.

Only Hollesley and Rendlesham have populations of more than a thousand. The other villages have remained small, and the decline in congregations means that it is becoming increasingly difficult to raise comparatively huge sums. For instance, a small parish like Butley needs to find £8,000 each year to cover its major cost, the Parish Share required by the Diocese, plus insurance, heating, lighting and sundry items. Extra money has to be raised for running repairs to the ancient fabric and in order to re-thatch the nave a special appeal will soon be necessary.

As elsewhere in the county, there is increasing emphasis on collaborative ministry. The Rector and three priests each serve a cluster of parishes, supported by a ministry team composed of retired clergy, ordained local ministers, readers, a lay pastor and numerous lay elders.

In addition to raising much-needed funds, the little churches of the Triangle extend a welcome to all sections of the community through concerts, art exhibitions, craft fairs, floral displays and coffee mornings. As one-by-one, the school, the post office, the shop and the pub close down, the parish church has become increasingly important in maintaining a village identity, a sense of community and a link with the past.

Story from a Gravestone

Chapter 19

One cold winter's afternoon the authors went to look at the weathered gravestones in Boyton churchyard, little expecting to be able to flesh out information contained in the burial registers of the parish. Few of the hundreds of people buried there over the centuries have a surviving stone, while those that do survive are often all but illegible. Occasionally relationships and epitaphs supplement bare names and dates.

Inside old churches a few more elaborate memorials may be anticipated. With Victorian renovations many of these disappeared, so that researchers have to depend on antiquarian descriptions. Boyton church was completely rebuilt apart from the tower in 1870, and its old inscriptions removed. Fortunately David Elisha Davy made a full record of Suffolk churches he viewed during much of the first half of the 19th century. On a visit to Boyton, he carefully transcribed the memorial to a youth from London who drowned in the Ore in 1771.

Our walk that day led to the story of a young man who went to sea from here.

The Battle of the Saints

The microcosm of the three manors of Butley, Boyton and Tangham can only occasionally be detected as directly in touch with great events in the outside world.

A postscript added to Robert and Mary Barber's weathered tombstone in the quiet

Boyton churchyard revealed that their only son was at the centre of one of the bloodiest naval actions of the 18th century. The words, *'and Robert their only son who was lost at sea Ville de Paris September 1782 in the 29th Year of his Age'* were the clues. It was apparently a French ship – merchantman or warship? What could Robert be doing on a foreign vessel? The local newspaper, which his two sisters must have anxiously scanned for news throughout that summer of 1782, unfolds for us, just as it did for them, the saga of events in which Robert was involved. Surviving copies of the *Ipswich Journal* show just how closely literate Suffolk folk were able to follow what was happening in London, and even on the other side of the world.

England was at war with France. At that time sugar from the West Indies contributed massively to the economic prosperity of both nations. The Caribbean inevitably had become a theatre of conflict between the two countries. The French had naval superiority and in the previous year their fleet had blockaded Yorktown, securing an American victory in the War of Independence and a letter of thanks from George Washington. They were poised to seize the British possessions in the West Indies when Admiral Rodney surprised their fleet and won a decisive British naval victory, known as the *Battle of the Saints*, on 12 April 1782.

News reached London five weeks later. At Orford the churchwardens paid a shilling for a thanksgiving prayer for the victory and a full report appeared in the *Ipswich Journal* on 25 May. It described graphically an action which lasted from 7am to 6pm, involving 5,500 French of whom 1,300 were on board the pride of their navy, the 110-gun *Ville de Paris*. She was battered by the British flagship *Formidable* which fired nearly 80 broadsides into her. Finally *Barfleur*, the other 90-gun British ship, joined in, sending shot *'which passed through both sides of her'*. When *Ville de Paris* finally struck her flag to the *Formidable* there were only three men alive and unwounded on her deck. One was the commander-in chief, Admiral Comte de Grasse, who had to lower the colours himself.

The marines who boarded her found the decks so full of dead and mangled bodies that, as Rodney reported in his despatch *'the scene was the most shocking that imagination can conceive'*. Added to the human carnage there were the remains of the cattle, sheep and goats which all French warships had on board because, unlike the British, they enjoyed a diet of fresh meat. A sister ship, *Glorieux*, had been easily captured when her terrified cattle broke out of their pens and stampeded, causing havoc on the gun-deck in the heat of the engagement.

The *Ville de Paris* was carrying 12 chests of money to pay for the subsistence of troops who were going to attack the British island of Jamaica. The captured cash amounted to £20,000. With great good sense Admiral Rodney then and there shared this out proportionately, so that, for instance, captains each received 450 Maria Theresa dollars, the international currency of the day, and the common men just one dollar. Reading the report, Robert's relatives will have been pleased to realise that

Model of the Ville de Paris in the Museum at Grasse.

Beautifully carved naval engagement on the memorial of James Saumarez who captained the Russell *in the Battle of the Saints.*

he would have received a share, although they could only pray that he was alive and unwounded.

The aftermath

For the rest of the year the newspaper carried reports from the fleet and focused on what was happening to the captured flag-ship. It was no secret that there was frantic activity repairing hulls and rigging from naval stores which had been shipped to the West Indies in anticipation of this kind of need. As was standard practice, Admiral Rodney commissioned the captured ships into the British navy. He gave command of *Ville de Paris* to Captain Fanshaw of the 2nd-rate *Namur*. To command a 1st-rate was every officer's dream, but the largest warships needed more manpower than the Navy could muster. Fanshaw had to make do with such men as could be spared from other ships and Robert Barber was one of these. The crew would have their work cut out to get her home safely. She had been so weakened that her heavy guns were taken off and lighter armament from the battered 3rd-rate *Shrewsbury* was transferred to her.

All the French prisoners were well treated and they were distributed amongst the fleet. Despite his *hauteur*, noted by Admiral Rodney, the Comte de Grasse was courteously entertain-ed on his voyage to England.

The high mortality among the French wounded puzzled Rodney, especially as he had ensured that they were cared for like his own. He observed that seven out of ten Frenchmen died of lock-jaw. No doubt the explanation for this is that tetanus bacteria flourished in the dung of the live animals on the French decks, infecting wounds.

Unfortunately the badly damaged vessels took much longer to repair than anticipated. They finally set sail from Port Royal dangerously late in the year, six men o' war with a fleet of 80 merchantmen. An officer on another prize, *l'Hector*, wrote home complaining of the very bad pumps on French ships. They were all to have need of them in the hurricane they later met off Banks, Newfoundland, on 6 October.

Most ships were dismasted and seven merchantmen foundered. When *l'Hector* fell in with *Ville de Paris* she was alone. Her main and mizen masts were broken and she was in a bad way. *L'Hector* laid by until thick fog separated them. She herself was in an even worse way with water washing over the decks. Her lookouts left their posts, went below and literally drank themselves to death on rum and wine. Fortunately a merchant-man picked up some survivors.

The crew of *Ville de Paris* was not so lucky. The last report of her was published in November. She had managed to reach Scottish waters where a merchant captain had met with her off the Western Isles. There was four feet of water in her hold and all her masts and rigging were gone. On 14 December the *Ipswich Journal* faced up to the melancholy fact that, along with her com-panions, *Centaur* and *Glorieux*, *Ville de Paris* had been lost

Robert's body was of course never found, and the laconic words added to his parents' tombstone probably reflect all that his two sisters were ever told officially. Because they had no formal notification of their brother's death, the manorial court could not transfer his copyhold land to the sisters.

The antiquarian, Davy, recorded that the manor court held at Valley Farm near Boyton Ford was *'defeated by a homager'* re-fusing to present to the court the death of Robert Barber. The homager, whose name is not recorded, alleged that the inscription on the gravestone was not sufficient evidence. As a result, the transfer of Robert's copyhold land was delayed for several years. Such uncertainties were not uncommon and must have caused some disruption to the management of farms and trades.

Robert's early involvement with the sea

Robert's parents came from well-to-do farming stock. Following the death of her first husband, his mother, Mary, was married in Boyton to Robert Barber from Pakefield, up the coast near Lowestoft. She was a Benington, daughter of Ann and Thomas who were tenant-farmers of Street Farm, later Neutral Farm, Butley, plus a farm in Boyton leased from the Mary Warner Trustees. Robert was an only son, born in 1753, and two daughters followed. The children were to inherit the lease of the Boyton farm after the death of their mother and £200 plus interest.

Something more about young Robert's seamanship is incidentally derived from Davy's voluminous notes. At the time of his visit there was a memorial in Boyton church-yard to Samuel Darkin, who drowned at the age of 23, although the epitaph did not reveal that Robert Barber was with him at the time. Samuel was the son of John Darkin of London who had lost several sons at sea and, to avoid a similar calamity befalling Samuel, had placed him with Robert Barber, senior, to learn farming. By a sad irony the latter was a skilled boat-builder as well as a farmer, and Samuel and Robert junior were starting out to sail one of his boats to Harwich in May 1771, when a sudden squall capsized the boat in the River Ore. Whereas Robert swam ashore, Samuel drowned and his body was not found for a fortnight. The boat was recovered after the accident and sold. It must have been a superb, lightly-built vessel since it was to win the Doggett's Coat and Badge race on the Thames at least once. Davy transcribed Samuel's now lost epitaph,

Ah Youth, unwarned to shun the watery way
Beneath whose treacherous flood Death
ambush'd lay
Twice seven revolving days its ample bed
Shrin'd the pale corse, long sought with
anxious dread.
At length, recovered from the tossing wave
These cold remains may find a peaceful grave.
From your blessed realms, Oh may thy happy
shade
Well pleas'd survey this debt to Mem'ry paid.

Notwithstanding this disaster, Robert's father put his son to sea, *'Because he was proficient in navigation so as to be able to keep a ship's reckoning'*. Davy adds that he was pressed into the navy after being a merchant seaman.

Missing seamen return

Whereas Robert Barber died at sea, Richard Cooper unexpectedly returned to Butley after many years serving as a marine during a later war with the French. His father, also Richard, had made his will 19 years before his death in 1800. He left his copyhold cottage and three acres to his wife and after her death to his brother John. He failed to appreciate the consequences of not changing his will once his children were born. His wife died in February 1815 and the copy-hold passed to a nephew, John Cooper.

The Doggett's Coat & Badge Wager depicted in an old print.

The race still takes place between London Bridge and Chelsea, originally against the tide, but now with it, and is the oldest continuous sporting event in the country, if not the world. The founder, an Irish comedian named Thomas Doggett, emigrated to London in 1690 and became a stage manager. He had the brilliant idea of founding the race in the year 1715 as a tribute to the Hanoverians after George I had ascended the throne. Thomas presented a coat and badge to be rowed for by six watermen in the first year of their freedom.

Watermen were once the equivalent of taxi-drivers, licensed to row passengers along and across the Thames. In the early years the competing boats were four-seater passenger wherries and this must have been the craft built by Robert's father at Boyton which capsized in the Ore.

Wash Cottage was once a public house at a natural stopping-place beside the former ford over the Laneburgh river. The modern name for the river does not occur in old documents, and the lower portion was formerly called 'Boiton Eie'.

However, shortly afterwards Richard re-appeared and in April the banns were read in Butley church for himself and the widow Sarah Bartrum. The manorial court record explains that Richard was born after his father made his will, had entered the marine service and had not been heard of for many years. Faced with his appearance in person, the Court had no option but to remove the copyhold from John Cooper and grant it to Richard and Sarah. Following Richard's death in 1839 his daughters, Emma and Martha, immediately sold the premises for £40, a contrast with the sisters of Robert Barber, who appear to have made every effort to retain his copyhold.

Davy noted the escapade of another Boyton resident. This was Joseph Evans, whose father, Arthur, kept a public house at Boyton Ford during the Napoleonic wars. Joseph was serving aboard a French privateer. When it was captured, he used an alias to avoid identification. However, in Yarmouth he was recognised by a seaman from Woodbridge. The identification was confirmed by Edward Long of Capel, who was living at the almshouses at the time of Davy's visit. Joseph Evans was convicted and sentenced, but, on appeal by his father, he was pardoned.

Conclusion

Naturally it was the large tenant farmers, such as Thomas Ablitt of Butley Abbey, who had the capital to invest in seagoing vessels. In 1795 he had a share in the *Two Brothers* of Woodbridge. In 1807 he also owned shares in *Good Hope* with two neighbours, namely, Robert Benington who was a relative of Robert Barber and John Woolnough, both gentlemen farmers of Boyton. Some trades-people also had cash to invest. Thus the Boyton dealer and chapman, Henry King, was a part owner of *Providence*, while Nathaniel Beedon of Butley Mills in 1835 had a share in the *Ida,* a 64-ton sloop. Their activities may have been entirely legitimate, but some were engaged in smuggling and their names were recorded only if they were apprehended or their vessels were seized.

Despite their coastal location, remarkably little information for the manors of Butley, Tangham and Boyton concerns sailors or fishermen. Wills and manorial court records are seldom concerned with labouring men. From incidental references to boats or fishing-gear, it is clear that the sea provided a secondary source of income for some farmers, for example John Candler, Edward Cleydon and John Medowe, all of Boyton.

Some Boyton fishermen

Where boats are today beached on the Boyton shore opposite Orford Ness there were fishermen's shacks in Tudor times:

'On this salt marsh divers cottages are sited and built which are for the lord's use for certain fishermen to be held at his will.'

About 1600, John Norden painted John Cowper's shack on the shingle of Orford Ness.

Extract from the will of John Candler, 1510:

'to Robert Candler my brother 3s 4d in the buying of a manfare of sparling net.'

George Arnott explained manfare as a net to hold a thousand fish, while sparling nets were suspended below the surface of the water.

Extract from the will of the wealthy farmer, John Medowe, of Boyton, 1550:

'To Edward Medowe my brother and to Richard Moss my brother-in-law my bote with anker and kabyll, maste, seyle and orys.

To Thomas Medowe the mariner my nets which are in Norfolk if they come home.'

Smuggling and the Wrong Side of the Law

Chapter 20

The Suffolk coast faces the Low Countries. Lacking access roads, the deserted little creeks especially lend themselves to smuggling. Today it is drugs and illegal immigrants, but in the past, wine and brandy, tobacco, silks and lace – luxuries desired by both men and women. The Excise stationed soldiers here to intercept smugglers, but so many people benefited from contraband that smugglers could rely on being tipped off when they were about. No doubt, as on the Sussex coast at Rye, fishing boats were constructed with secret spaces where small items could be stowed. Liquor was not so easy to conceal or carry. The tracks of carts taking it to inland destinations could be obliterated by flocks of sheep driven by complicit shepherds.

The upper reaches of Butley Creek and the Froize were reputed to be the haunt of smugglers. Watercolour painted by Anne Paterson Wallace who lived at Ferry Farm.

There were certainly smugglers in the Sandlings, and their activity escalated in the course of the 18th century. H.A. Tripp notes that by 1720 smuggling had reached such a height on this coast that in one night six vessels ran cargoes and 300 men were waiting ashore to receive them. Later in the century the *Ipswich Journal* is the place to look for contemporary factual accounts. An incident at Orford in the winter of 1784 shows that some gangs were out of control:

On 28 February it was reported: *'a seizure of 160 half ankers of gin [680 gallons] was made at Orford, being part of the cargo of a smuggling cutter that bulged near that place; upon which the smugglers rescued their goods, and in the scuffle two of the officers were much wounded.*

After the smugglers were gone, the officers made another seizure of goods out of the cutter, lodged them in a house in that town, and sent to Saxmundham for a party of dragoons; but about twelve at night, a gang of about thirty smugglers, all armed, broke into the room where the goods were lodged, and carried them off in

triumph.' It is clear that the boat was so heavily laden that when she grounded her sides opened up, 'bulged', forcing the smugglers openly to rescue their contraband.

The following month no fewer than 6,380 gallons of recovered *'foreign Geneva'* were auctioned at Southwold, Colchester and Aldeburgh, plus nearly 1,000 gallons of brandy, 13 gallons of rum and 39 lbs of roasted coffee.

The most exciting reported incidents have been recounted a number of times. One of the most memorable was retold by local writer, George Ewart Evans, in *Ask the Fellows Who Cut the Hay*. Tunstall men were members of the notorious Hadleigh gang who landed a cargo at Sizewell Gap in June 1778. Shortly afterwards at Tunstall's *Green Man* two of them, who had nearly killed an informer by appalling ill-treatment, were caught when a servant girl named the man to whom she had lent the cork stuffed into the informer's mouth. They were sentenced to two years' imprisonment in Ipswich Gaol.

Inland at Earl Soham near Framlingham,

A tombstone in Tunstall cemetery commemorates two less lucky members of the Hadleigh gang. They were suffocated by fumes on 22 June 1778.

Robert Debney's father farmed nearby Plunkett's Farm and William Cooper was probably the miller's son. The gang had constructed a vault six feet deep on a farm on Leiston Marshes. Here they stashed their contraband gin, tobacco and tea. The vault was concealed below a muck-heap. When Robert and William entered it the methane overcame them.

Their epitaph presumes the reader knows the facts:

'All you dear friends that look upon this stone

Oh! Think how quickly both their lives were gone;

Neither age nor sickness brought them to decay,

Death quickly took their strength and sense away

Both in the prime of life they lost their breath…'

Unloading a barge at Orford Quay. Detail of a watercolour by Emmeline Rope c.1880.

the surgeon, William Goodwin, had plenty to say about smuggling in his journal. In February 1785 he recorded that no fewer than 3,700 gallons of spirits passed through the village. Almost everyone *'from the highest to the lowest'* was involved in smuggling or buying contraband. Liquor and tea merchants no longer sought further orders because so much was being smuggled. At this time private gin and tea shops were to be found in every parish. In Butley the Ferry-house probably fulfilled this function, since in 1776 a pensioner from the Boyton almshouses was fined one shilling for tippling there. Unlike Woodforde, the Norfolk parson who colluded in the activity, Goodwin was delighted to record that lowered duties and the success of the King's cutters in capturing smugglers' vessels was resulting in *'this shameful business'* being nearly at an end. In this he was mistaken.

A number of the larger farmers in the Triangle had shares in sloops, schooners and brigs of between 40 and 125 tons. The Woodbridge *Port Books* show that a few were built in the North-East but most on the Deben or Orwell. They engaged in coaling and other coastal trades, and occasionally were apprehended for carrying contraband. For instance, William and Thomas Waller with Henry Edward, all farmers in Sutton, had shares in *Resolution,* a square-sterned sloop of 40 tons which was seized in September 1802 at Woodbridge. The

following spring it was condemned in the Exchequer *'for smuggling practices'* and sold.

Successful smugglers might turn their profits to legitimate purposes. Such a man was Richard Chaplin who later in life was a well-to-do farmer in Sudbourne. Nothing shows better the extraordinary status of smugglers than his advertisement in the *Ipswich Journal* in August 1785 in which he openly announced that he was giving up his smuggling activities. In 1833 he died a gentleman at the age of eighty two.

George Culham of Orford

In 1797 George Culham of Orford made his will as he lay abed in the *Bird-in-Hand Inn* at Stratford, Essex, apparently following a violent incident. He described himself as a farmer. However, his will and inventory reveal other operations. He owed nearly £1,000, but his assets were largely suspect and his executor had great difficulty in sorting out his affairs. The bills presented by a range of lawyers, tradesmen and house-keepers fit the picture of a leader of a smuggling gang based in Orford with widespread activities and distribution in the area of Earl Soham, Cretingham and Easton.

In addition to his large undecked sailing boat, he owned the *Daphne* with which he had captured a Dutch vessel. Although Culham was claiming a reward for taking the prize, the High Court of Admiralty had not yet adjudicated. Since then the *Daphne* had been *'condemned for illicit practices'*. An out-standing insurance claim of £400 for goods lost on the *Mary Ann* while *en route* to Hamburg was in doubt since the vessel might have fraudulently foundered at sea. Culham owned a house in Orford, and was building another one. He was also the tenant of a farm and house on Havergate Island.

The house on Havergate Island painted by Emmeline Rope c.1880. There was a house on the island before 1787.

Buttons Farm. The little white farmhouse, set back from Capel Street and backing on to marshes, takes its name from the Button family. Both Jonathan junior and Samuel were seamen. Jonathan, a master-mariner, owned *Molly*, a 30-ton cutter built in 1786. He was caught smuggling by Captain Carr of the Excise cutter, *Badger*. *Molly* was seized in 1818 and her papers taken. The brothers also owned the 18-ton smack, *Oak*, which, significantly, they gave up about this time.

His executor had to sell the furniture and stock 'under a distress for rent'. The island would have provided perfect cover.

A smuggler's retreat

It is difficult to separate fact from fiction in the popular story published by the Reverend Richard Cobbold in 1845. However, its factual basis cannot be doubted. Reports in the *Ipswich Journal* show that the Cobbold family had a servant girl named Margaret Catchpole, and a letter from her to Mrs Cobbold survives. It was written in 1800 just before she was transported to Australia. According to Richard, the man behind the smuggling operations into which Margaret was drawn due to her love of Will Laud, was Captain Bargood, five of whose crew on the *Alde* were Butley men. He rented 'Green Cottage', which was one of the places 'always kept neat, and ready for his occupation, by a dame whom he permitted to live in it rent-free, paying her something extra for house-keeping'.

There are several contenders for this cottage. Indeed Vera Noble claimed it was *The Oyster Inn* and others that it was the cottage at the head of the creek, now the *Froize Inn*. However, as described in the novel it lay 'close to Butley Abbey', a description which best fits the cottage tucked

out of the way below Oak Wood and facing Capel Green. Today Capel Green consists of Green Farm and a pair of brick cottages, but a century ago there were dwellings on three sides of the green. William Large, the Butley wheelwright born in 1881, knew of Green Cottage because it had once belonged to one of his family. Eliza Cooper was his grandmother and the cottage hard by Oak Wood was owned successively by members of the Cooper family.

Among the family documents surviving in Australia is an indenture dated 1817, between William Cooper and Francis Smith Cook, for the lease of the cottage for three years. Francis Cook is described as a merchant, an unusual occupation for someone living in a tiny and remote hamlet. It makes the most intriguing connection with the character given the name of Captain Cook in the novel. He lives at the cottage prior to a voyage to 'cheat the Hudson's Bay Company of a good cargo of skins' when Captain Bargood decides 'something may be done in the fur-trade this winter.' It is possible either that the two Cooks are the same man, or that the known merchant dealt in contraband as well as legitimate merchandise.

Capel Green would be an ideal hideaway, screened as it is by woodland. It lies at a distance from *The Oyster Inn*, yet a straight

Isaac Johnson's undated draft map of Capel Green named W. Cooper and Cook (arrowed) on the plot below Oak Wood.

Door now rehung at the bottom of the stairs in The Oyster Inn.

track, the ancient 'Royal Highway', connects the two, enabling a wary eye to be kept on any troopers resting there. In the Men's Kitchen there used to be two doors with circular openings at eye level, over which were sliding panels. These were said to facilitate watching any troopers installed by the fire and sufficiently mellow to forget their duties. Below the older eastern side of the building there is a cellar with outside access and an internal stair. No doubt this was always the 'official' cellar, but a large carefully constructed portion lies under the Men's Kitchen. It may once have been separate and used to store contraband.

The Excisemen

Smuggling became profitable in the early 18th century when high duties were imposed. Initially it was countered by private contractors using swift cutters. They were employed by the Customs and needed very fast boats in order to intercept the smuggling runs. For its part, the Treasury was aware that Dutch herring boats operating off the East Coast were bringing smuggled goods with them and were responsible for thousands of gallons of gin reaching the English market. Thus the response to complaints from the Dutch that Excise officers were raiding their ships and drinking their *'personal gin'* was of a sarcastic nature.

The presence of Excisemen and their families living in Butley during the last decade of the 18th century is vouched for by entries in the baptismal records of the parish. John Black is described as an Exciseman, when he and his wife, Rosannah, had their two children baptised in Butley church in 1792 and 1794. He was followed by Harris Thompson, and his wife Elizabeth, who had three children baptised between 1799 and 1800. We know that he was an Exciseman because he is listed as such on the Land Tax records for the year 1799. He paid £4 in each of the two hundreds, Loes and

Plomesgate within which Butley lay, but it is not clear why Excisemen were assessed for a land tax.

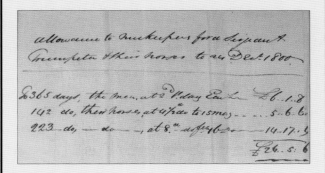

Yeoman cavalrymen were lodged at inns like the *Oyster*. The account (above) shows that in 1800 an innkeeper might receive an allowance of 2d per day per man, and between 4½d and 8d per day for each horse.

Sergeants at this time were paid 2s 11d per day and trumpeters 2s 4d, but both might have 2½d per day deducted in order to have extra feed supplied for their horses.

Yeoman Cavalry Sergeant James Lambert had difficulty in spelling his claim for subsistence on 5 June 1798:

	s	d
For the trumpeter Corn	0	9
to is diner	0	10
to my mare Shoues	0	6
to won night Quarters at Wainford	1	3
to Corn at Difrants times	0	9
	4	1

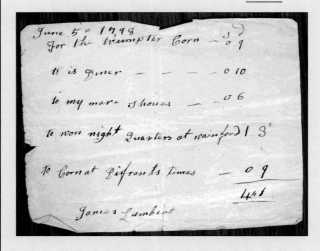

In the Sandlings no other village had an Exciseman listed among its inhabitants in 1799. However, the tax relating to the towns of Orford and Aldeburgh does indicate that Excisemen were stationed there. Orford had six or so 'officers' taxed between £5 and £10, and in Aldeburgh there was a similar number of men who were taxed on their salary, paying between £2 and £10. The tax was at the rate of 4s in the pound, which would make the salary of Harris Thompson £40 a year. This is not a large amount, especially after tax, and the Riding Officers had to supply their own horses.

However, they were awarded a share of every seizure of contraband, and some may even have connived with the smugglers for a reward. Were Excisemen stationed in Butley because it was a centre for smuggling, or because it was a central point within the peninsula between the Deben and the Alde rivers?

Something of our presumed smuggler, Francis Smith Cook, can be gleaned from the parish records and a will. His mother, Mary Cook, was housekeeper to Francis Smith, yeoman, of Capel, who died in 1783. The child's baptism was noted as *'Francis b.s. of Mary Cook, widow'*, meaning he was her base or bastard son. He was four when his father left him his house and lands. Francis Smith also bequeathed £40 to his widowed

Only revenue cutters were allowed to have extra long bowsprits. This was to enable them to outsail smugglers.

mother and £30 to be shared by his four unmarried sisters.

After he dropped the 'Smith' according to the parish and census records, Francis went on to marry Ann Minter, a widow, in 1820. She was 51 years of age, and he was nine years younger. He was now respectable, an agricultural labourer when the census was taken in 1841, while she attained the great age of 88 before dying in Capel in 1857.

Was Mary Cook the housekeeper for Captain Bargood's gang?

Some of the action in the Margaret Catchpole story takes place in this area: Orford Ness, Havergate Island, Butley, Sudbourne, Boyton and Bawdsey. Thus here

A burglary in Butley Street

A single incident involving a gang of three labourers and a mariner must have shocked the whole of Butley. The new shop erected by the grocer, Joseph Till, was broken into at midnight in 1836 and bank-notes and cheques, coins, and a bag of tobacco were stolen. What we see here is the later shop built when the Hazelwood family moved to Butley Street from High Corner.

Joseph Till's shop was in White Row, the three-storey cottages on the extreme left where a woman stands in the doorway. An Exciseman was said by Will Pettitt (born 1884) to have been lodged next door to the shop.

beside Butley Creek with its woods and reed beds we are in true Catchpole country.

The events told in *The History of Margaret Catchpole* took place during the last few years of the 18th century, precisely the time when Mrs Cook occupied the cottage on the Green. As a former housekeeper she was an ideal woman for Captain Bargood to place rent-free in a cottage to be used by himself or his captains when required. On this basis her bastard son Francis is even more likely to have been a member of Barwood's gang. Although Margaret's story ends, where Suffolk is concerned, with her transportation, smuggling continued to be based in Capel as Jonathan Button's capture in 1818 shows.

Critics maintain that the Reverend Richard Cobbold invented most of the story of Margaret Catchpole apart from her theft of a horse, escape from Ipswich Gaol and the letters she sent from Australia. Tantalisingly in the story it was a John Cook who stole the horse from the Cobbolds and made her ride it to London. Perhaps our tale indicates there are more facts contained in the novel than have been allowed.

In May 1974 Wesley Hazelwood found a button on his allotment opposite his shop, and took it to William Pettitt, then aged about ninety. He identified it as having come from the jacket of a Preventive Officer. Will was born in Butley and after World War I he was the village postman for many years. He said his father told him that two officers had lodged at *The Oyster* and one in the Street.

Poaching

In Butley and its surrounding four parishes during the period 1802 to 1825 only one man was convicted of poaching and taken to the House of Correction in Theatre Street, Woodbridge. Theft is recorded of farm animals, timber, clothing and money – a mere 22 offences in total for the same

period. A Gedgrave shepherd was convicted for allowing his sheep to stray into a cornfield (400 years earlier the manorial court would have simply fined such an offence). Thomas Catlin charged Hannah Snayling, his 15-year-old apprentice, with acting in an indecent manner with divers men in his service. She did not learn from her punishment for six years later the Governor of the House similarly charged her along with three other young women.

The introduction of the new Poor Law and the 1831 Game Act quadrupled the number of convictions. It criminalised men and boys, some as young as ten, all of whom were sent to the House of Correction. In the 11 years between 1831 and 1842 when it closed there were 47 convictions from the five parishes of which 36 were for poaching. The sons of Tokley Caley, who was a Butley shoe-maker, were very active poachers. One who was a persistent offender was sent to Ipswich Gaol; he served one month for poaching, three months for a second offence, but only 20 days for removing *'a live fence'* (hedge) from Neutral Farm.

Four hundred years of smoking *in* The Oyster

Research done for the Tobacco Manufacturers Association at football grounds, revealed that 41% of empty packets, discarded by Ipswich Town supporters, had not been taxed. This was the highest percentage in the country. Tobacco has always been one of the easiest commodities to bring illegally into the country.

Walter Raleigh brought the weed back with him from the New World and smoking rapidly became popular. Until 1638 tobacco had to be imported via London and, not surprisingly, pipes were manufactured there first. King James I disliked the habit intensely and published a tirade against it in 1604. The nicotine-stained ceilings of public bars used to bear witness that men were not deterred.

The Great Oyster, as Butley's pub was then known, was no exception. Fifteen clay pipe-bowls which have been dug up in Oyster Field chronicle changing fashions in their shape from 1600 until the late 19th century. The earliest are so small that it is hard to see

Vic has a collection of small finds from the allotments and Oyster Field. His smallest pipe does not have rouletting round its barrel-shaped bowl and is the earliest of a group of four which predate 1640. A group of three has larger bowls and can be dated between 1660 and 1710. A smooth-bowled bowl with a leaf pattern flanking the mould-seam is a common form and dates to the period 1780-1820.

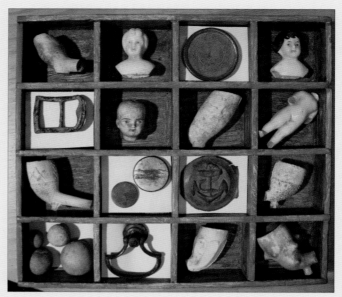

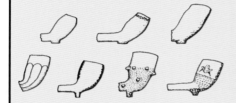

why King James was offended by the smoke they made.

Towards the end of the 16th century tobacco had become less expensive and pipe-bowls were much larger. By the 19th century a large number of elaborately decorated bowls were in circulation: leaves, flutes, acorns, spikes and Masonic emblems decorate local examples from Oyster Field. In the 19th century clay pipes were supplied to landlords by the tobacco companies and given away to purchasers of tobacco. They were said to be too hot until the bowl turned brown when they were 'all right'.

It has taken 400 years for public opinion to swing round, leading to a ban on smoking in public places. James would be amused to see people having to stand outside the bar door these days in order to enjoy a cigarette, but glad to know that his concern about passive smoking is now taken seriously. What he could not foresee when he introduced licenses for public houses was that a ban on smoking would endanger the very survival of small pubs. Supermarkets, not smugglers, are nowadays the source of cheap alcohol with which publicans cannot compete. This, together with drink-driving laws, has forced many serious and not-so-serious drinkers to tipple at home, as a result of which social life in the village is becoming that much the poorer.

Appendix

Butley's elusive parsons

Many parish churches display lists of their previous incumbents taken from diocesan records. However, Butley's living was in the gift of Butley's priors and successive lay rectors until the last century and the names of those appointed were not recorded at Norwich. On the other hand rectors inducted by the Bishop served the churches of Boyton and Chillesford and their names were inscribed in the *Liber Inductionum* (1526-1629). When, as quite often happened, the rector of Boyton, or in later years of Chillesford, was also the perpetual curate of Butley it enables the incumbent to be identified.

Before the Dissolution the churches of Butley, Capel and Gedgrave were served by chaplains or canons appointed by the Prior. Occasionally their names can be found witnessing charters or parishioners' wills, or, much later, in various directories. Since they were not appointed by the Bishop, precise dates for their ministries are unknown. The dates given below show when an individual parson was active in the parish.

pre-1171	Ernald	1740	Jonathan Dorling
c. 1200	Alexander	1754	Christopher Jeaffreson
1485	William Potoke	1776	Samuel Hingeston
1489	Thomas Framlingham	1780	Joseph Sharpe
1518	Robert Chippenham	1783	William Bradley
1521, 1528	Thomas Sudbourne	1784	Peter Lathbury
1528	Dionysius Metcalfe	1790	Samuel Mortimer
1529, 1534	Robert Chippenham	1791	John Black
1538, 1544	Henry Johnson	1844	Samuel Hobson
1553	John Burkett	1855	Robert Kidd
1567	Thomas Agas	1868	F. Hobbins
1578, 1579	Daniel Devis	1874	Goodwyn Archer
1584	Robert Howlett	1880 - 1897	William Edwards
1587	William Tay	1898 - 1899	C. J. Eland
1590, 1606	Thomas Reddrich	1899 - 1923	Charles Wanstall
1610	John Baldwyne	1924 - 1938	Thomas Thomas
1624	Samuel Perse	1938 - 1967	Arthur Snell
1631, 1640	Nathaniel Ferian	1968 - 1976	Martin Lewis
1654	Francis Jacob	1976 - 1979	David Wall
1676	— Weldon	1979 - 1982	J. L. Baillie
1686	Richard Howlett	1983 - 1994	Daniel Gray
1705, 1723	Zephaniah Eade	1997 - 2005	Robert Clifton
1735	Reginald Eade	2005 -	David Murdoch
1735	— Chilton		

Rectors of Boyton

The list expands that published by Colin Maycock in 1993.

1297	Stephen de la Prise	1609	George Cariebe
1353	William de Playford	1617 - 1647	Edward Oliver
1354	Roger at Brigge	1648	John Clubb
1354	John Fraunceys	1652 - 1663	Walter Clopton
1383	Roger Boys	1676, 1686	Edmund Sugden
1433	Richard Orford	1697	Samuel Pulham
1442, 1458	Robert Bawdesey	1720	Richard Golty
1468, 1477	William Wulpet	1733, 1751	James Welton
1483	John Plomer	1764	Samuel Hingeston
1509, 1512	William Prestall	1798	William Cole
1526	Robert Wurnatt	1807	William Norford
1528	Nicholas Oxburgh	1807	William Aldrich
1529	James Carre	1837	James Coyte
1530	William Prestawe	1840	William Aldrich
1533, 1534	Hugh Birkbecke	1865	George Hoste
1535	John Fynche	1886	James Clowes
1538	Nicholas Palmer	1891	Adam Washington
1551, 1558	Richard Nicholson	1911	Joshua Davies
1553	Henry Johnson	1945	Frederick Dunn
1566, 1572	Thomas Agas	1951	George Sherlock
1572	Richard Wardroff	1957	William Groom
1573 - 1608	Daniel Devis	1967	John Gates

Notes to chapters

Numbers in bold refer to bibliographic entries in A.V. Steward's, *A Suffolk Bibliography* (ed. P. Northeast), published by the Suffolk Records Society in 1979.
An author's name followed by a date refers to an entry in the Bibliography.
A key-word followed by a date in parentheses refers to an entry in the Documentary Sources.

Preface
Clyatt portraits - **5535**
Luttrell Psalter - Millar, 1932: fo. 163 b

1
p. 1   Dugdale, 1661
p. 2   Orford Castle - Potter *et al.*, 2002
        Augustinians - Knowles, 1974
        Ranulph's views reported by Ralph of Coggeshall - Brewer, 1873: 244
        foundation - Evelyn-White **4457**, XI: 1-6
        Gilbert - Stevenson, 1875; Brewer, 1873: 244, 45
p. 3   layout - Agas (1594)1, 2; Myres **4459**: 242-59
p. 4   layout - Naunton lease (1538)
        Johnson, note on draft survey (1780)
        'wharf' - Ward-Perkins in Myres **4459**: 260-64
        Roy Collins' recollections
p. 6   charters - Mortimer, 1979
        location - Evelyn-White **4457**, XI: 1-6
p. 7   Rielie Green - Agas (1594) 15-17
        history - Myres **4459**: 182-89
p. 8   wool export - Evans, 1936
        Memorandum re Belhomme (1341)
        West Somerton hospital - Mortimer, 1980
p. 9   Luttrell Psalter - Millar, 1932: fo. 163 b
        Brommer suicide - Dickens **4454**: 25
p. 10   finances - Dickens **4454**: 15

2
p. 11   heraldry - MacLachlan, 2005
p. 12   images - Norden, (1600-02): XII
        Baret (c. 1493-1508)
        Rush - MacCulloch & Blatchly **510**, 36: 101-14
        flooding - Dickens **4454**: 34; Myres **4459**: 185, 226-27, 260; Boyton register (1383) 8.
p. 13   Visitations of 1514, 1520, 1526, 1532 - Jessop **1822**
        Manning's later offices - Copinger **459**, IV: 143
p. 14   image - Norden, key map (1600-01) detail
        wills: Thomas Manning (1544) – NRO 204 Whyteffott;
            Robert Haughfen (1539) – IC/AA1/10/95;
            William Barfote (1539) - IC/AA1/10/100;
            John Awod (1542) - IC/AA1/12/338.
        Butley Priory surrender (1938)
        Household List - Dickens **4454**: Appendix I
p. 15   wills: William Cokeson (1540) – IC/AA1/11/93;
            Thomas Punte (1540) – IC/AA1/11/45.
        Hollond accounts (1450)

p. 16   Household List - Dickens **4454**: Appendix I
        Naunton, William, lease (1538)
        Valor Eccl., 1817, III: 418-22
p. 17   spices - Leiston account (1305)
        Taxatio: **1480**
        wills: John Jaye (1541) – IC/AA1/12/82;
            William Cokeson (1540) – IC/AA1/11/93.
p. 18   Chorographer - **351**
        wills: Agnes Mawling (1558) – IC/AA2/18/326;
            Thomas Punte (1540) – IC/AA1/11/45.
        Case of arson (1540)
p. 19   images - (top) after Ford, 1945;
            (lower left) Blatchly, 1975
        Town of Woodbridge to Cromwell (1538)
        Campsey Dissolution inventory- Haslewood, **510**,
                VIII: 83-116
        will: Agnes Sawer (1550) – IC/AA1/14/48
        Geyton indent - Coales, 1987; Davy - J 400/15
        papal licence (1398)
p. 20   image (top)- Millar, 1932: fo. 176 b
        licence of free warren (1292)
        Butley court roll (1388)
        Broom Close - Agas (1594): fo. 2
        warreners - Dickens **4454**: Appendix 1
        lodge - Bond, 2004: 181-82:
        cunny money - Staverton court notebook [n.d.]

3
p. 23   images -after Biblio. Ambrosiana, codex G 301;
        grant to William Forth (1544)
        Suffolk clothiers - Amor **510**, XL: 417-26
        will: William Forth (1504) - TNA PCC 19 Holgrave
        Classis Movement - Collinson *et al.*, 2003
        marriage register - St Denis Backchurch (1538)
        Hadleigh Charity (1547)
p. 24   Mary I's reign - Duffy, 1992; Garrett, 1938.
        It is unlikely to be a coincidence that John Burkett, parson of Butley, gave up his tenement in Butley in April 1553 - Butley Court roll
        Boyton Manor, grant of reversion (1545)
        will: William Forth (1559) - TNA PCC 7 Mellershe
p. 25   Frances' gowns - Certificate (1563); bequest of Marie Glemham (1571) - TNA PCC 40 Holney
        Mansion-house - Hawes **4966**
p. 27   inventory -Forth (1601)
        image - Norden, J. key map (1600-01) detail
        Deputy Lieutenants' meeting (1588)
        engraving made in 1738 - see page 55

Glossary

Advowson	Right to present a clergyman to the bishop for induction to a benefice.
Almoine ryvett	Flexible light armour with retractile plates sliding on rivets.
Arras	Figured tapestry named after the town near Lille.
Bailiff	Agent who collects rents or manages estates.
Baronetcy	Patent or rank of lowest hereditary titled order.
Bastinado	Stick, staff or truncheon.
Batfowling	Knocking game birds from their perches at night.
Blodwit	Fine for shedding blood.
Buckheading	Pollarding.
Caliver	Light matchlock musket.
Carpet	Furniture covering of piled cloth.
Carucate	Notional area of land, approximately 120 acres.
Champion country	Unenclosed countryside.
Chantry	Chapel or altar endowed for the singing of masses for its founder.
Corselet	Defensive armour covering the body.
Crag	Pleistocene ferruginous shelly sand.
Cunny	Coney, adult rabbit. Prior to the 18th century the word rabbit was reserved for the young.
Demesne	Land reserved by the lord for his own use.
Distrain	To confiscate a person's land or goods to force him to meet an obligation.
Dowry	Property or money brought by bride at marriage.
Encroachment	Illegal occupation of land belonging to the lord.
Entailed	Settled on persons successively, so that it cannot be bequeathed at will.
Ferdwita	Fine for failing to do military service.
Fichtwit	Fine for fighting.
Flemenefrenthe	Fine for harbouring fugitives.
Frankpledge	System by which each member of a tything was responsible for every other, a tything being ten households.
Free warren	Right to keep or to hunt game.
Fulling	Process of cleansing and thickening a cloth by beating; fulling mill.
Furred	Trimmed, or lined, with fur.
Gelding	Castrated horse.
Glebe	Land attached to a clergyman's benefice.
Gilt	Young sow.
Hamsoca	Right of a lord to judge forcible entry with violent assault.
Harness	Protective leather jacket worn by bowmen and billmen.
Heckling	Processing fibres using two combs preparatory to spinning.
Hengenwita	Fine for failure to raise hue and cry.
Holbard	Halberd, combination of spear and battle-axe.
Hundred	Subdivision of county or shire having its own court.
In-chief (*in capite*)	Land held directly from the monarch.

Indenture	Legal document between parties with edges indented to prevent fraud.
Infangen-theof	Right of a lord to pursue and hang a thief caught in the act.
Inning	Reclamation of inundated land.
Interregnum	Specifically, the Commonwealth Period.
Jointure	Property provided for a wife during widowhood.
Keep	Small cupboard.
Knight service	Obligation of military service to a superior lord.
Kyne	Cows.
Last	Medieval measurement based on stowage space between the ribs of a ship.
Layer	Field of grass or clover.
Lockeram	Coarse, loosely woven linen.
Manfare	Net capable of holding a thousand fish.
Mark	Unit of monetary value, not a coin, worth 13s 4d.
Marl	Agriculturally valuable soil consisting of clay and carbonate of lime.
Messuage	Landholding including a dwelling.
Minority	Under age for legal purposes.
Missal or manual	Catholic service book.
Murrain	Infectious disease in cattle.
Necessary	Commode or chamber pot.
Nuncupatative will	One declared orally not in writing.
Penal bond	Loan which, if not repaid by the due date, is doubled.
Plantation	Deliberately planted woodland.
Recusant	One who refused to attend Church of England services.
Reversion	Passing to ultimate grantee.
Seme	Measurement of weight, capable of carriage by a pack-horse.
Shackage	Right to run sheep on stubble of the demesne.
Shot	Young pig.
Slay	Instrument used in weaving to beat up the weft.
Socha et sacha	Right of a lord to retain fines and profits from administering justice.
Solar	Upstairs chamber.
Sorrel	Reddish brown.
Sparling	Sprats.
Staple	Market where foreign merchants were permitted to buy specific products.
Suffragan bishop	Assistant to diocesan bishop.
Synod	Assembly of clergy.
Tathe	Land manured with sheep droppings.
Tenement	Land which is held by any form of tenure, and may include a dwelling.
Tenter	Frame on which cloth was stretched after fulling.
Tester	Canopy of wood or cloth over a bed.
Terrier	Register of landed property showing holdings, services and rents.
Tithe	Tenth part of the harvest levied to support the clergyman.
Trental	Thirty masses said for the dead.
Trundle	Low bed on wheels which can be stored under a high bed.
Twill	Fabric with 2:1 weave.
Vellum	Calfskin treated so as to be suitable for writing on.
Ward	Underage heir whose deceased father held his lands in-chief.
Warpeni	Payment in lieu of guard duty.
Warren	Piece of ground in which rabbits are bred, or abound.

Note on Currency and the Calendar

Before decimalization the coinage used was the pound (£), the shilling (s.) and the penny (d.). The pound comprised 20 shillings or 240 pence. One third of a pound was 6s. 8d, not a coin, but an amount which occurs frequently in accounts and bequests.

There have been two main methods of dating legal and ecclesiastical documents in England over the centuries. One was based on the regnal year and the other on the relevant day in the calendrical month. However, the year ran from 25 March to the following 24 March. Thus 1 March 1740 becomes 1 March 1741 by modern reckoning. A change occurred in 1752 with the introduction of the dating method used today.

An added complication in old documents is the use of saints' days combined with regnal years in preference to calendrical dates. For instance, the Feast of St John Baptist, Michaelmas, and the Annunciation refer to 24 June, 29 September and 25 March, respectively.

Land was measured using the acre (0.4ha.), consisting of 4 roods divided into 40 perches.

Bibliography and further reading

Agas, Radulph, 1596, *A Preparative to Platting*. London.

Bailey, M., 2007, *Medieval Suffolk*. Woodbridge

Beck, Cave, 1657, *The Universal Character*, Frontispiece. London.

Bendall, Sarah, 1997, *Dictionary of Land Surveyors & Local Mapmakers of Great Britain & Ireland 1530-1850*. London

Beresford, J.B.(ed.), 1963, *The Diary of a Country Parson*. Oxford

Besse, Joseph (ed.), 1753, *A Collection of the Sufferings of the People Called Quakers*

Bethan, W., 1801, *The Baronetage of England*, vol. I. Ipswich

Black, Robert, 1966, *The Younger John Winthrop*, Columbia, USA

Blackwood, G., 2001, *Tudor and Stuart Suffolk*. Lancaster

Blake, Robert, 1994, *Melton - a Changing Village*. Woodbridge

Blatchly, J., 1975, Mid-14th-century indents at Hollsley and Westleton, Suffolk. *Trans Mon. Brass Soc.* 47-50

Blatchly, J., 2004, *John Kirby's Suffolk: his Maps and Roadbooks*. Woodbridge

Bond, J., 2004, *Monastic Landscapes*. Stroud

Brewer, J.S. (ed.), 1873, Speculum ecclesiae in Geraldi Cambrensis Opera, IV. *Records Soc.,* XXI

Britton, Frank, 1987, *London Delftware*. London

Clark, Kenneth, 1974, *Another Part of the Wood*. London

Coales, J., 1987, *The Earliest English Brasses, Patronage, Style and Workshops. Trans* Mon. Brass Soc., London

Cockburn, E.P., 1881, *The Wickham Market Workhouse. Wickham Market*

Cockayne, G.E. (ed.), 1900-05, *The Complete Baronetage*, 5 vols (reprinted 1983, Gloucester)

Cockrill, L., 1987, The Suffolk punch: the Crisp family and Chillesford. *The Suffolk Review,* New Ser. 9: 15-18

Collinson, P., 1967, *The Elizabethan Puritan Movement*. London

Collinson, Patrick *et al.* (eds), 2003, *Conferences and Combination Lectures in the Elizabethan Church 1582-1590*. Church of England Records Soc. Woodbridge

Connard, Jane, 1982, Butley Ferry Farm - 1914. *The Lady*, 11/11/1982: 870-92

Dillon, Viscount, 1905, *An Almain Armourer's Album*. London

Dovey, Zillah, 1999, *An Elizabethan Progress*. Stroud

Duffy, E., 1992, *The Stripping of the Altars*. London

Duffy, S. & Hedley J., 2004, The Wallace Collection's Pictures. London

Dugdale, W., 1661, *Monasticon Anglicanum*. London

Evans, A. (ed.), 1936, Pegoletti, F. La Practica de la Mercatura, *Med. Acad. of America*, 24. Cambridge, Mass.

Dymond, D. & Martin, E., 1989, *An Historical Atlas of Suffolk*. Ipswich

Evelyn-White, H.G., 1905, An unpublished rent roll from Butley Priory. *East Anglian*, XI: 1-6

Fenwick, V., 1984, Insula de Burgh: Excavations at Burrow Hill, Butley, Suffolk. *Anglo-Saxon Studies in Archaeology & History*, 3: 37-54

Fenwick, V., 2008, Elizabethan flood defences on Orford Ness. *Orford & District Local History Bulletin,* 10: 1-5

Firth, J. d' E., 1954, *Rendall of Winchester*. Oxford

Fraser, A., 1974, *King James VI of Scotland I of England*. London

Ford, E.B., 1945, *Butterflies*. London

Garrett, Christina, 1938, *The Marian Exiles*, Cambridge

Gathorne-Hardy, J., 1959, Iter litoralis. *Transactions Suffolk Naturalists Society*, 11: 123-37

Greenwood, J., 2006, *Quakers in Woodbridge*. Woodbridge

Grose, F., 1773-77, *The Antiquities of England and Wales*. London

Harrup, V., 2007, The making of a gentleman. *Orford & District Local History Bulletin*, 8: 7-9

Harrup, V., 2009, George Cullum, the noted smuggler. *Orford & District Local History Bulletin*, 12

Hewitt, John, 1991, *Two Horse Power*. Lavenham

Hopper, Peter, 2004, *Suffolk's Historic Farms*. Derby

Kirby, J., 1735, *The Suffolk Traveller*. Reprinted 2004. Woodbridge

Kirby, J., 1736, *Map of Suffolk*. Reprinted 2004. Woodbridge

Kleuber, A.J., n.d., *The Story of the Suffolk Baptists*. London.

Knowles, D., 1976, *The Religious Orders in England*, vols I-III. Cambridge

Mac Culloch, D., 1986, *Suffolk and the Tudors*. Oxford.

Mac Culloch, D., 1999, *Tudor Church Militant*. London

MacLachlan, Peter, 2005, Heraldry at Butley Priory. *The Blazon*, 77: 3-11

Maycock, C., 1993, *Charity, Clay and Coprolites*. Mary Warner's Charity, Boyton

Miles-Cadman, C.F.(ed.), 1913, *Poems by Suffolk Children*. Woodbridge

Millar, E. G., 1932, *Facsimile of the Luttrell Psalter* - Add MS 42130: 46e. London

Mortimer, R. (ed.), 1979, *Leiston Abbey Cartulery and Butley Priory Charters*. SRS Ipswich

Mortimer, R., 1980, The Prior of Butley and the lepers of West Somerton. *Bulletin Institute Historical Research*, 53: 99-103

Norden, J., 1607, *The Surveyor's Dialogue*. London

Pinney, R., 1984, *Smoked Salmon and Oysters*. Orford

Pobst, P. E.(ed.), 1996, *The Register of William Bateman*. Woodbridge

Potter, V., Poulter, M. & Allen, J., 2002, *The Building of Orford Castle*. Orford

Rackham, Oliver, 1986, *The History of the Countryside*. Dent

Salter, H.E. (ed.), 1922, *Chapters of the Augustinian Canons*. Oxford.

Saunders, H.W., 1932, *History of the Norwich Grammar School*. Norwich

Saunders, J. B., 1970, *Mozley and Whiteley's Law Dictionary*. London

Scarfe, Norman (ed.), 1988, *A Frenchman's Year in Suffolk, 1784*. Suffolk Records Society, XXX. Woodbridge

Sheail, John, 1971, *Rabbits and their History*. Newton Abbot

Stevenson, J. (ed.), 1875, *Chronicon Anglicanum of Ralph of Coggeshall*, Rolls Series. London

Stone, L., 1993, *Broken Lives*: 25. Oxford

Timmins, T.C.B. (ed.), 1851, *Suffolk Returns from the Census of Religious Worship*. Woodbridge

Torrance, W.J., 1978, *The Story of St Osmund Bishop of Salisbury*.

Usher, R.G.(ed.), 1905, *The Presbyterian Movement in the Reign of Queen Elizabeth Illustrated by the Minute Book of the Dedham Classis*. London

Watson, F.J.B., 1965, The great wood party. *Apollo*, LXXXI: 480-81

Webber, R., 1980, *The Peasants' Revolt*. Lavenham

White, W., 1844, *History, Gazeteer and Directory of Suffolk*. Sheffield

Williams, Perry, 1998, *The Later Tudors, England 1547-1603*. Oxford

Williamson, T., 2005, *Sandlands. The Suffolk Coast and Heaths*. Macclesfield

Winthrop, R.C., 1864, *The Life and Letters of John Winthrop*. Boston, USA

Documentary Sources

General:
Aldeburgh Register of Ships (1824-40) - IG 2/1/1
Calendar of State Papers - HLR 941 RS120
Coroners' Inquests - indexed by surnames and places, 1767 to 1932
Dasent, J.R., 1896, Acts of the Privy Council, New Series, XIII
David Elisha Davy's records on microfiche. Wilford Hundred - J 400/15
Domesday Book. Suffolk (2 vols). Phillimore, 1986. Chichester
Fitch, M., 1964, Index to Administrations in the Prerogative Court of Canterbury, IV: 1596-1608
Lay Subsidy Return, 1524, Suffolk Green Book, X.
Orford Borough Records - EE5
Overseers of the Poor Records - ADA 11
Quaker records - microfiche J 424/3. Burial in the orchard (omitted from fiche) -
                                                              TNA RG 6 Book 1077: 55
Rye Register of British Ships 1855-1894 - E. Sussex Record Office RSS/4/1/1
Smith, L. and D., 1995, *Sudden Deaths in Suffolk 1767-1858; 1859-1920*. Ipswich
Valor Ecclesiasticus, vol. III : Caley, J. and Hunter J. (eds), 1817. London
Woodbridge - House of Correction records (1802-1842)
Woodbridge Quarter Session records (1665-1676). Index - B 105/2/7
Woodbridge Port Records - E 190; IG 2/4/1

Abbreviations:
BL	-	The British Library, London
BRO	-	Suffolk Record Office, Bury St. Edmunds
CUL	-	Cambridge University Library
IRO	-	Suffolk Record Office, Ipswich
NCC	-	Norwich Consistory Count
NRO	-	Norfolk Record Office, Norwich
PCC	-	The Prerogative Court of Canterbury
SAC	-	Suffolk Archdeaconry Court
TNA	-	The National Archives, Kew (formerly Public Record Office)

All records cited are held at Ipswich Record Office unless otherwise attributed.

Manorial Records
Boyton court rolls - GB 412: 6331 and HD 1538/171/ 14-15
Boyton Minute Book (1793) - GB 412 : 6331 Box 4
Butley court rolls - HD 1538/171/1-9 and 14-15
Butley court books - HB 26: 8039/7-8
Butley court book (1702-49) - BRO E1/4/2
Butley court books (1625-30); 1635-82 - BL Add. MSS 23,923
Butley and Tangham loose papers (1682-1749) - BRO EI/4/2
Kettleburgh Manor Court Book - Kent Family History Society, Record Pub., 75; fiche in IRO
Naunton Hall court book - HB 26 8039/32
Staverton with Bromeswell court books (1586-1923) - HB 10: 427/1/1-10
Staverton with Bromeswell court notebook (n.d.) - HB 10: 427/612/1

Staverton court notebook (n.d.) - HB 10 427/907
Tangham court book (1654-82) - BL Add. MSS 23,956
Tangham court books (1713-37) - BL Add. MSS 23, 955; 23,957
Tangham court rolls - HD 1538/171/11-15
Tangham court book - HB 26: 8039/9

Tithe maps:
Butley (1846) - P 461/53. Apportionment - FDA 53/A1/1a
Chillesford (1841) - FDA 63/A1/1. Apportionment - FDA 63/A1/1a

Parish registers - births, marriages and deaths:
Butley from 1785
Boyton from 1538
Chillesford from 1740
Wantisden from 1708
Bishops' transcripts fill in gaps: Butley (1693-1784); Chillesford (1698-1739); and Wantisden (1705-1707)
Other parish registers consulted:
Benhall; Great Finborough; Elsing, Norfolk; Great Stambridge, Essex; Orford; St Margaret's Ipswich; Rendlesham; Sudbourne.
St Denis Backchurch, 1538-1754. Harleian Society, London, 1878

Other sources in date order
Final concord between William Prior and Robert de Blanchville (1198) - Cal. Feet of Fines 10 Ric.
Licence of free warren (1292) - TNA Chart. Rolls Edw I, 59
Leiston Abbey, account roll (1305) - HD 371/4-5
Belhomme, Thomas, memorandum of pleadings (1341) - HD 1538/172/8
Yield of turbaries in the north of Butley Manor (late 13th cent.) - TNA SC6/1005/7, 8, 10, 12
Boyton Manor, register and customs (1383) - GB 412:6331
Papal license to wear bishop's regalia (1398) - Cal. Papal Registers V: 162
Butley Priory rent roll (14th cent.) - CUL MSS Add. 7871
Codex G 301, Biblioteca Ambrosiana, Milan (1421)
Fulbourn, Walter, Survey of Bawdsey Manor (1437) - BL Add MSS 23,948
Hollond, John, accounts of (1469) - HA49/F1/1
Commission de Walliis et fossatis (1478) - TNA Cal. Pat. Rolls, 1476-85: 112
Baret, Henry, accounts of (*c*.1493-1508) -HD 1538/406/25; 26
Liber Inductionum (1526-1629) - FAA 27/1
Butley Priory Household List (1538) - TNA S.P. I. 129/394 (2)
Butley Priory surrender (1 March) - TNA Cal SP Dom 1538: 393
Town of Woodbridge to Cromwell (1538) - TNA Cal SP Dom, 432
Naunton, William - lease of Butley Priory to, (July 1538) - TNA L & P Hen VIII xiv (I): 603
[C 66/696]
A case of arson: Denny and Punt (1540) -TNA STAC 2/25/218
Depositions regarding Ore fishing rights (1540) - EE5/7/13
Stallboat dispute: charges against Lord Willoughby. Star Chamber (1540) - EE5/7/1; EE5/7/4; EE5/7/6
Heigham Marsh MS (1544) - HB 83: 988/6
Grant to William Forth of lands in Butley and Capel (1544) - TNA E371/325/X-XIV
Cleydon, Edward *c*. Thomas Spicer and others - Star Chamber (1545) - TNA STAC 2/10/52
Forth, William *c*. William Redham (1545) - TNA C1/1177/65
Grant of reversion of Boyton Manor to William Forth & Richard Moryson (1545) - TNA E371/366
Hadleigh Market Feoffment Charity (1547) - Hadleigh archives O4/A/01
Forcible occupation of a fishery at Boyton (1545) - TNA Star C.P., Hen VIII, 10: 52-53

Forth, William c. William Willoughby - Court of Chancery (1549) - TNA C1/1220/28-31
Forth, William c. William Willoughby - Extract of Court award (1549) - EE5/7/30
Willoughby, Lord, charges for attack on Thomas Spicer (1553) - EE5/7/12
Replacement of Orford church roof (1562) - EE5/6/65
Certificate issued in accordance with Statutes - HD 1538/12 fo. 1
Depositions regarding Lowdham Marshes (1568) - HB 83:988/6
Terrier of Boyton Manor (1568) - GB 412: 6331
Agas, Radulph, plan of Tangham (n.d.) [c. 1573]- BL Egerton 2789B
Forth, Robert, Bill of complaint of (n.d.) [c. 1573]- TNA C2/Eliz/F5/9
Sone, Priscilla c. Richard Wingfield - Star Chamber (1575) - TNA STAC5 S16/2; S55/28; S70/32;
S84/28
Chillesford, extract from manorial court roll (1576) - HD 1538/183/10
Grimston, Harbottle, infant c. Richard Wingfield - Court of Chancery (1585) - TNA C2 Eliz G14/58
Deputy Lieutenants' meeting (1588) - TNA SP12/208(23)
Inventories taken at Costessey Hall & Wingfield Castle (1590-1599) - NRO JER/271, 55 x 1
Wingfield, Anthony to Earl of Shrewsbury (1590) - Talbot Papers, Lambeth Palace Library
Blenerhasset, Samuel c. Edward Derehaugh, Court of Chancery (1591) - HB 83: 988/6
Wingfield, Anthony, Acquittance to Henry Wingfield (1592) - HA93/5/170
Evidence touching Mr Michael Stanhope his lands...(1592) - HB83:988/5
Forth, Elizabeth, to Sir Robert Cecil (1593) - Hatfield House, Cecil Papers 22/87
Forth, Elizabeth, to Frances Jerningham (1593) - NRO JER/357/55x2
Forth, Robert, c. Henry Jernegan - Court of Requests (1593) - TNA REQ2/27/45
Agas, Raduph, Survey of Manors of Butley, Boyton & Tangham (1594) - BL Egerton
2789A
Norden, John, An Ample and Trew Description of the Estate of Sir Michael Stanhope (1600-02) -
V5/22/1; EE5/11/1
Norden, John, Key map to his 'Ample and Trew Description' (1602) - HD 88(996)
Forth, Frances, to Lionel Tollemache (1602) - BL Egerton MS 2,410 fo.11
Manor of Sudbourne - bailiff's accounts (1606) - V5/18/10.1
Forth, Henry, Inquisitio Post Mortem(1614) - TNA WARD 7/53/218.
Records of licensed properties (1617-20) - Bucks Record Office D/X 648
Stanhope, Sir Michael, memorial inscription, Sudbourne church (1621)
Indenture of Thos Symley to John Fiske blacksmith (1626) - EE5 9/9-21
Indenture of Avern Glover to Thomas Trusson and his wife (1630) - EE5 9/10
Forth, William, mortgage arrangements of (1632) - GB 412: 6331 Box 4.
Leases of Butley ferry (1632; 1638) - BL Add Ch. 10,287; 10,289
Sale of the Manor of Boyton (1634) - GB 412: 6331 Box 4
Covenant between William Forth and Francis Warner (1634) - GB 412:6331 Box 4.
Forth, William and Anne, lease to Sir William Harvy of Ickworth (1638) - BL Add Ch 10,289
Clyatt c. Devereux Court of Chancery cases, including the 1655 family settlement - TNA C/10/211/15;
C/10/215/22
Archdeaconry of Suffolk Allegations (1663/64) - FAA/1; Précis by V. Redstone and H. Ogle (1931)
Hearth Tax return (1663) - TNA E179/257/15
Woodbridge Quarter Session records (1665-1676). Index - B 105/2/7
Jointure for Anne Warner (1675) - GB 412: 6331 Box 4
Liber Visitationis, Wilford and Orford Deaneries (1686) - FAA/6/11
Depositions taken at Rotterdam (1693) - TNA E134/5 W&M/East 27
History of the Jerningham Family from (c.1700) - NRO JER/302a 7b, 55 x 1
Hooke, J., indenture of bargain and sale (1704) - BRO E1/21
Devereux Edgar's Commonplace Book 1703-1716 - HA247/5/4
Devereux Edgar, indenture between (1705) - E3/10/51
Repair of Butley church (1706) - NRO E1/4/2
Spencer, Henry, quitclaim to Edward Spencer of lands in Butley, Capel and Boyton (1707)- HD172/15

Clyatt, Frances, to Edward Spencer (1716) - BRO Suffolk Collections 4 Butley
Abstract of deeds relating to Mrs Clyatt's estate in Butley (1723) - HD1538/172/10
Kirby, John, Book of plans of 5 farms [c. 1730] (n.d.) - HD 427/1
Warner Trustees' contract with potters (1744) - GB 412: 6331 Box 4
Warner Trustees c. Duchess of Hamilton (1748) - GB 412/6331 Box 4
Bounds of the Parish of Wantisden (1747-1832) - HB17:2719/21
Leases of Valley Farm, Butley (1774; 1792) - in private possession
Johnson, Isaac, Draft plans of Butley Estate (1780-1830) - Greenwell Family Archives
Log of *Namur* (1780-82) - TNA ADM 52/ 2418
Log of *Barfleur* (1781-83) - TNA ADM 52/2160
Admiral Rodney, letters from Leeward Islands (1782) - TNA ADM 1/314
Ships' Logs for the Battle of the Saints (1782) - TNA ADM 52/211/3
Washington, George, letter from, in Musée de Grasse (1783)
Goodwin, William, surgeon and farmer of Earl Soham, Diary of (1785-1809) - HD 365/1
Johnson, Isaac, journal (1791-96) - HD 11:432
Coroner's Inquest (1791) - HB 10/9/7/13
Survey of glebe for rector of Boyton (1791) - FC163/03/2
Forth, Nathaniel Parker, A plain statement of facts... (n.d.) [18th cent.] - BL Add MS 65,152
Johnson, Isaac, survey of Ashe Park for J. Rivett, Esq. (1796) - HA 10:50/18/12.3(5)
Transfer of Butley copyhold land to Peter Isaac Thellusson (1803) - HB 83: 1004/24 (pt) 1 no. 191
Woodbridge House of Correction records (1802-1842). Quarter Session records and card index
Street Farm, Butley, sale of (1803) - HB 83: 1004/25
Rendlesham, account of game killed (1807) - HA11/B1/3/17
Chillesford, map of (1841) - HD 628/7
Inquest on Mary Tibbenham (1845) - HB 10/9/59/6
Butley Vestry Minute Book (1856) - held by parish clerk
Neutral Farm: Sale of Street Farm, Butley (1884) - HB 26: 8039/8
Clouting, William, blacksmith, account book (1860-76) - HC 406/1/1
Hazelwood, Robert, farm stock of, (1896) - in private possession
Coroner's Inquest (1897) - EC 5/40/48
Large Family collection (19-20th cent.) - in private possession
Oyster Inn: inventory and sale particulars (early 20th cent.) - in private possession
Church Farm, Chillesford, sale catalogue (1919)
Forth Papers; correspondence, vol. VIII (n.d.) - BL Add MS 65,146
Sudbourne Baptist Church History. Anon. (n.d.) in private possession
MacCulloch, D., 1977, *Power, Privilege and the County Community*. Ph D thesis, Cambridge University
Rackham, Oliver, 2000, Lecture at Millennium Celebration of Trees. Wantisden

Index

Places are in Suffolk unless otherwise named.

UNTOLD TALES
FROM THE SUFFOLK SANDLINGS

Valerie Fenwick
and
Vic Harrup

PRICE: £25

Payment can be made by cheque payable to: Butley Research Group.
Or buy on-line from www.butley-research-group.org.uk
PayPal® available.

Postage within the UK costs £3.95 for one book and £5.95 for two or more.
All other areas are charged according to weight.

I enclose payment of £ ....

Name ....

Address ....

.... Post Code ....

Delivery address (if different) ....

.... Post Code ....

Contact Number / Email ....

Butley Research Group
Church Farm House, Blaxhall, Suffolk IP12 2DH